RÉSUMÉ POWER
Selling Yourself on Paper

Tom Washington

Mount Vernon Press
Bellevue, Washington

Cover design: Charles Fuhrman, Forest Knolls, California
Typesetting: Steve Wozenski, Fairfax, California

ISBN 0-931213-06-1

Library of Congress Cataloging in Publication Data:
Washington, Tom, 1949-
Resume power.
Bibliography: p.
1. Resumes (Employment) I.Title.
HF5383.W316 1984   650.14   84-20779

Acknowledgments

To my parents I owe more than words can state. Their love and support, demonstrated in so many ways at so many times, made this book possible.

Advice for improving the book came from many sources. Each person who reviewed the manuscript not only provided ideas for improving it, but also a dose of encouragement. The rough edges were knocked off and many significant improvements resulted. For their advice, encouragement, and friendship, I thank Michael Badger, Jody Burns, Diane DeWitt, Richard French, Michael Grubiak, Roxanne Legatz, Ivan Settles, and Nat Washington, Sr., my advisor and confidant. Jody Burn, Charles Clock, and Jack Porter were particularly helpful with the resume research.

While obtaining a master's degree in counseling at Northeastern Illinois University, I received a great deal of help and support, especially from two outstanding professors, Jim Fruehling and Mac Inbody.

And Mabel. Mabel Thompson made me a writer. Her love of conciseness and hatred of dead verbs had a profound impact on me.

Finally, a deep thank you to my dear wife Lois, who put up with more than anyone should have to. She read, critiqued, and offered help when I needed it. I love you.

—Tom Washington

How This Book Can Help You Get A Job

A TOP-QUALITY RESUME can net you interviews at a rate ten times greater than your competitors. This book will help you write that resume. *Resume Power* not only will help you write an interview-getting resume, it also provides practical and effective advice covering all phases of the job search. Nowhere can you find a book so packed with proven strategies which have enabled people to find better jobs, at higher pay, and in less time than they had thought possible.

Developing a top-quality resume is dependent not on writing ability but on knowledge and time—knowledge of how to write a resume and market yourself, and time to write, revise, and write again. A mediocre resume takes most people three to four hours to write. An outstanding resume requires six to eight hours. Those three or four extra hours could be the best investment you ever make.

A top-quality resume not only leads to more interviews, but will also produce more job offers. By taking the extra time to review your work experience and accomplishments, you'll be sharper in interviews and appear more confident. Your resume can actually guide the interview and enable you to answer questions that help make you look good. An effective job search begins with a top-quality resume.

Since 1981 I have been researching what makes effective resumes. During that time I have completed some of the first scientific research to determine what really attracts employers to applicants. To date the studies have covered secretaries, engineers, and recent college graduates. The studies have exploded such myths as the belief that resumes must be only one page in length. While more studies are needed, the results of the studies already completed will enable you to write a top-quality resume. We now know, for example that a resume with results, not just duties, will obtain more interviews. Additional findings will be described throughout the book.

RESULTS YOU CAN EXPECT

Writing a top-quality resume is not difficult, but it does take time and careful thought. This book is designed so that you can quickly absorb the information you need to write a resume that gets results. It takes you through the process step by step and answers questions as they arise. It covers key points that are not even mentioned in other resume writing books, points that can make the difference between getting or not getting an interview. If you follow my advice and take enough time to write and edit, you can obtain interviews at a rate ten times greater than competitors with typical resumes. This figure is based on an actual survey of former clients.

Once you have completed your resume, you may still want professional advice. Career Management Resources can edit and help you strengthen your resume. (See page 232 for more on editing.)

Happy Writing!

Contents

Part Two

FINDING THE JOB THAT'S RIGHT FOR YOU

Part Three

WINNING AT INTERVIEWING

Appendix

RESUME EDITING

Part One
Creating A High
Impact Résumé

A Top-Quality Resume

The eye is drawn quickly to your name to establish your identity. ——————————

A clear objective reveals that you are focused and creates a positive impression. ———

The qualifications —————— section sells you in ways that the job description alone can't do. The section summarizes your strengths and experience and sets the tone for what the reader will discover about you.

Training ——————— demonstrates growth and proficiency.

Both job descriptions —————— are filled with results. Results sell you to an employer and reveal much more about your potential than duties alone.

The job descriptions —————— are short and concise, highlighting key points. Short job descriptions invite the employer to read thoroughly and help maintain interest.

Effective layout invites employers to read your resume thoroughly.

BRIAN SANCHEZ
11918 NE 147th
Kirkland, Washington 98034
(206) 821-3731

OBJECTIVE: Management opportunities

QUALIFICATIONS

Strong management and marketing background. Experienced in controlling costs and meeting budget guidelines. Proven ability to increase sales and productivity. Recognized as an excellent trainer and motivator.

EDUCATION

BA - History, Western Washington University (1987)

PROFESSIONAL TRAINING

Negotiating Skills, Simpson & Associates, 16 hours 1992
Professional Selling Skills, Sales Professionals, 24 hours 1991
Supervising People, IPC Group, 16 hours 1990

EMPLOYMENT

Arco, Seattle, Washington, 6/90-Present

FIELD CONSULTANT - Work closely with ten AM/PM Minimart units to increase sales and profit margins. Hire and develop store managers. Took six corporate stores from a "poor" rating in 1989, to the top rating in 1991 and 1992. Prepare monthly and annual budgets and have full responsibility for profit and loss of each store. Have increased sales in stores over 12% per year, the second highest district average in the Northwest Region.

Eddie Bauer, Seattle, Washington 9/87-6/90

ASSISTANT FLATPACK MANAGER - In the Eddie Bauer Distribution Center, oversaw the unpacking, pricing, and inventorying of merchandise. Directly supervised a staff of 20. Through effective training increased productivity of the unit by 18%.

The Importance Of Your Resume

A TOP-QUALITY RESUME can net you interviews at a rate ten times greater than your competitors. This book will help you write that resume. My advice is presented in great depth for a reason—a resume is not *just* a resume. The impact of an effective resume goes far beyond the simple act of mailing it in response to want ads. There are, in fact, at least six benefits to writing a top-quality resume:

1) You will get more interviews when responding to want ads and when sending unsolicited resumes;

2) Your resume becomes your calling card and helps people remember you, while also enabling them to contact you and refer you to others;

3) Knowing you look good on paper builds self-esteem;

4) You will be better prepared for interviews;

5) Because it emphasizes results, your resume will guide your interviews and enable you to focus on your most positive experiences;

6) It will help your prospective boss justify the decision to hire you.

I am going to show you how to create a resume that has real impact. You will be making dozens of decisions as you construct your resume; the information and examples provided will enable you to make the right decisions and will enable you to make them quickly. There is no single "right" way to do anything, but I can assure you that if you follow the advice, you will have a resume that looks good, reads well, and most importantly, has impact.

Remember, a resume is not just a resume. It represents you. Take the time to create a resume that presents the best you have to offer. A resume won't get you a job, but it can help get interviews. Or, put another way, a good resume won't get you a job, but a bad one will cost you jobs. Set your mind on spending whatever time it takes to produce a resume that truly sells you.

What Makes A Top-Quality Resume?

You never get a second chance to make a good first impression.
—Unknown

Eye Appeal

A resume must be visually appealing. Lasting impressions can be formed during the first five seconds your resume is read. That's how long it takes someone to view the layout, observe the quality of the typing and printing, and note the color and quality of the paper. Of course most of this takes place on an unconscious level. Resumes are usually scanned the first time through. If the reader detects misspellings, smudges, poor-quality typing or printing, clumsy or verbose writing, or a confusing layout, the resume may be set aside after just ten or twenty seconds. The result—no interview.

Positive Tone

The top-quality resume presents you in the best possible light, yet does not exaggerate your qualifications. Every item is selected carefully to promote you in the eyes of the employer. Unflattering facts are not hidden, they are either left unmentioned or carefully turned into positives. The resume that concentrates on strengths helps you obtain interviews. Make positive statements about yourself; throw false modesty aside.

Impact

Write with impact. Impact is achieved with tight, concise phrases using action verbs. Impact is achieved when you accurately describe and *project* your desired image. Your full potential will come across only when you write with impact. Effective writing requires plenty of editing and rewriting—something even best-selling authors must do. The effective resume provides valuable information quickly and is easy to read. Each sentence expresses a fact, impression, or idea which will help sell you. All unnecessary words and phrases have been removed. Concise writing is appreciated by all employers and reveals much about your ability to communicate.

Results

An effective resume is filled with results and accomplishments. You've got many results, and when described properly, will cause employers to want to meet you.

RESUME PRINCIPLES YOU NEED TO UNDERSTAND

The Laws of Resume Writing

There are no laws when it comes to resume writing, but there are principles that generally work. When I feel strongly about a principle or approach I'll tell you. But any rule or principle can be ignored if doing so will help sell you to employers.

How to Begin

Before your resume is completed, you will have made dozens of important decisions. This chapter is designed to help you make those decisions quickly and easily. Each section of a resume is explained in detail and you'll learn when and how to use each section, as well as how to write it. Examples and options are provided. You'll know what will work best for you. Examples throughout the chapter explain and demonstrate particular points. Read pages 6 to 71 quickly. Then return to study each section as you begin to write that portion. Highlight examples that are especially applicable to you.

How Interview Decisions Are Made

Have you ever wondered how employers decide who will get interviews after they've placed help wanted ads? A good job will typically attract 75–200 resumes. An employer who has a batch of resumes on her desk will usually scan each one for 5–25 seconds and place each resume in either the "I'm interested" pile or the "reject" pile. When screening resumes, people are usually looking for reasons to reject. That's why even one typo can be a killer. A resume which contains obvious typos, spelling errors, grammatical errors, or verbose writing, will most likely end up in the reject pile. Those who obviously lack the necessary background for the position will also end up in the reject pile.

Out of 80 resumes, perhaps only 20 will be placed in the "I'm interested" pile. Those 20 will be read, with one to five minutes devoted to each. Out of the initial 80 resumes, ten will generally make it through this screening process. Of the ten or so who are called, perhaps six will be invited for interviews.

There is one type of resume that gets through this process nearly every time—the one that sells potential. That's the resume you need to write. I will show you techniques you can use to create a resume with this kind of impact. I'll take you through each section of a resume and show you how to pull all of the pieces together.

Stating Your Objective

MOST RESUMES should have an objective, but avoid the common mistake of trying to cram too much into the objective with statements such as, "Seeking responsible accounting management position with a large progressive firm offering opportunity for growth and promotion, where skills in human relations and effective written communications will prove beneficial." These types of objectives are trying to combine an objective with a qualifications summary, but the combination simply does not work. The objective sounds trite. It's better to use a simple objective and then get creative in producing an effective qualifications summary.

Before starting your resume, write out your objective. Later you can change or delete it, but having an objective will keep you focused while you write. Objectives such as "Bookkeeper," "Chemist," or "Construction Superintendent" can be very effective.

Stating an objective on your resume demonstrates focus. People naturally respect you if you know what you want. A resume that says, "I'll do anything, just give me a job" will get you nowhere. If your objective states "Sales Representative" but you have never been one, everything that follows must demonstrate your *potential* for that position.

Simple objectives usually work best:

Computer Programmer
Senior Accountant
Flight Attendant
Secondary Teacher — Drama, English, ESL
Sales Manager

In the above cases, the people knew exactly what they were looking for and so they used an exact job title. If this is your case, and the title is recognized by all people in your field, use a specific job title. However, if you are considering one of several positions which are all closely related, you might try something like this:

OBJECTIVE: Office Manager/Administrative Assistant/Executive Secretary

In this example, all three types of positions—Office Manager, Administrative Assistant, and Executive Secretary—are similar. A person who is qualified for one is often qualified for all three. In fact, what one company calls Administrative Assistant, another might call Executive Secretary. This person just wants a good job with a good company, and would enjoy any of the three types of jobs. If only "Office Manager" is listed as the applicant's objective, however, an employer with an executive secretary opening might overlook the resume.

You should never pair unrelated job titles as "Secretary/Sales Representative," "Teacher/Real Estate Agent," "Flight Attendant/Bookkeeper." It's okay to be looking for both positions at the same time, but you would need two resumes with two different objectives to do so.

Sometimes an exact job title is *not* advised. This is particularly true in management. If you are currently a personnel manager considering positions such as Training and Development Specialist, Director of Training and Development, and Vice President of Human Resources, you might want to create an objective which incorporates all of these titles such as "OBJECTIVE: Human Resource Management." Using the term *management* does not limit you to a specific job title, while "Human Resource" is specific enough that it is clear you have focus.

Use an objective if your goal can be easily stated with a job title or a descriptive phrase. Occasionally you will find it better to omit an objective and let your cover letter and the tone of your qualifications section indicate your goal. I use an objective for approximately 85% of the resumes I help people write. I frequently recommend multiple versions of a resume where the only changes occur in the objective and in the qualifications section. For example, if you were interested in both sales *and* marketing, you would have two versions of your resume, one with a "Sales" objective, and the other with a "Marketing" objective. One resume would be directed to sales managers and the other to marketing managers.

The Qualifications Statement

THE QUALIFICATIONS SECTION is a summary of your background and strengths. It includes positive statements about you that would be difficult to express in any other section of a resume. Since it is designed to sell your most marketable abilities and experiences, the statements must catch and hold the reader's attention or the section will be skipped. Covering too many points will also result in the section being overlooked.

The qualifications statement can do more than any other section to create a favorable impression of you and will set the tone for the rest of the resume. It can greatly strengthen your perceived worth since employers reading your resume will constantly be asking what you can do for them. Give them positive answers in those first few seconds by creating a qualifications section which truly sells you. This section should capture the *essence* of what you want to sell. Any point which is not crucial should either be eliminated or considered for inclusion in your cover letter.

Studying the following examples will help you understand the function of the qualifications section. A job has been included with each qualifications example to help you see how they fit together.

Example #1

OBJECTIVE: Marine Sales

QUALIFICATIONS

Outstanding sales record. Highly knowledgeable in all facets of sailboats, powerboats, commercial fishing vessels, and marine hardware. Strong ability to introduce new product lines to distributors, dealers, and boat builders. Top-selling rep in the country for four major marine manufacturers.

EMPLOYMENT

Bellkirk Marine, San Diego, California 6/87 to Present

MANUFACTURERS' REPRESENTATIVE - Represent 27 lines covering California, Nevada, and Arizona. Increased the number of accounts with distributors, dealers, and boat builders from 35 to 96 and have increased sales 85%. Since 1989 have been the top-selling rep for four major manufacturers.

Qualifications section example #1 includes a summary and an accomplishment. It starts off with a simple but bold statement: "Outstanding sales record." It then goes on to describe the areas of expertise. The top accomplishment (being the top-selling representative in the country for four manufacturers) has been included twice—in qualifications and the job description. It is a valuable statement worth repeating.

Example #2

OBJECTIVE: Grocery Management

QUALIFICATIONS

Strong management background. With a 21-store district, increased profits 32% and oversaw the construction of four new stores. During 17 years in management, coordinated the grand openings of 13 stores and produced some of the most profitable new stores with three different chains.

EMPLOYMENT

Fine Food Centers, Tulsa, Oklahoma 5/85 to Present

DISTRICT MANAGER 9/88 to Present. Responsible for profit and loss analysis, wage and salary administration, merchandising, store layout, advertising, and buying for 21 stores in the district. Supervised the remodeling of five stores and the construction of four stores. Developed in-house cleaning and repair services, saving $150,000 annually. Through improved merchandising and customer service, increased sales per store 28% and profits 32%.

Qualifications section example #2 begins with a bold statement: "Strong management background" and then proceeds to back it up *with proof.* Immediately you realize this person has been very successful and you want to know more about her. One fact comes right out of her current position (the 32% increase in profits). The second statement (concerning the success of 13 store openings) is a summary that comes from her entire management background. If this summary had not been stated so clearly in a qualifications section it might have been easily overlooked, even during a careful reading of the entire resume.

Writing Your Qualifications Section

Write your qualifications section last. It is the most difficult section to write and requires the most care. Once you have the employment section completed you will know better what needs to be included in your qualifications.

As you prepare for writing the qualifications section, review the resume and determine what points should be covered in it. Use qualifications to introduce yourself to the reader and to give an overview of why you are qualified for your stated objective. To do this ask yourself, "Why would I be good at this occupation?" Or if you already have experience ask yourself, "What makes me successful in this field?" Remember, in qualifications it is permissible to repeat or paraphrase points made elsewhere in the resume.

If you have strong work experience, you will probably want a short qualifications section. If you are seeking to break into a new field, qualifications is usually the best vehicle for bringing in related experiences and selling an employer on your potential.

While relatively short, the qualifications section is often the most difficult to write. Because it can strengthen the overall effectiveness of the resume, it deserves a great deal of attention and effort. An hour spent writing and editing your qualifications section is not too much.

I like short, hard-hitting qualifications sections. I try to capture the *essence* of what will impact employers. As a result, most qualifications sections I write are one paragraph with three to five lines. If there are two distinct areas which need to be sold then I may have two paragraphs with three to five lines each. People making career changes or those seeking positions without having the traditional background, may need three or four paragraphs to bring out all of their related experience. Even so, the emphasis should still be on conciseness and impact.

Essence is not easy to achieve, but the impact of your resume will be significantly strengthened when you succeed. Identify those qualities and areas of experience that an employer absolutely needs to know about you—those critical points. While there may be many points you want an employer to know about you, usually only two or three are critical. Sell those effectively and the employer will feel he or she must meet you.

Write A Qualifications Sketch

To write an effective qualifications section, begin by writing a "qualifications sketch." List the key strengths and assets that you want to convey to employers. After writing your qualifications sketch, determine which are critical and which are not. Simply scratch out those which are not critical and use the critical ones to compose your qualifications section.

The qualifications sketch of a quality control manager might look like this:

1. Ten years in quality control. Familiar with all techniques that have been developed for the electronics industry.

2. Saved money and reduced rejects for three different companies.

3. I work well with other department heads, particularly production, and coordinate and cooperate well with them rather than work against them.

4. I've developed creative programs that really work.

5. I like my work and enjoy a challenge.

6. I'm always looking for a better method, technique, or system; I'm open to new ideas from others.

7. I'm an excellent supervisor. I train my staff well, I listen to them, I maintain high morale, and productivity is always high.

8. I'm hardworking, loyal, reliable, creative, and efficient.

The final version of the quality control manager's qualifications section might read like this:

QUALIFICATIONS

Strong experience in quality control gained during ten years in supervision and management. For three electronics manufacturers implemented new quality control programs which decreased rejects at each plant by at least 23%.

Develop excellent relations with all department heads and work well with production personnel.

Excellent supervisor. Consistently increase productivity of quality assurance personnel, and through effective staff training, increase their technical capabilities.

If you review the eight points the person originally wanted to cover, you'll notice that everything is included here either directly or by implication (points 5 and 8 were covered implicitly). By reading the qualifications section in the context of the entire resume, you would certainly pick up that he enjoys a challenge and that he is hardworking, loyal, reliable, creative, and efficient.

In writing qualifications sections there is a tendency to use the words *strong* and *excellent,* such as "Strong experience in quality control . . ." and "Excellent supervisor." Both are excellent words, but try not to overuse them. I've searched the thesaurus and just haven't found many good substitutes. I rarely use the word *good* because it just isn't strong enough. I occasionally use the word *outstanding,* but it can seem too strong, so use it selectively.

Other phrases can also be used to make a point. If you use "Excellent experience" in one paragraph, you could use "Broad experience," "Broad background," or "Excellent background," in the next. Don't be bothered if you use the word *excellent* three times, but use substitutes to avoid using it excessively. Excellent is often the best word because it is not as humble as *good,* nor is it too strong, as *outstanding* sometimes seems.

I often start a qualifications paragraph with a short statement, such as "Excellent management experience," then I back it up with further details. In this case the follow-up might be "Consistently obtain high productivity from employees," or "Consistently implement new techniques and procedures which increase productivity and lower costs." Another effective backup statement would be: "Proven ability to turn around projects which are behind schedule and over budget." Whatever general statement you make should be explained or reinforced with details. Look at the resumes on pages 83, 99, 106, and 107 and notice how percentages or other statistics have been included in qualifications. This can be very effective but is not always necessary or possible, particularly if you are making a broad statement about your entire career.

Notice how effective the various back-up statements can be when they are paired with the beginning short statement.

Excellent management experience. Consistently obtain high productivity from employees.

Excellent management experience. Consistently implement new techniques and procedures which increase productivity and lower costs.

Excellent management experience. Proven ability to turn around projects which are behind schedule and over budget.

Broad banking background with strong managerial and technical expertise. Always a top producer with the ability to establish strong, long-term customer relationships.

Strong background in trucking gained during 20 years of management experience. Recognized for ability to significantly increase market share and quickly increase profitability. At each terminal achieved one of the best on-time records in the industry.

Opening with a short statement provides impact. It hits the reader and makes the person want some evidence, which you will provide in your very next sentence. Of course, you need to be able to verify anything you say, such as

"Consistently obtain high productivity from employees," either in other sections of your resume or in a personal interview.

To write effective qualifications statements study several examples. Analyze them to determine what makes them effective. When you're through writing a qualifications statement, compare what you have to some of the examples. If you're not pleased, set the resume aside for a day. You'll return to it later with a fresh perspective. Let others see it and get feedback from them. Don't use the qualifications section as filler. Include only those points which you really think will sell you.

Some people just can't come up with a good qualifications section. If you fall into that category, do what you can to improve the qualifications section, but finish the resume so you can get it out to the right people. In such a case I would recommend that you wrap it up with a short summary of 15–25 words without trying to make any hard-hitting statements. Here's an example.

OBJECTIVE: Programmer/Analyst

QUALIFICATIONS

Excellent background in data processing gained during eight years in programming and systems analysis.

Even though this qualifications section lacks punch, it serves a purpose. As soon as an employer sees an objective, he immediately asks himself what makes this person qualified. By seeing the word *QUALIFICATIONS* followed by a statement, the employer instantly assumes the person *is* qualified and goes on to seek evidence in the education and experience sections.

You can use this way out if you have difficulty with your qualifications, but use this approach only after you've spent at least two hours working solely on qualifications. Once you've used your resume for a while, try working on qualifications again. You'll probably have some new thoughts, and it may come together after all.

Education

EDUCATION SHOULD USUALLY APPEAR on the first page right below qualifications. If you have a college degree or a certificate in a technical field, it should be obvious why you would want education to appear early in the resume. You can design the section so that just a glance will tell the reader what degree(s) or certificate(s) you hold. Perhaps you don't have a college degree or a certificate but have very strong experience in your field. In that case, you would still place education right after qualifications because you'll want the reader to see quickly that while you don't have a great deal of education, you have a wealth of qualifying experience.

There are a number of reasons for placing education on the first page of your resume. For one thing employers are curious about education. If education does not appear on the first page they will often flip immediately to the second page. Also, not putting your education on the first page can give the impression that you are "hiding" or "burying" your education. For these reasons, I rarely place education at the end of the resume, although it can be placed at the end of a one-page resume.

I like to see education right after qualifications. Most readers will merely glance at education and notice only that a person has a degree. The more curious will note the school, major, and year of graduation. Since employers are curious about education, and since the section takes only 3–6 seconds to read, I believe it belongs at the top.

Occasionally education is left off entirely. This most often happens when a person with 20 or more years of experience in his or her field lacks a college degree and simply decides to leave it off. One option is to include an education section which lists professional seminars as well as any college courses taken.

A top-quality resume must be easy to read. The first example below is easy to read and you obtain the key information almost instantly. The next two education sections are difficult to read. Notice the difference.

Easy to read:

EDUCATION

B.A. - Business Administration, University of Washington (1978)

The above example represents the best way of describing a college degree. "B.A."—instantly a reader can see that you hold a degree. The next most important fact is your major, then your school, followed by the year of graduation.

The following bad examples show you what *not* to do:

Hard to read:

EDUCATION   <u>Butler University</u>, Indianapolis, Indiana.

Received a B.A. in Business Administration in December, 1979. Curriculum emphasized Marketing and Financial Management, with field of specialization Real Estate. Grade point average 3.21.

Harder to read:

<u>EDUCATION</u>

Central Michigan
<u>University</u>

Mount Pleasant, Michigan

September 1975   <u>Bachelor of Arts</u>, Majored in Sociology with
        to   a minor in Psychology
June 1980

Both are hard to read. The reader has to look carefully just to learn whether the person has a degree.

HOW TO BEST DISPLAY YOUR EDUCATION

The following section reveals the best way to show your education, depending on just what your educational background is. Highlight or place a mark by the one that matches your situation.

High School Graduate, No College

EDUCATION

Graduated - Roosevelt High School, Chicago, Illinois (1976)

Some College, No Degree

If you have attended college, there is rarely a reason to include your high school.

EDUCATION

University of Nevada, Las Vegas, Business, 136 credits (1974-1977)

In the example above, credits were included to show that although a degree program has not been completed, the person was at least a serious student, accumulating 136 of 180 quarter credits necessary to graduate. A major is given to show the emphasis of study. When determining what major to include, try to make sure it is related to the type of work you're seeking. If you have 20 or more credits in each of three fields, pick the one which will best sell you.

Certificate From A Technical School

EDUCATION

> Certificate - Welding Technology, Davis Technical School (1975)

or

EDUCATION

> Certificate - Computer Programming, Sims Business College (1975)
> Graduated - Norcross High School, Norcross, Pennsylvania (1972)

No Degree, Attended Several Colleges

Some people have acquired credits at four or more schools. If this is your situation, you need not list all schools on your resume; it may give the impression of instability.

EDUCATION

> Cheboit Junior College, Castlerock Community College, Riverside Community College, 98 credits.

The person in the above example actually attended three other colleges, which are not mentioned because only a few credits were obtained. The credits are included in the total, however. Attendance was very sporadic over a ten-year period, so no dates are given. There is usually no need to mention the cities and states where the colleges were located.

No Degree, Two Colleges Attended

EDUCATION

> Northeastern Illinois University, Business, 70 credits (1974-76)
> University of Illinois, Circle Campus, Business, 30 credits (1972)

No Degree, No or Few College Courses Taken

EDUCATION

> Total Quality Management, Dreyfuss & Assoc., 24 hours (1991)
> Implementing Just in Time, Bob Huston & Assoc., 40 hours (1989)
> The Problem Employee, Dreyfuss & Assoc., 8 hours (1988)
> Principles of Management, University of Texas, 5 credits (1985)
> Motivating Employees, Dreyfuss & Assoc., 16 hours (1984)
> Introduction to Marketing, University of Texas, 5 credits (1981)

This person has been taking seminars for years but has little formal education. He has taken college courses for personal benefit, but not with a degree in mind. By combining seminars with a few college courses, this type of education section works well and demonstrates that he is a growth-oriented person.

Degree, Two Or More Colleges Attended

Unless you have a special reason for including all of your schools, list only the college you graduated from. If you got an Associate of Arts (A.A.) and then moved to a four-year college, still mention only the four-year college. Everything else is superfluous. Since you did not attend four years at the college mentioned, state only the year of graduation.

EDUCATION

B.S. - Physics, Rhode Island University (1976)

Will Soon Graduate

If you will graduate in just a few months you might show education like this:

B.A. - Political Science, University of Arizona (June 1994)

In the above example the assumption is that the resume has been written in the spring of 1994, and you are scheduled to graduate in June, 1994.

If you expect to graduate in the coming year, but don't know which quarter, you might express it this way:

B.A. - Chemistry, University of Texas (Expected 1994)

Another possibility would be:

Economics, University of Maryland, B.A. to be completed by June 1994

Bachelor's Degree Plus Graduate Studies, But No Graduate Degree

EDUCATION

Graduate Studies, Public Administration, University of Georgia (1976-78)
B.A. - Political Science, University of Georgia (1971-75)

or

M.S. Program, Psychology, UCLA, 30 credits (1977-1979)
B.A. - Psychology, Eastern Washington University (1972-1976)

Recent College Graduate, Little Work Experience

You may want to include some of your coursework to demonstrate the extensiveness of your training. If you are a liberal arts graduate seeking a management trainee position, you could list economics, accounting, and business courses. The person with a technical degree is also often benefited by listing courses. Although the reader knows your major, that information alone is not always adequate. For the person with few summer or part-time jobs, listing coursework will make your resume, and therefore your experience, look fuller.

In the following example, the person was looking for an entry-level position in advertising.

EDUCATION

B.A. - Journalism/Advertising, University of Hawaii - 3.39 GPA (1992)

Coursework included: Advertising Copywriting, Public Relations Writing, Media Planning, Media Representation, Production Graphics, Advertising Layout and Design, Media Aesthetics, Principles of Design, Principles of Color

Graduate Degree(s)

In the first two examples below the people merely listed their degrees. The third is the same except that the person chose to include his thesis. A more elaborate description of the thesis can be very effective. It could be described right after the thesis title, or an entire section could be devoted to it called "THESIS."

EDUCATION

M.A. - Counseling, UCLA (1972-1974)
B.A. - Psychology, Oregon State University (1966-1970)

EDUCATION

Ph.D. - Industrial Psychology, Stanford University (1975-1977)
M.A. - Psychology, Northwestern University (1972-1973)
B.A. - Sociology, Northern Illinois University (1967-1971)

EDUCATION

Ph.D. - Physics, University of Washington (1984-1987)
  Thesis: Interlinear Regression Analysis of Wave Length Dichotomy
M.S. - Physics, University of Washington (1979-1982)
B.S. - Physics, University of Manitoba (1975-1979)

All But Dissertation

If you have completed all requirements for a graduate degree, except for the dissertation or thesis, it might read:

Master's Program, Physics, Iowa State University, completed all but dissertation (1978-1981)

or

Master's Program, Physics, Iowa State University, completed all coursework (1978-1981)

TIPS FOR STRENGTHENING YOUR EDUCATION SECTION

The following tips will help you put the finishing touches on your education section.

Listing Major and Minor

You may want to list both your major and minor if you believe the minor will also help to sell you. In the case below the person wanted to become a labor relations negotiator and felt the economics minor strengthened her credentials.

EDUCATION

B.A. -   Major: Industrial Relations. Minor: Economics. Syracuse University 1971

Degrees And Abbreviations

If you hold a B.A., B.S., M.A., M.S., or Ph.D., it is best to abbreviate since everyone knows what they stand for. Many people are not familiar, however, with B.F.A. (Bachelor of Fine Arts), so it is better to spell out the term. The same is true of M.P.S. (Master of Professional Studies), B.B.A. (Bachelor of Business Administration), and others. Almost everyone knows A.A. stands for Associate of Arts, but many do not know A.S. stands for Associate of Science or that A.T.A. stands for Associate of Technical Arts. If you think some people will not know what your degree stands for, spell it out.

When to Use GPA (Grade Point Average)

Generally GPA is listed only if it is over 3.0. GPA usually is dropped from your resume after you've been out of school for five years. By that time your work record will reveal much more about you than your GPA. It's interesting to note that most follow-up studies have revealed virtually no correlation between a high college GPA and success on the job. Many who were mediocre in school begin to shine only when they enter "the real world."

When to List Honors

If you graduated with honors or with a title like Cum Laude or Summa Cum Laude, you could include it like this:

EDUCATION

B.A. - Cum Laude, History, Brigham Young University 1968-72

City and State of College

The city and state in which your college is located is usually not included in your resume. This is particularly true if your college is well known in the region in which you are conducting your job search. If you think employers might be curious, however, include the city and state.

Order of Schools

Normally schools are listed in reverse chronological order, beginning with your most recent school. Typically this would also mean that your highest level degree would appear first.

Whether to List Major

People should usually include their major, even if that major did not directly prepare them for the field they are now in. There are presidents of Fortune 500 companies who graduated with degrees in history or literature. I say keep your major in, but if you feel strongly about removing it, it might look like this:

B.S. - Southern Illinois University (1982)

Professional Training

IT IS GENERALLY BEST to separate education from training. Training usually includes seminars and workshops, but can also include college courses taken to help you perform better in your field, but which are not part of a degree program. Seminars include those sponsored by your employer and those offered by outside consulting firms at your place of employment. You should also list seminars and workshops you've attended away from your place of employment, paid for either by yourself or your employer. Even if you have received college credit for such courses, you would normally include them under training rather than education. Glance at the example below and you'll see why it's a good idea to separate training from education.

EDUCATION

    Total Quality Control, Rainier Group (24 hours) 1987
    Terminating Employees, Human Resources Inc. (8 hours) 1985
    B.A. - Business, University of Colorado 1980
    Supervising Difficult Employees, Townsend & Assoc.
      (10 hours) 1979

If you hold a degree, you want the reader to spot that fact instantly. In the example above, the B.A. is hidden by the seminars. It would look better this way:

EDUCATION

    B.A. - Business, University of Colorado 1980

PROFESSIONAL TRAINING

    Total Quality Control, Rainier Group (24 hours) 1987
    Terminating Employees, Human Resources Inc. (8 hours) 1985
    Supervising Difficult Employees, Townsend & Assoc. (10 hours) 1979

Listing workshops and seminars can help demonstrate your professional growth. But as valuable as seminars are, be selective about those you choose to include—be sure they are relevant. If you took a course in estate planning, but that knowledge will be of little or no value for the job you're seeking (restaurant management, say), it's better to leave it out.

Usually you should state the seminar title, the name of the organization that put it on, and the year you attended. If most of your seminars lasted a half day or more, it would be useful to show the number of hours spent in class. If your company sent you to seminars in different cities, it can be beneficial to list those cities. It demonstrates that your company thought highly enough of you to invest in out-of-town workshops.

Some seminars have catchy titles that really don't describe their content. If "Make The Most Of Yourself" was really about time management, it should be written as: "Time Management, Simms and Associates (1989)." Feel free to alter seminar titles so the reader will understand their content. Review the following:

MANAGEMENT SEMINARS

Managing People, Harvard Business Workshop, four days (1992)
Motivating Employees, Bob Collins & Associates, two days (1990)
Management and Human Relations, California Institute of Technology,
124 hours (1987)

❖

SEMINARS

Financial Management for Closely Held Businesses, 40 hours,
Seattle-First National Bank (1992)
Construction Cost Improvement, 20 hours, Nevett & Associates(1991)
Scheduling, CPM, 20 hours, Nevett & Associates (1990)
Real Estate Syndication, 10 hours, NW Professionals (1990)
Construction Estimating, 30 hours, Lake Washington Vo-Tech (1989)
Closing the Sale, 12 hours, Roff & Associates (1987)
Goal Setting/Richer Life, 18 hours, Zig Ziglar (1986)

Employment

Every job is a self-portrait of the person who did it. —Unknown

FOR MOST PEOPLE the employment section will be the longest section of the resume. Employment has four main purposes: 1) it reveals your career progress; 2) it describes duties and responsibilities; 3) it describes results and accomplishments; and 4) it accounts for where you've been and for whom you've worked.

Employment history should not be just a recitation of duties and responsibilities. You have a definite goal in mind: you want employers to sense your future worth to their organizations. Everything in your resume should demonstrate your ability to master the type of job you are seeking. Include whatever information will create that sense of value; exclude whatever information will not.

Describing results and accomplishments in each job you've held will do more to reveal your capabilities than anything else. Each job description should consist of concisely described duties and at least one accomplishment. The employment section should begin with your most recent position and move backward in reverse chronological order.

Writing effective job descriptions can be difficult, but I've developed techniques which will ultimately save you time and produce a better resume. The most important technique is to begin by creating a *job sketch*.

USING JOB SKETCHES TO STRENGTHEN YOUR RESUME

*If I had eight hours to chop down a tree, I'd spend the first six
sharpening my axe. —Abraham Lincoln*

A job sketch is simply a listing of all the major duties you've performed in each job, plus a brief description of special projects, and an analysis of the results you achieved in each job.

Before you even begin to write your resume, write a job sketch for each job you intend to list in the employment section. Since developing the use of job sketches in 1981, I have seen the quality of clients' resumes improve by at least 50%. Job sketches work because they help prevent writer's block. Without a job sketch a person is forced to stare at a blank sheet of paper or a blank computer screen. Suddenly the person is under real pressure to produce. The questions come flooding in—"where should I start, what's important, how much space should I devote to each job?"

A job sketch prevents that type of pressure and panic. Instead of beginning by staring at a blank page, you begin your resume with each job sketch in front of you. And each job sketch covers everything that could go into the resume.

You produced each job sketch under low stress conditions because you were merely writing down everything that came to mind, not worrying about spelling, grammar, sentence structure, or polished writing. In other words, you were not trying to write a resume.

With your job sketch before you, it is much easier to decide what the key points really are, and what emphasis you should give to each one. Because your job sketch is so complete, you will have more information than you will actually put into the resume. But that's okay. Information which is not used may be great material to bring up in your interviews.

To produce each job sketch, review the job in your mind and then list major duties, less major duties, and even selected minor duties which might be relevant for the type of position you are seeking. Those minor duties may have taken up less than 1% of your time, but may be critical in demonstrating that you at least have exposure in a key area.

After you've listed job duties, think about any projects you worked on. Then write a brief description of them, including their results or outcomes. A project is anything that has a definite beginning and ending. Bookkeeping includes certain things that are done daily, weekly, monthly, quarterly, and yearly—bookkeeping is not a project. Analyzing the present bookkeeping system and recommending and implementing changes would be a project. Some occupations consist of repetitive duties that rarely or never involve projects. People in occupations such as engineering, programming, chemistry, and consulting, continually move from one project to the next.

Thinking through all of these duties, responsibilities, and projects for all of your jobs will take one to three hours, but taking the time now can make the difference between a mediocre resume and an outstanding one. If you save each job sketch, you will never have to go through this process again, except as you add new positions.

The key to a good job sketch is to simply write whatever pops into your mind. Don't worry about grammar or spelling, just get your thoughts on paper. Go for volume. Write quickly. Don't filter out or neglect to put something down because you think it is insignificant. Remember, only a small portion of your job sketch will end up in the resume, but you need plenty of data to work with.

As you read the sample job sketches, and the job descriptions that resulted from the sketches, notice the impact that results have. After reading the polished version of the job descriptions, you will have the definite sense that these two people are very good at what they do.

The following job sketch of an insurance claims adjuster is thorough and detailed. It took about 30 minutes to write. Once this person was ready to start her resume, it practically wrote itself.

INSURANCE CLAIMS ADJUSTER

Read each new claim file and determine which ones to act on first.

Call claimants or the insured party to clarify what occurred and set up appointment to inspect car, write an estimate, or meet injured parties.

Go to body shop to write estimate and negotiate final cost with manager. Haggle about how many hours to give for straightening frame, fender, quarter panel, etc. Use crash book figures for time necessary to remove and replace parts, to paint panels and for cost of parts. Threaten to take car to another shop if can't reach a compromise. Come up with creative and cheaper ways for car to be repaired such as splicing in entire front or rear section.

Totals—if totaled, use *Blue Book* to calculate value. Negotiate if necessary with claimant or insured to determine amount to be paid. Get bids from Midwest Auto Auction and award car to highest bidder. Arrange to turn over title to new owner after getting payment.

When injuries have occurred visit accident scene and draw picture, visit surrounding stores or homes to locate witnesses, get statements. Get recorded statements from claimant and insured. Go to hospital if necessary and explain that I want to make a fair settlement. Try to settle on first visit for small sum and get signature on release statement.

Collect all medical and hospital bills. Request diagnosis from treating physician. Determine real extent of injury, estimate what the case should settle for, and request an adequate money authorization from supervisor to settle.

Visit claimant and negotiate—explain why injury isn't worth as much as claimant thinks it is.

Negotiate with attorney by mail or phone. Explain any circumstances which weaken claimant's case, i.e., question of who was really at fault or extent of injury.

Results

1985 Set record for most claims settled in one year.

1985 Out of 15 adjusters, 3rd lowest average cost per collision settlement, 2nd lowest average bodily injury settlement.

This person had three years' experience as a claims adjuster and was looking for another claims position with an insurance company. The final version of the job description—just 77 words—is given below.

CLAIMS ADJUSTER - 6/83-7/86. Handled a full range of property damage and personal injury claims. Wrote estimates on damage to claimant and insured vehicles, disposed of total losses, and handled claims on comprehensive coverage including stolen cars, tires, and glass breakage. Investigated accidents and settled injury cases with claimants and attorneys. In 1985 set record for most claims settled in one year. Out of fifteen adjusters, had third lowest average cost per collision settlement and second lowest average personal injury settlement.

The job sketch below is written somewhat differently from the previous one. It's included to show you that there is no set way to write a job sketch.

SENIOR TECHNICIAN

A. Test printed circuit boards, end items, and systems according to test procedures set by engineering. Troubleshoot down to component level.

B. Interface with clinical personnel if problems occur with functionality of units, kits, etc. Identify problems and suggest solutions.

C. Interface with design and R & D engineering regarding fit, form, or functional flaws or problems. Suggest solutions. On the Y235 scanner, suggested solutions which reduced time to produce prototype by four months. On the U454 scanner, identified a problem which would have cost over $200,000 to fix in the production phase.

D. Interface with production, test, and assembly personnel to ensure a proper production flow.

E. Work with Quality Control on functional as well as cosmetic problems. Fix if necessary or show why QC documents are wrong or why specifications should be changed. Changes in specifications typically speeded up production by 10–15%.

F. Work with Material Control to ensure parts are available when needed. Expedite shipments when necessary.

G. Assist engineering in setting up pre-clinical trials for prototype products.

H. Check out functional test procedures for Test Engineering to ensure they are correct, practical, and understandable.

I. Review printed circuit board schematics and assembly drawings and make corrections where necessary.

J. Keep and maintain a file of all new product test procedures, drawings, specifications, and parts lists. This has improved access and use of all data and saves approximately 200 man-hours per year.

Notice how points in the final job description were taken right out of the job sketch, in some cases with only minor revisions.

SENIOR TECHNICIAN - 3/87 to Present. As Senior Technician for this manufacturer of CAT scanners, test printed circuit boards, end items, and systems, and troubleshoot down to component level. Rework failed equipment. Work closely with clinical personnel and design engineers to identify problems and suggest solutions. Identified and resolved a problem with one product which would have cost over $200,000 to fix in the production stage. Interface with Quality Control and frequently recommend changes in QC specifications. Recommendations typically speed up production by 10–15%.

Assist Engineering in setting up preclinical trials for prototype products. Review test procedures established by Test Engineering to ensure tests are understandable and workable. Review PC schematics, assembly drawings, and parts lists, and make corrections where necessary. Developed and currently maintain a file of all test procedures, drawings, parts lists, and specifications, which has significantly improved access and use of the data, saving approximately 200 man-hours per year.

While the data and information you produce for your job sketch are important and useful, the very process of writing the job sketch also serves several valuable functions. It makes you recall *all* the duties and functions of the job and allows you to choose the most important ones for your resume. It also causes you to relive some of the experiences and makes them more vivid. What's more, it helps you recall accomplishments and results. In addition, the very act of remembering, sorting through, and writing down all of your duties, accomplishments, and experiences, prepares you for interviews.

As you write your job sketches, it is important that you make the most out of each one of your accomplishments. The next section on accomplishments will show you how to do that.

ACCOMPLISHMENTS

To write an effective resume you should look for ways to insert accomplishments into your job descriptions, special projects, and qualifications. This section will provide you with the techniques to create real impact in your resume through the use of accomplishments and results.

Accomplishments separate achievers from nonachievers. Duties alone cannot do this. Consider two people, each with ten years of experience and identical job titles. Applicant A has not had an original idea in three years. The drive and initiative that propelled A upward is gone. Applicant B, however, has demonstrated significant accomplishments each year and still exhibits great enthusiasm. Only accomplishments will distinguish over-the-hill applicant A from full-of-potential applicant B. Accomplishments make you seem more like a real person and create strong impressions. Stressing accomplishments in a resume is important for everyone, but it is absolutely critical for the person changing careers; those accomplishments will prove your potential for success in the new career.

Employers make hiring decisions based on your perceived potential. Experience is frequently used to measure potential, but it is often a poor yardstick. Employers certainly want people who can come in and handle the job from day one, but other factors are also important. Employers are willing to train someone if they feel that person has the potential to become a better employee than the one with more experience. Potential is best demonstrated through accomplishments.

Accomplishments do not have to be big, knock-your-socks-off types of experiences. They are merely experiences in which you made a contribution. An employer who clearly sees that you've made contributions that go beyond just doing your "duty," immediately assumes that you will continue to make contributions in the future. That's potential. But it's not enough to have achieved certain accomplishments or to possess potential. You must present them in your resume in ways that bring them to life. Your competitors, in fact, may have accomplishments even more impressive than your own, but if they fail to describe them in their resumes, it's the same as if they did not have them. And if they don't list them in their resume, they probably will not describe them in interviews. This gives *you* the advantage.

Ideally, you will list one or more significant accomplishments for each job you've held. For some jobs, however, this is not practical. Perhaps you held the job for just a short time, or didn't enjoy the job and performed below your full potential. With jobs like these, provide only short descriptions so that the reader will concentrate on the more important jobs you held.

Describe accomplishments concisely and concretely so that they'll have impact. Every employer seeks people who can increase profits, decrease costs, solve problems, or reduce the stress and pressure they face. Specific information such as percentages and dollar figures, make accomplishments more tangible and impressive. Compare these two statements: "Implemented new personnel policies which increased morale" and "Implemented new personnel policies which reduced absenteeism by 27% and reduced turnover by 24%." The specific figures given in the second sentence make the accomplishment seem more impressive and real.

You're probably thinking, "I know my idea saved time and money, but I have no idea how much." In this section I'm going to show you how to arrive at your figures. In many cases they will be estimates, but use company records to verify your figures whenever they are available. One of my clients used printed reports to verify his 63% increase in tons of aluminum sold during a two year period. Those figures were impressive in the resume; during interviews he was able to elaborate.

Arriving at a percentage or a dollar figure when you have no verifying figures requires creative thinking and sometimes creative guessing. You would not want to exaggerate the accomplishment, but you can calculate figures to the best of your knowledge. The following example illustrates how this can be done.

Saving Money in Alaska

Roger wanted to leave Alaska, where he had repaired heavy construction machinery. He felt he was a top-level mechanic but could think of no evidence to prove it. After talking with him a bit, I discovered he was constantly developing new tools and finding easier ways to make certain repairs. One of the tools he made helped him install a $500 part by aligning it perfectly in place. Without the tool the part was sometimes misaligned, but there was no way to tell until the part was clamped in; by then it was too late, the part would crack. Roger estimated he replaced the part 30 times per year and would have cracked two of them without the tool. About 20 other mechanics with similar duties copied his tool. We figured he and the 20 others each saved about $1000 annually. So on the resume we stated that he saved $20,000 per year with his tool. Actual savings may have ranged from $18,000 to $25,000 per year; we chose $20,000 as the most likely. If an employer asks Roger to verify the figure, he can explain how it was calculated. Employers have always been satisfied with his explanation. In an interview all you need to do is explain how you arrived at the figures and state that they're accurate to the best of your knowledge.

Using Results To Create Impact

It's great when you've got computer printouts or company documents to prove what you are claiming, but few people have that type of documentation. Nevertheless, I have never had a client tell me that their claims were not believed.

Accomplishments which cannot be translated into dollars or percentages can still have impact. Statements such as "Selected as employee of the month," or "Brought the product to market five months ahead of schedule." can have a powerful effect on employers.

In the following sample job descriptions, notice that accomplishments are described very briefly. Elaborate on your accomplishments at the interview, not in the resume.

In the Memory Academy example below notice the impression you gain, even though no figures are used. You will quickly recognize that she is responsible, creative, hard-working, and an excellent supervisor and trainer. She is the type of person who is always looking for ways to improve programs and systems.

Memory Academy, Dallas, Texas 5/85 to 6/87

OFFICE MANAGER/EXECUTIVE INSTRUCTOR - Office manager of a 14-person office with direct responsibility for ten. Developed and wrote detailed manuals for each position and created a smooth functioning office. In 1986 redesigned the teaching techniques of the memory course. Instructors immediately experienced better results and received enthusiastic ratings from clients.

Her key accomplishment came from improving the teaching techniques at the Memory Academy. With the recognition of an accomplishment comes a better understanding of her as a person. You know that she cared about her job and invested her energy in making the business more effective and successful.

Accomplishments are loaded with powerful information. One fifteen-word accomplishment can say more and have more impact than one hundred words of a job description. Look at the following two examples and notice the impact of the accomplishments. Imagine what the impact would be without them. I have italicized key parts of the accomplishments, for your benefit. The italics did not appear in the original.

Des Moines Trust & Savings, Des Moines, Iowa 9/87 to Present

BRANCH OPERATIONS MANAGER - Managed operations at three branches and supervised 20 employees. *Overcame serious morale problems* by working closely with the branch staffs and providing better training and supervision. Within the branches *absenteeism was reduced 42% and turnover 70%.* Customer service and marketing of bank services were strengthened. Based on customer surveys, the *customer service rating improved from 74% good or excellent, to 92%.*

❖

Central Mortgage 5/79 to Present

DIVISION MANAGER, Missoula, Montana, 9/87 to Present. Opened the Missoula office and set up all bookkeeping and office systems. Within ten months *became the number-one home mortgage lender* in the Missoula area and *obtained 54% of the mortgage market and 68% of all construction loans.* During five years *averaged 48% profit on gross income, the highest in the company among 33 offices.*

The following example vividly illustrates the need for accomplishments. The first version lacks both accomplishments and impact. The revision ultimately sold the person into a good position.

Before

SALES REPRESENTATIVE - 2/88 to Present. Develop and service established accounts as well as new accounts. Set pricing structures after determining the market. Responsible for the district's western Orange County territory. Sales have increased each year.

After

SALES REPRESENTATIVE - 2/88 to Present. In the first three years moved the territory from last in the district to first among ten territories. Aggressively went after new accounts and have significantly increased market share in the territory. By 1991 became the number one sales rep in total profits and have maintained that position. Profits have increased an average of 30% annually.

Is there any question which resume would result in an interview? In the second job description, you get a sense of a salesperson who is successful, works hard, has excellent product knowledge, and knows how to get a sale. It makes an employer want to meet him to learn if he is as good in person as he seems on paper.

Notice that the impression you get of the person is much stronger in the second version, yet it required just one more line than the first. This powerful effect can be created by presenting *what* you've done in jobs, rather than *how* you've done it. Tell *what* resulted from your efforts, but devote little or no space to describing *how* it happened. Accomplishments speak for themselves and you rarely need to go into detail regarding all the things you did to get your results. Save the details for an interview.

Sometimes you will want to *allude* to what was done without providing details. The bank branch operations manager presented earlier, provides a perfect example. She said, "Overcame serious morale problems by working closely with the branch staffs and providing better training and supervision. Within the branches absenteeism was reduced 42% and turnover 70%." How she got her result is merely alluded to with the statement, "Overcame serious morale problems by working closely with the branch staffs and providing better training and supervision." She did not go into detail about the morale problem, but simply stated it existed. And, she only alluded to *how* she solved it—working closely with staff and improving training and supervision. An employer who wants to know more will have to interview her.

In the resume below, a bank controller's job description does not do him justice. Because this was his most recent and most responsible position, more detail is required to show his potential. Although the second job description is longer, it is well-written and concise. It does not contain any unnecessary words. Everything mentioned is designed to sell him and give an employer a full view of his experience.

Before

CONTROLLER - Managed accounting department, seven-person staff; prepared financial statements and filed various reports with state and federal agencies; assisted and advised senior management concerning regulatory accounting, and tax ramifications of decisions and policies; worked with savings and loan divisions on operational and systems design; served as primary liaison with computer service bureau in Los Angeles.

After

CONTROLLER - Managed a seven-person accounting department and significantly increased productivity by simplifying procedures, cross-training staff, and improving morale. Prepared financial statements and advised senior management on regulatory, accounting, and tax ramifications of new policies and programs under consideration. Heavily involved in the research and planning of an investment "swap" program which resulted in a $5.3 million tax refund. Successfully directed the Association's response when the refund resulted in an IRS audit.

As financial division representative, worked closely with both the savings and loan divisions to increase interdivision cooperation related to new systems, operations, and customer service. Significantly improved communications with the Association's service bureau and implemented modifications in the general ledger system which streamlined operations and saved more than $20,000 per year.

The accomplishments he included were his increase in productivity, finding a unique approach for justifying a large tax credit and then defending it before the IRS, increasing cooperation among divisions in the bank, improving relations with the computer service bureau, and saving money on computer services. These accomplishments are likely to pique the interest of a targeted employer.

Results Sell People

Below are additional statements which effectively convey accomplishments. Read them to give you further ideas on how you might present your results.

Developed a new production technique which increased productivity by 7%.

Through more effective recruiting techniques, reduced terminations company-wide by 30% and turnover by 23%.

Edited a newsletter for an architectural association, with readership increasing 28% in one year.

Organized a citizen task force which successfully wrote a statewide initiative, adopted with a 69% favorable vote.

As chairperson for fundraising, developed a strategy which increased funds raised by 26% while reducing promotional costs.

Awarded Medal of Merit for contributions to the community.

Set a record of 46 days without a system failure.

Which/Which Resulted In

Accomplishments and results are powerful. Everything you've done on a job has had a result. When the result is positive *and* significant, it belongs in the resume. Train yourself to look for results. Remember, you don't need computer printouts to verify your results. Your own honest estimate is sufficient. If asked about it during an interview, just describe how you arrived at the figure and then go into more detail concerning how you accomplished it. Results sell you.

I've developed a simple technique which will help you identify your results as you write your job sketches. As you list a duty or a project, add the words *which*, or *which resulted in*, and then ask yourself what the duty or project resulted in. For example, "Wrote an office procedures manual" becomes, "Wrote an office procedures manual *which* decreased training time and billing errors." After you've taken time to quantify the results and to explain it more accurately, it will become, "Wrote an office procedures manual which decreased training time of new employees by 25% and reduced billing errors over 30%."

Later, after completing your job sketches, go through the process one more time. Review each duty and project to see if you forgot something as you were writing.

The words *which* and *which resulted in* force you to take all of your activities and accomplishments to their logical conclusion. With each duty or function you list, ask yourself whether you did it as well or better than others. If better, ask yourself how you know. This process will lead you to the logical end result. You should keep going back until you have determined what the most basic result is. Once you've identified all of the results from a particular experience, you can then determine which ones will have the most impact in your resume.

The problem I've observed is that people are often quite satisfied to come up with just one result from a duty or project. Many times, however, three or more results are actually lurking in that project just waiting to be discovered. Each one is important. Even if not all of your results get into your resume, they can become highly valuable in interviews.

When describing an accomplishment, be sure to include concrete information about its effect. Don't stop short. People often write in a way which they think demonstrates a result, but does not. For example, one person wrote, "Developed a scheduling system to better schedule production and reduce late deliveries." Through the use of the word "to" the person is merely implying that the *goal* was to improve scheduling and decrease late shipments. The statement does not tell us for sure that it was accomplished. Look what happens when we add *which*: "Developed a better scheduling system *which* improved production scheduling and virtually eliminated late deliveries." This is a stronger statement. There is now no doubt that the new system accomplished its goal and had a real impact on the operation.

Don't assume that just because a result does not come to mind immediately, that there is no result. People are often amazed when they go over their job sketches a second time, or when a friend helps out, that there were many more results than were initially visible.

Virtually all projects which had a successful conclusion contain at least one result. Some duties, however, do not have results; you simply did the work but did it no better and no worse than others. Still, you need to pause as you look over each of your duties from all of your jobs and ask yourself whether there could be a result hiding in there. The more you find, the more interviews you'll get, and with those interviews you'll sell yourself to the fullest.

CALCULATING RESULTS

To make the most out of your results you need to know how to quantify them. One reason we don't see more statistics in resumes is that people don't know how to calculate results, and then don't know how to use or describe them to their best effect. Usually all it takes is simple arithmetic and a little logic. I'm going to show you the methods for calculating percentages. Try to follow along, but in case it gets confusing don't worry, there are people out there who can help you. If you are at least able to pull some estimates together, you can locate friends or relatives who can help you in this critical area. I work with statistics frequently, but I still have to think twice before I can remember how to do the calculations. So, let's begin.

In the process of calculating results the first step is to identify all benefits, whether it was something improved, increased, or decreased. Start with the assumption that if you can identify it, you can quantify it. Quantifying results may require some guesstimating, but you can do it.

Review your job sketches to see what clues they might give you. Were there any functions that were left off the sketches that you now think might be valuable? Were there any projects that were not mentioned in your sketches? If a project achieved its goal, it almost assuredly had a result. That result can be quantified. Even if you think a particular result was too small to mention in the resume, still spend some time with it because it might be helpful in an interview. Since you are going to discuss a lot of things in interviews that are not included in your resume, you need lots of additional experiences to discuss. Being able to quantify them will enable you to score points.

EXAMPLES

Determining An Average Annual Increase

Often a person will bring about improvements over a period of several years. A good way to express this figure in a resume is to show the annual increase. Selling something would be a typical example. The following example shows how one client used an increase in sales to its best effect.

Susan increased sales in her territory over a five year period. Sales the year prior to her coming to the territory were $200,000. Her first year she increased sales to $240,000, then $275,000, then $300,000, then $310,000, and finally $350,000. Her first year increase was 20% since her increase of $40,000 is 20% of $200,000.

Mathematically it is figured this way:
$240,000 - 200,000 = $40,000
$40,000 \div 200,000 = .20$ or 20%

The second year her increase was 14%:
$275,000 - $240,000 = $35,000
$35,000 \div 240,000 = 14\%$

The third year the increase was 9%, the fourth 3% (a recession year), and the fifth 13%.

Over the five years she increased sales 75%. To get the average annual increase add the increases from each year and total them (20+14+9+3+13 = 59). Then divide by the five years to get the figure (59 ÷ 5 years = 11.8%) of an 11.8% average annual increase. For a resume it would be rounded off to 12%, or in the resume it could be stated, "Increased sales an average of 12% per year." Although she increased sales a total of 75% you cannot divide 75 by 5 to get the average annual increase.

Once the figures have been determined, a decision has to be made as to the strongest way to present the information. Sometimes the best way is simply to present the raw figures. In this case it would be, "In five years took sales in the territory from $200,000 to $350,000." If those figures did not have the impact she wanted she could say, "Took over a mature territory and increased sales 75% in five years," or "During a serious economic downturn in the region, increased sales an average of 12% per year."

Simple Increases

Simple increases might be figured according to the following method: In 1990 advertising revenue for a magazine had been $2,560,000. By the end of 1992 it had increased to $3,180,000. The percent of increase is 24% (3,180,000 - 2,560,000 = 620,000; 620,000 ÷ 2,560,000 = .242 or rounded off to 24%)

Simple Decreases

Simple decreases can be figured and expressed similar to the example below: A manufacturing supervisor reduced rejects (parts which did not meet specifications and were therefore rejected by quality control) from a rate of 6% to 2%. On resumes people often miscalculate such figures and might report that they reduced rejects by 4%, simply subtracting 2 from 6 and getting 4. Going from 6% to 2% actually represents a 67% reduction in rejects, however. The proper way to calculate this is 6 - 2 = 4; 4 ÷ 6 = .6666 or 67%.

Another common problem occurs if something was reduced from say 15 to 7. We'll say that the average daily absenteeism in a department has been reduced from 15 people per day to 7. Some will subtract 7 from 15 getting 8; then dividing 8 by 7 getting 1.14, which they translate into 114%. On the resume it might read, "Reduced absenteeism 114%." But nothing can ever be reduced by more than 100%, or to be more accurate, 99.9999%. Reducing something from 15 to 7 equals 53% (15 - 7 = 8; 8 ÷ 15 = .53) Logic tells you that absenteeism was cut by a little more than half so you know it will be slightly above a 50% decrease.

Large Increases

With large increases you must be careful when calculating percentages. Let's say production in a plant went from 10,000 units per year to 30,000 over a five-year period. It is easy to see that units tripled, so one would tend to say that production increased 300%. The problem is that it actually represents a 200% increase. Going from 10,000 to 20,000 was a 100% increase, and going from 20,000 to 30,000 was another 100%, for a total of 200%.

If calculating numbers is still difficult, don't simply decide not to include your results—get help. Those who know how to calculate such things will enjoy helping you.

ASSISTED IN

If you feel uncomfortable taking primary responsibility for a project, you can use the phrases, *instrumental in, key person in, played a key role in*, or *played an important role in*. It might read, "Played a key role in implementing a management-by-objectives program which increased productivity 14%."

In resumes I often see the phrase *assisted in*. I rarely use it because it tends to dilute the person's actual contribution. For example, Fred wrote "Assisted in developing a quality control program which reduced rejected circuit boards

24%." In this case, the other person working on the program was a peer who contributed less to the success of the program than Fred. A more appropriate description would be, "Developed a quality control program which reduced rejected circuit boards by 24%." During an interview Fred could explain that he was the primary, but not the sole developer of the program.

JOB DESCRIPTIONS

Job descriptions must be concise but complete. A common problem of resumes is that the job descriptions are too short and do not adequately describe duties, experience, level of responsibility, or accomplishments. As you begin, don't be concerned about limiting the resume to one page. While it is often assumed that a resume should be no longer than one page, my studies have verified that so long as it is well-written and concise, a two-page resume is perfectly acceptable, and for many people, essential.

Once you've completed your job sketches with duties, projects, and results, you're ready to write a rough draft of your resume. Start by stating your objective. Although the wording of the objective may change later, you know that everything which appears in the final draft must demonstrate your capability of performing the work defined by your objective.

Begin by reviewing your job sketch for your current or most recent position. What are the most important things an employer should know about the job? Try to eliminate some of the less important duties, but don't worry if your first draft seems a little too long. When you rewrite, you will be able to identify points that should be deleted or summarized more briefly.

From your resume the employer should be able to sense your positive attributes, such as diligence, efficiency, cooperation, effectiveness, and intelligence. Your duties must be adequately covered so that the employer will recognize the full range of your experience. The types of positions you will be seeking will determine which duties should be given the most attention. If employers will have no interest in a certain duty, it should be mentioned only briefly or not at all. Describing your duties effectively will help employers immediately realize that you are ready for more responsibility. Results and accomplishments will be the frosting on the cake that makes the employer want to meet you.

The examples below demonstrate these points. Read the job descriptions as the person had originally written them, then read the revision. Notice how the revisions were made and how they affected the impact of the information being presented.

Compare the following two versions of one woman's employment section. Notice how in the first version her descriptions are concise, but lacking in detail compared to the second version. Her second version provides a fuller, more vivid description of her experiences.

Also, as you study the revised job description, ask yourself what you know about the person that you didn't before. The revised job description is longer, but it had to be to adequately describe what she had done and to give an employer enough details to fully appreciate her capabilities.

Version #1

EMPLOYMENT

Employer	Wiggins Sportswear 1991-Present
Position	Marketing Coordinator
Responsibilities	Coordinate the entire clothing program
	Creating and utilizing Lotus spread sheets for marketing, production, and finance projections
	Market research
	Coordinating advertising with publication
	Work with outside contractors on special projects
	Fabric and notion research/purchasing
	Calculated preliminary and final costing of garment
	Approved bills relating to the clothing program
Employer	Broadway Department Store 1990 to 1991
Position	Salesperson
Responsibilities	Sales
	Interior layout and display
	Opening and closing the department
	Handling customer complaints and problems
	Issuing merchandise transfers

Version #2

EMPLOYMENT

Wiggins Sportswear, San Diego, California 4/91 to present

MARKETING COORDINATOR - Coordinate the production and marketing functions for a new line of active sportswear. Came into the project when it was two months behind schedule and in serious trouble. Worked with the designer to select colors, designs, and fabrics. Purchased fabric and accessories. Negotiated with two garment manufacturers to produce small lots, thus reducing the required unit sales to reach a break-even point. Worked out schedule arrangements with manufacturers and authorized any changes in specifications. Line was introduced on schedule with final costs one-third lower than originally projected.

Coordinated the production of the annual sales catalog. Designed order forms, verified prices, and consulted with graphics artists and printers. Had authority to make all necessary changes.

Set up the company's first computerized systems, using Lotus and other software to provide the first accurate year-to-date sales figures, as well as highly useful marketing, financial, and manufacturing projections.

Broadway Department Stores, San Diego, California 9/90 to 4/91

SALESPERSON - Sold women's clothing and had interior layout and display responsibilities. Selected as Employee of the Month for December in this store of approximately 190 employees. Selected on the basis of sales, favorable comments from customers, and taking on added responsibilities.

The revised version is slightly longer than the original, but because it provides more background, you get a clearer picture of her capabilities. By mentioning a project that was behind schedule and in serious trouble, her ability to complete it on schedule and under budget makes the accomplishment especially meaningful. Her original resume contains only a brief list of duties and gives you no information regarding whether she had been successful. The revised job description conveys a sense of her potential. It shows that she was given a lot of responsibility and that she handled it well. It suggests to the reader that she has some very interesting stories to tell about her experiences at Wiggins; but those details will be saved for the interview.

The experience at Broadway did not receive as much space because she has no intention of returning to retail work. The experience does, however, demonstrate valuable background which pertains directly to her career in marketing. It is important that she was able to demonstrate that she was successful even though it was a short-term job. Simply listing her duties provides no clues about the quality of her work, and could lead an employer to believe that she did not do well. Mentioning that she was employee-of-the month proves that she was valuable. By mentioning the basis for the award—sales, comments from customers, and taking on responsibility—she demonstrates to the employer that she was judged outstanding in each category.

As you write your resume, look for ways to tell your story that convey your value and your successes. Even if you were fired from a job it is possible to show that you were valuable. Do that by stressing what you did well; simply ignore your problem areas.

The next job description comes from a youth counselor. One of his earlier positions was as supervisor for a parks department. In the first job description you get nothing but a dull list of duties. He is a very interesting person with an excellent background, but the first version of the job description fails to convey this.

Version #1

> SUPERVISOR — Portland Park Department, Portland, Oregon 5/88-7/89. Overall responsibility for staff, facility, and program at a neighborhood community center; supervising, hiring, training, and recruitment; program planning, implementation, and evaluation; record keeping, budgeting, grant writing, and analyses; work with schools, local, state, and federal agencies in a variety of capacities; direct service including teaching, training, and work with adults and youth in social, educational, cultural and athletic programs; community and business presentations.

As you read the revised job description below you'll get the sense that here is a person worth meeting. There's a personal touch evident in this version that is lacking in version 1.

Version #2

Portland Park Department, Portland, Oregon 5/88 to 7/89

> SUPERVISOR - Developed and promoted social, educational, cultural, and athletics programs for the community. Contracted with consultants, instructors,

and coaches to provide instruction in dozens of subjects and activities at the Browser Community Center. Interviewed and hired instructors, and conducted follow-up assessments to ensure top-quality instruction. Personally taught several courses and coached athletic teams. In three years tripled participation at the Center and took it from a $1,400 deficit to a $12,000 profit.

The revised job description presents a person who has goals and ideals. It's clear that he really cared about what he did: he got involved, he took action, and he got results. This more vital, caring tone is created by using action verbs like *developed* and *promoted.* You feel the action. The programs that the community really wanted didn't exist so he went out and *developed* them. Since people don't come flocking to programs they don't know about, he *promoted* them. And he not only planned programs he also taught some. He even coached several athletic teams. This demonstrates that he is an action-oriented person in good physical shape. The ultimate result of all this effort was a tripling of participation, yet his original job description did not even mention it.

Writing a top-quality resume takes time. From these examples you can see why. Also, describing oneself in positive terms is difficult for most people, yet it is necessary. Write your job descriptions and then keep editing until they approach the examples you find in this book. Everyone can do it, but it will take time and thought. Just remember that taking the time will pay off in interviews and job offers. And that's what you're after.

EMPLOYMENT FORMAT

The format you choose for your employment section can make a big difference in the visual appeal and readability of your resume. I have tested formats extensively and find that the format below is the one that most employers prefer.

EMPLOYMENT

Balboa's Steak House 7/89 to Present

GENERAL MANAGER, Miami, Florida, 10/91 to Present. Took over a troubled restaurant which had had six managers in two years and had incurred losses each month during that time. Resolved serious morale problems, instituted an effective training program, and redesigned the menu. During the first nine months increased lunch revenue 38% and dinner 29%. Losses were eliminated within two months and a consistent profit margin of 14% has been maintained.

ASSISTANT MANAGER, Ft. Lauderdale, Florida, 7/89 to 10/91. Redesigned the menu and helped introduce wine sales. Provided extensive staff training which enabled the restaurant to become number one in wine sales in the chain of twenty restaurants. Purchased all food and supplies.

Saga, Inc., Tallahassee, Florida 9/87 to 6/89

STUDENT MANAGER - For this college cafeteria, prepared food, scheduled part-time workers, purchased supplies, and oversaw lunch and dinner lines.

Following are sample treatments of various types of work histories. One of them should conform fairly closely to your own.

Same Company, Three Positions, All in the Same City

EMPLOYMENT

Douglas Bolt Company, St. Louis, Missouri 8/79 to Present
<u>V. P. PURCHASING</u>, 7/88 to Present. ....

....

<u>DIRECTOR OF PURCHASING</u>, 5/85 to 7/88. ....

....

<u>MANAGER, STOCK PARTS PURCHASING</u>, 8/79 to 5/85. ....

....

....

Same Company, Three Positions, Three Different Cities

EMPLOYMENT

Horizon Gear 8/78 to Present
<u>REGIONAL SALES MANAGER</u>, Houston, Texas 7/89 to Present ....

....

<u>DISTRICT SALES MANAGER</u>, Atlanta, Georgia 3/85 to 7/89. ....

....

<u>SALES REPRESENTATIVE</u>, Little Rock, Arkansas 8/78 to 3/85. ....

....

In a situation like this you might want to indicate where the headquarters is located. In that case you would show it as: Horizon Gear, Chicago, Illinois 8/78 to Present.

One Position With Each Company

EMPLOYMENT

Shannon Electric, Garden City, Michigan 5/87 to Present
<u>INSTALLER</u> - ....

....

....

Preston Electric, Detroit, Michigan 6/84 to 5/87
<u>INSTALLER</u> - ....

....

....

Work for a Subsidiary or Division of a Major Company

EMPLOYMENT

Antac, Inc., Subsidiary of A&R Industries, Buffalo, New York 5/77 to Present

It is seldom necessary to specify the parent company. If you choose to, however, this is the easiest way to do it.

PRIOR EMPLOYMENT

A prior employment section is particularly useful if you are trying to shorten your resume or de-emphasize your earlier jobs. A prior employment section is an effective way to explain how you've gotten to where you are, without making the employer spend a lot of time reading about it. Other titles for this section include *Previous Employment, Prior Experience,* or *Additional Experience.*

The example below shows the most commonly used format for the prior employment section. The Assistant Purchasing Manager position is the sixth job description position on his two-page resume.

> ASSISTANT PURCHASING MANAGER - 3/77-5/78. Set up and developed an inventory control program to reduce inventory and operating costs. Over the next year reduced inventory by 20%.
>
> PRIOR EMPLOYMENT
>
> Counterperson, Zenith Electronics, Los Angeles, CA 3/76-3/77
> Expediter, Hughes Aircraft, Los Angeles, CA 4/74-3/76
> Parts Manager, High Lift Equipment, Long Beach, CA 9/72-4/74

In the example above, the person has included title, name of company, city and state, and dates. Generally this information would be included. In the remaining examples, however, you will see how personal taste varies. I generally include city and state, but if it seems like unnecessary detail for some distant jobs, feel free to leave city and state off.

In the example below, the person provides the job title, name of employer, and dates, but not the city and state.

Example (starting with the person's fifth position on a two-page resume):

> National Computer Stores, Spokane, WA 5/86-6/87
>
> SALES REPRESENTATIVE - Sold hardware and software for this IBM authorized dealer. Consistently exceeded monthly sales goals.
>
> PRIOR EXPERIENCE
>
> Food Service Specialist, Johnson Nursing Home (8/84-5/86); Cook, Boyd's Restaurant (7/82-8/84); Cook, Iron Pig Restaurant (6/81-7/82)

In the following example the individual did not feel it necessary to give specific time periods or list the names of employers.

Example (starting with the person's seventh position on a two-page resume):

> Xytelin Electronics, Mountain View, California 1967 to 1969
>
> INTERNAL AUDITOR - Discovered weaknesses in the parts inventory control procedures and recommended remedial action. Responsible for quarterly and yearly audits.
>
> Prior Experience, 1960 to 1967: Airline Internal Auditor, Cost Clerk, Production Scheduler.

In the example below, the person listed dates, but did not list employers.

Example (starting with fifth position on a one-page resume):

Department of Social Services, Winston-Salem, North Carolina 3/70 to 4/71

<u>ELIGIBILITY SPECIALIST</u> - Assisted families in obtaining all of the Medicaid benefits they were legally entitled to. Provided psychological and social support services.

Previous Experience:

Cashier/Hostess 1/69 to 3/70; Sales Clerk 6/68 to 1/69; Long Distance Operator 7/66 to 6/68.

The remaining examples will simply give you more options.

PRIOR EMPLOYMENT

<u>CASHIER</u> - Pay Less Drugs, Elgin, Illinois 5/66 to 11/67
<u>CASHIER</u> - Don's Rexall, Carbondale, Illinois 4/65 to 5/66
<u>STOCKER</u> - Jewel Foodstores, Peoria, Illinois 9/62 to 3/65

<u>Previous Employment</u>

Truck Driver (1963-1967); Warehouseman (1963); Machine Repairman (1962-1963)

Sometimes a person will choose not to describe all the positions with a particular company, especially the first company employed with. The person below has worked for Boeing since 1972.

<u>PRODUCTION INSPECTOR</u> - 3/80-4/82. Performed final interior, flight line modification, and wing line inspections on Boeing 767 aircraft. Verified that the production department installed assemblies according to specifications.

Prior Boeing positions: Assistant Production Inspector 4/77-3/80; Tooling Inspector 5/75-4/77; Jig Builder 3/72-5/75.

TIPS FOR WRITING EFFECTIVE EMPLOYMENT HISTORIES

The Job Description Summary

It is often helpful to begin your job description with a summary, or an overview of what you did. It typically consists of a string of items and is very effective in helping a reader quickly understand what you did. A job description summary might look something like this:

Research databases and create surveys to analyze trends and to identify opportunities for improving customer support strategies.

For this sign manufacturing company, prepared financial statements and supervised payroll, billing, and accounts receivable personnel.

Directly responsible for all phases of investment analyses, development, and property management of properties.

39

Coordinated all aspects of the Early Childhood Special Education Program, including hiring and training of staff and support professionals, and the design and implementation of curriculum.

Supervised and trained a lending staff of four in credit and business development efforts.

Interviewed, counseled, and educated patients and families preceding and following open-heart surgery.

Even before learning the details in the rest of each job description, the reader has a good overview of what the person did. It is fine to start off with "Responsible for ..." but don't overuse it. Notice that only one of our examples started with "responsible for ..."

Several Jobs Within One Company

Sometimes a person will have five or six changes in job title within one company, during a 4–6 year period. Frequently the person was promoted and kept all or most of the previous responsibilities, and then added others. To describe each job separately would be redundant and unnecessary. Look for any two jobs which were *essentially* the same, and treat them as one.

What To Call Your Employment Section

There are a variety of words and phrases you can use to head your employment section: *Employment, Employment Experience, Work Experience, Professional Experience, Employment History, Work History,* and *Experience* are all good terms. I typically use *Employment,* and sometimes *Professional Experience.* Each of the terms is a good term so pick the one that feels right for you.

Dates

Dates should be used on nearly all resumes. If you have no time gaps between jobs or short gaps, you should usually use the months and years you started and left. If you have long gaps, you can indicate the year you started and the year you left.

When to use month and year (example: 5/87-3/93):

1. No gaps in employment.
2. Short gaps of less than five months.
3. One gap of over five months several years ago.

Employers prefer to see month and year and may wonder if you are hiding anything by omitting months. On the other hand, if you reveal long gaps between jobs, employers may question your perseverance and dedication. With this in mind, decide what is best for you.

Location Of The Job

Your resume should indicate the city and state you actually work in, not the location of your company's national headquarters. If you work out of your home, include your city as your location; if you live in a suburb, include either the name of the suburb or the more familiar name of the large city you live near.

Clarifying What Your Company Does

If you work for General Motors, General Electric, or Boeing, there is no need to explain what the company does. If your employer is Eastside Masonry Products, it is also unnecessary to elaborate because the company name explains its type of business. If you work for SLRC Corporation, though, you may want to explain in the resume. Handle it this way:

SLRC Corporation, Montgomery, Alabama 5/88 to Present

SALES REP - For this producer of food additives, opened up a new territory and have increased sales an average of 32% each year.

Or this way:

CBD, Inc., Boston, Massachusetts 1988 to 1992

SALES REP - Increased sales 20% each year for CBD, the Northeast's second largest distributor of electronic components.

Scope Of The Job

The scope of a job includes such things as the products and services of the company, size of company in terms of gross sales, the size of your department in terms of people and dollar budget, the budget you personally work with, and the number of people supervised. It is useful to include the scope of the job if doing so will clarify your level of responsibility or any other key point. To describe the scope of a job you might say, "Managed all finance, accounting, and data processing functions for this $80 million manufacturer of outdoor equipment." Or you might say, "Supervised a staff of four supervisors and managed a department budget of $1.2 million."

How Much Detail And Space Should You Give?

Principles (not laws) to keep in mind: 1) Your current or most recent position is described in the greatest detail as long as it is similar to the type of job you are seeking. Each preceding job is described in slightly less detail. 2) If the job you held three jobs ago is closest to what you're seeking, devote the most detail to it. 3) Jobs held many years ago and jobs that have nothing to do with what you want to do in the future can usually be described in two or three lines, or handled through "Previous Employment."

How Far Back Should Your Descriptions Go?

If you are a college graduate, go back as far as your first full-time job after graduation. If you went to work right after high school, go back to your first full-time job. If you've had a lot of jobs, you can write about your four to six most recent positions, but also include a previous employment section, which merely lists prior positions without descriptions.

Although some of your earlier jobs may not be applicable to your current occupation, employers are still curious about where you've been. Such positions require only a very straightforward two- or three-line description of duties. Or, you might present this information in a prior employment section where you would include your job title, employer, and dates, but would not use any job descriptions.

If you feel certain that it would be detrimental to include all of your jobs, simply do not list those in the most distant past. If you do so be sure not to show dates for education, or any other section which would give away your age or would indicate that some positions are missing.

Current Job Is Less Valuable Than A Prior Job

Generally, it's wise to devote less space to a current, but less valuable job, and more space to an earlier, more relevant job. Another option can be effective: you can separate your experience into two segments, calling one "Related Experience" and the other "Additional Experience."

The related experience section would come first and would generally have the greatest detail. Except for the fact that you have two employment sections, Related Experience and Additional Experience, it is a standard reverse chronological resume. Within each category you should list jobs in reverse chronological order and show the correct dates. Showing the information in this way makes it clear to the employer that even though you are using an atypical format, all jobs have been covered. More importantly, it means that the employer will read your relevant experience first.

Special Projects/Activities/Awards

A SPECIAL PROJECTS SECTION can be especially effective for a person with valuable experiences which did not occur on a job. Career changers, recent college graduates, and women reentering the work force can benefit from including a special projects section. The section can also be labeled *Selected Projects, Accomplishments, Achievements, Activities, Projects, Noteworthy Projects, Selected Accomplishments,* or *Noteworthy Accomplishments.* Volunteer experiences with clubs and associations, as well as special projects performed as part of a course, can be presented in this section.

Use these examples as guides to determine whether a special projects section will strengthen your resume.

In the example below, the person had been at home rearing children since 1973. Her special projects section helps make it obvious that she is very capable and energetic.

SPECIAL PROJECTS

As President of PTA, increased parent participation by 26% and funds raised by 34% over the previous year. (1989)

As a United Way fundraising team leader, exceeded the quota by 22%. Honored at banquet as Team Leader of the Year. (1982)

A project or accomplishment seldom requires over 45 words—20–30 words is usually best. Do not try to describe the project in detail—concentrate on results. When writing out each accomplishment in the first draft, feel free to describe it in 50-70 words. Then rewrite it by concentrating on results and include just enough detail so that the reader will understand what you did. Save all other details for an interview. List the projects and accomplishments in reverse chronological order and include the year.

The person below had been active in community affairs for several years and was seeking the directorship of a city-run agency for youth. His employment experience alone would not have even gotten him an interview.

SELECTED PROJECTS

Wrote news articles and special features for *Troy Herald, Outdoor News,* and *College Forum.* (1988-1991)

Lobbied for and obtained Troy city council support for three community parks. Played a key role on the planning committee and helped obtain matching federal funds for this "model project." (1989)

Participated as a guest expert on disadvantaged youth for a public affairs radio talk show. (1988)

Organized a basketball camp for disadvantaged youth in Troy, and obtained $55,000 in corporate and city funding. Got four coaches and seven college players from three surrounding colleges to donate one week to the program. (1987)

Below is a special projects section used by a 40-year old woman reentering the work force after completing an MBA. She had held one part-time research position in the last ten years.

SPECIAL PROJECTS

Developed and coordinated budgets for YWCA and Big Sisters Program, Newark, 1983-1986.

Developed highly successful parenting, exercise, and personal growth programs for the Newark YWCA, 1982-1985.

Planned and coordinated programs for the League of Women Voters, Newark, 1981-1983.

Chaired "The Mayor's Conference on Aging," Newark, 1982.

The following example was written by a teacher who was seeking a position in private business and needed to demonstrate non-classroom abilities.

SPECIAL PROJECTS

Interned for Omaha National Bank during the summer of 1992. Received assignments working with retail credit, corporate loans, and trust departments. Developed and completed a survey which determined customer needs. (1992)

Supervised the senior class store which sells school supplies, tickets, jackets, and sweaters. The store maintained a profit each year under my management, something it had never done previously. (1986-1992)

Supervised the research and publication of the Omaha "Volunteer Directory," which helped draw new volunteers into dozens of agencies. (1987)

Developed an intern program to allow students to work in nursing homes and schools for the retarded. Dozens of students gained new skills and several now work in geriatrics. (1985-1992)

Organized record-breaking blood drives and won trophies each year from 1984 to 1988. No other school came close to matching the high percentage of students who willingly donated blood. (1984-1988)

Sometimes other section titles such as "Honors and Awards," "Publications" or "Activities" will work better than "Special Projects." This recently graduated college student had only one special project to describe so she combined it with an award and called the section, "Awards and Publications."

AWARDS AND PUBLICATIONS

Chairperson, Task Force on Teaching Quality. Investigated teaching evaluation methods at Reed College and published position paper which helped initiate change in tenure decision policies. (1991)

Senior Class Inspirational Person-of-the-Year Award. (1987)

Licenses/Certificates

ANY LICENSES you hold that are necessary or valuable in the field you are seeking should be listed. Be selective, though. Only list certificates and licenses which are relevant to the new position. Mentioning a real estate license when you want to be a purchasing agent for a tool manufacturer would not add to your qualifications and might cause the employer to wonder whether your preferred career was selling real estate or purchasing.

LICENSES

First Class FCC Radio Telephone Operator (1979)
Commercial Instrument Pilot rating (1978) 840 hours flight time
Private Pilot (1977)

(Electronics technologist and sales rep who flies to see customers)

LICENSES

General Electrical Administrator Certificate, California (1982)
Journeyman Electrician License - California, Nevada, Arizona (1981)
Commercial - Instrument Pilots License (1980)

(Electrician who would like to do some flying for his employer)

CERTIFICATION

Standard Elementary and Secondary, Idaho. Lifetime 1986.

(Teacher)

LICENSES

FCC, 1981

(Broadcast journalist who needs a Federal Communications Commission license to operate on the air)

Associations/Memberships/ Professional Affiliations

INCLUDING ASSOCIATIONS and memberships can demonstrate you are keeping up to date in your profession and that you have developed useful contacts. For the person making a career change, listing memberships can demonstrate you are serious in making a shift in career direction. Use these categories only if they are relevant and will help you. An engineer might use the following:

PROFESSIONAL AFFILIATIONS

American Chemical Society (1982-Present)
American Institute of Chemical Engineers (1980-Present)

Belonging to associations and professional organizations may mean only that you paid the annual dues, or it could mean that you are active in the organization. If you want a one-page resume and you are three lines over, affiliations can be sacrificed. The section provides interesting, but not usually crucial, information. List any offices held. The examples below can be used as guides. Do not list an affiliation unless you believe its adds credibility or value to your resume. Organizations you are no longer a member of or no longer active in are usually not mentioned, unless you held an office.

Use the examples below as guides for presenting information regarding affiliations.

MEMBERSHIPS

Pacific Northwest Personnel Managers Association (1986-Present)
American Society for Personnel Administration (1985-Present)

ASSOCIATIONS

Homebuilders Association, member 1979 to present
    Officer 1985 to present
    Associate of the Year 1983
Board of Realtors, member 1975 to present
    Chairperson, Legislative Committee 1985-87
    Chairperson, Political Affairs and Education 1979-81

ASSOCIATIONS

Southeast Community Alcohol Center
    President, Board of Directors (1987)
    Member of Board (1977-Present)
Northwest Nurses Society on Chemical Dependency
    Treasurer (1987-1989)
    Member (1983-Present)

Publications

A LIST OR DESCRIPTION of publications can be used to demonstrate expertise in a particular field. Listing publications can also demonstrate your abilities in researching, interviewing, and writing. If you are widely published, include only your most relevant articles.

Publications include articles in newspapers, newsmagazines, trade journals, professional journals, school papers, anthologies, or just about anything in printed form with a circulation over 50.

PUBLICATIONS

"The Arts in Seattle," *The Weekly*, July 27, 1992
"Marketing A Symphony," *The Conductor*, April, 1988
"Will Bach Be Back?" *Symphony News*, November, 1986

PUBLICATIONS

"The Dismantling of Student Loans," University of Kentucky
   Daily, 1992
"Tenureship Under Attack," University of Kentucky Daily, 1992
"An Hour With G. Gordon Liddy," University of Kentucky Daily, 1991

PUBLICATIONS

"Robots and Production," *Chrysler Employees Newsletter*, 1990
"Automation and Its Impact on Blue Collar Workers," paper presented at the annual Industrial Psychologists Symposium, 1988

If you are going to use a special projects section and have only one publication, you could include the publication with your projects. For example:

SPECIAL PROJECTS

Volunteer Probation Counselor, King County - 1986 to Present
Authored an environmental article published in *Ecojournal* - 1990

Personal Information

USING A PERSONAL DATA SECTION has become outdated. During the past 15 years resumes have gone from virtually always having a personal data section, which included such information as age, marital status, height and weight, and health status, to an almost total extinction of such a section. Women began excluding it from their resumes about 15 years ago and men have followed suit. Equal Employment Opportunity legislation also helped hasten the trend. It was never a very helpful section, but it was traditional to include it.

In the 1930s and 40s it was traditional to include religion and the national origin of parents in a personal data section. It was assumed that employers wanted to know and therefore it should be included. Actually, including this information merely gave employers greater opportunity to discriminate. My recommendation is to exclude it as a section. Sometimes, however, it is useful to use a section called "Personal." It can be used to cover bonding, security clearances, citizenship, willingness to relocate or travel, and any other aspects that might not fit in other categories of a resume.

Bonding

Mention you are bondable if your type of work requires it. Essentially, anyone who does not have a prison record is bondable. Bonding is a type of insurance employers take out on employees who handle large amounts of money. If an employee heads to Mexico with thousands of dollars, the employer collects from the bonding company.

Security Clearance

Many people in the military, and civilians working on military projects, have been given security clearances, typically "Secret" or "Top Secret." After leaving the military, it quickly lapses and a new investigation is conducted before reestablishing a security clearance. By including your security clearance, however, you're really saying, "My honesty and integrity were verified by a very thorough investigation; you, too, can trust me." If you held a security clearance within the last ten years, it may be helpful to mention it. Indicate the years it was active. An alternative is to mention your security clearance in your military job description.

Citizenship

Include this information only if you believe an employer might question your citizenship, or if you especially want to let an employer know that you are a U. S. citizen. If you are not a U. S. citizen, you may want to state "Permanent

Resident" or indicate your status. There is no need to specify "Naturalized U.S. Citizen;" simply say "U.S. Citizen," or possibly "U.S. Citizen since 1978." Other terms could be "Canadian Citizen since 1959," or "Valid Green Card."

Health

I suggest not listing your health status. Everyone always states "Excellent Health" anyway, so it really has no purpose.

Relocation

If you are willing to relocate and you are contacting national or regional firms, state this in the personal section or merely state at the bottom of the resume, "Willing to Relocate."

Activities

Whether you should include activities or interests is open to debate. Some insist that anything not demonstrating work-related skills or background should be excluded. Others feel a discussion of activities can become an interesting topic of conversation and helps the candidate to be remembered. Both sides make good points. I sometimes include activities because it can make a person seem more real. Select your interests and activities carefully; use only those in which you really are active. Jogging is an excellent activity to include, but don't list it if you run only occasionally.

With each activity you select, ask yourself what impact it will have on an employer. Unless you believe most employers will view it positively, do not include the activity.

Give a consistent picture of yourself. Decide what image you want to convey and then select the appropriate activities. Office workers are wise to state interests that indicate a highly energetic personality.

ACTIVITIES

Strong involvement in marathon running, skiing, and scuba diving.

❖

ACTIVITIES

Actively involved in golf, jogging, and camping.

❖

INTERESTS

Enjoy making exotic breads, creating stained glass windows, and dance exercise activities.

Saying It With Impact

PRODUCING IMPACT through your words is crucial in a resume. Knowing which action verbs, adjectives, and adverbs to use and how to use them will significantly strengthen your resume. This section will cover all of these points and show you how to bring it together in your resume.

ACTION WORDS

A resume should sound alive and vigorous. Using action verbs helps achieve that feeling. "I changed the filing system" lacks punch and doesn't really indicate if the system was improved. "I *reorganized* and *simplified* the filing system" sounds much better and provides more accurate information.

Review the sentences below to get a feel for action words. Then quickly scan the words in the following list and check any you think you might want to use in your resume. Don't try to force them in; use them when they feel right.

Conducted long-range master planning for the Portland water supply system.

Monitored enemy radio transmissions, analyzed information, and identified enemy strategic and tactical capabilities.

Planned, staffed, and organized the intramural sports program for this 1,200-student college.

Produced daily reports for each trial and made sure documents and evidence were handled properly.

Presented seminars to entry-level secretaries and worked to increase the professionalism of secretaries in the county system.

Improved the coordination, imagination, and pantomime techniques of adults through mime and dance training.

Allocated and dispensed federal moneys to nine counties as board member of the CETA Advisory Board.

ACTION VERBS

Accomplished	Adjusted	Apprised	Assigned
Achieved	Administered	Approved	Assimilated
Acquired	Advanced	Arbitrated	Assisted
Acted as	Advised	Arranged	Assured
Activated	Allocated	Articulated	Attained
Active in	Analyzed	Ascertained	Attended
Adapted	Applied	Assembled	Audited
Addressed	Appraised	Assessed	Augmented

Authored	Culminated in	Executed	Inspired
Authorized	Cultivated	Expanded	Installed
Balanced	Customized	Expedited	Instigated
Blended	Dealt	Experienced	Instilled
Bought	Decided	Experimented	Instituted
Brought	Decreased	Explained	Instructed
Brought about	Defined	Explored	Insured
Budgeted	Delegated	Expressed	Integrated
Built	Delivered	Extracted	Interfaced
Calculated	Demonstrated	Fabricated	Interpreted
Carried out	Derived	Facilitated	Interviewed
Catalogued	Designated	Familiarized	Introduced
Chaired	Designed	Fashioned	Invented
Clarified	Detected	Filed	Investigated
Classified	Determined	Finalized	Judged
Coached	Developed	Financed	Justified
Collaborated	Devised	Fixed	Kept
Collected	Diagnosed	Followed up	Kindled
Commanded	Directed	Forged	Launched
Commended	Discovered	Forecasted	Led
Communicated	Dispatched	Formed	Lectured
Completed	Dispensed	Formulated	Lifted
Compared	Displayed	Found	Lobbied
Compiled	Dissected	Founded	Localized
Composed	Distributed	Functioned as	Located
Computed	Diverted	Gained	Logged
Conceived	Documented	Gathered	Maintained
Conceptualized	Doubled	Generated	Managed
Condensed	Drafted	Governed	Marketed
Conducted	Dramatized	Graduated	Mastered
Conserved	Earned	Grouped	Maximized
Consolidated	Edited	Guided	Mechanized
Constructed	Educated	Handled	Mediated
Consulted	Eliminated	Harmonized	Merged
Contacted	Employed	Harnessed	Minimized
Contracted	Enacted	Headed	Moderated
Contributed	Encouraged	Hired	Monitored
Controlled	Enforced	Identified	Motivated
Convinced	Engineered	Illustrated	Negotiated
Converted	Enhanced	Imagined	Nominated
Cooperated	Enlarged	Implemented	Observed
Coordinated	Enlisted	Improved	Obtained
Corrected	Ensured	Improvised	Offered
Correlated	Equipped	Increased	Opened
Corresponded	Escalated	Indexed	Operated
Corroborated	Established	Influenced	Optimized
Counseled	Estimated	Informed	Orchestrated
Created	Evaluated	Initiated	Ordered
Critiqued	Examined	Inspected	Organized

Originated	Quadrupled	Revamped	Substituted
Overcame	Questioned	Reversed	Succeeded
Overhauled	Raised	Reviewed	Summarized
Oversaw	Ramrodded	Revised	Supervised
Participated	Realized	Revitalized	Supplied
Perceived	Received	Revived	Supported
Perfected	Recognized	Saved	Surpassed
Performed	Recommended	Scheduled	Surveyed
Persuaded	Reconciled	Screened	Synthesized
Piloted	Recorded	Secured	Systematized
Pioneered	Recruited	Selected	Tabulated
Placed	Rectified	Separated	Taught
Planned	Redesigned	Served	Tested
Played	Reduced	Serviced	Traced
Predicted	Reevaluated	Set up	Trained
Prepared	Referred	Shaped	Transacted
Prescribed	Refined	Shifted	Transcended
Presided	Regulated	Shipped	Transcribed
Presented	Rehabilitated	Simplified	Transferred
Prevented	Related	Sold	Transformed
Printed	Remodeled	Solidified	Translated
Prioritized	Rendered	Solved	Treated
Processed	Reorganized	Sorted	Tripled
Procured	Repaired	Sparked	Underwrote
Produced	Replaced	Spearheaded	Unified
Programmed	Reported	Specified	Updated
Projected	Represented	Spoke	Upgraded
Promoted	Reorganized	Staffed	Utilized
Proposed	Researched	Standardized	Validated
Protected	Reshaped	Started	Verified
Proved	Resolved	Stimulated	Vitalized
Provided	Responded	Straightened	Won
Publicized	Restored	Streamlined	Worked
Published	Resulted in	Strengthened	Wrote
Purchased	Retrieved	Structured	

DESCRIBING RESULTS WITH KEY ACTION VERBS

The typical resume merely lists duties and does little else to sell the person. One of the best ways to sell yourself is to describe accomplishments in terms of *results*. While duties are often represented by phrases such "Responsible for...," results are frequently conveyed by using the verb *developed*. For example, one might say, "Developed a secretary's manual which explained hundreds of procedures and significantly reduced clerical errors." This person's duties were typing, filing, and answering phones, so to show that she stood above the rest, she demonstrated results.

When describing projects and results, one of the best words to use is *develop*. More than any other word, it seems to be so useful and it clearly expresses what a person wants to convey. While *develop* is an excellent word, when used three or four times in a resume it becomes overworked and loses impact. You'll need substitutes. The most common are

Created	Instituted
Designed	Introduced
Established	Set up
Implemented	

Other verbs that may be appropriate substitutes for develop in certain circumstances would be

Built	Fabricated	Originated
Composed	Fashioned	Perfected
Constructed	Formed	Pioneered
Coordinated	Formulated	Planned
Cultivated	Generated	Prepared
Devised	Installed	Produced
Elaborated	Introduced	Refined
Enhanced	Organized	Revamped

Here are examples that demonstrate how to describe results in various situations. In parentheses are words that could have been used instead of *develop*.

Developed (devised, prepared, produced) a creative financing/purchasing package to obtain 1900 acres of prime California farmland.

Pioneered a mime program for gifted children age 8-12.

Developed (designed, established) training programs for new and experienced employees and supervised the new employee orientation program.

Set up apprenticeship programs for five skilled trades at the Physical Plant Department.

Developed and implemented an information and referral service for consumer complaints and human rights issues.

Coordinated the company marketing effort, including advertising and promotions.

VERB TENSES

Describe your current job in the present tense. For all previous jobs, write in the past tense. You may need to describe an event in your current job, such as a project that has already been completed. In that case, use the past tense to describe the project while using the present tense in the remaining portions of your current job.

Example:

STORE MANAGER - 6/90-Present. Oversee total operation of the store, supervise and schedule employees, and complete monthly profit and loss statements. Designed a new inventory system which has saved over $10,000.

Since the inventory system was designed over a year ago, it must be described in the past tense.

USING ADJECTIVES AND ADVERBS

Adjectives and adverbs are words that describe actions and things. Used appropriately, they can enliven a resume and describe more accurately what you did. While using adjectives and adverbs can add sparkle to a resume, if overused, they can actually weaken a phrase. Notice how they change the tone of the sentences below. In each example the second sentence has more impact.

1. Worked with industrial engineers.

    Worked <u>closely and effectively</u> with industrial engineers.

2. Initiate and develop working relations with local, state, and federal agencies.

    Initiate and develop <u>outstanding</u> working relations with local, state, and federal agencies.

3. Establish rapport with customers.

    <u>Quickly</u> establish rapport with customers.

Here are more examples of how to use adjectives and adverbs effectively:

Dealt <u>tactfully</u> and <u>effectively</u> with <u>difficult</u> customers.

Presented technical material in <u>objective</u> and <u>easily understood</u> terms.

<u>Consistently</u> maintained <u>high</u> profit margins on all projects.

<u>Significantly</u> improved communications between nursing administration and staff.

Completed <u>virtually</u> all apartment units ahead of schedule.

<u>Continually</u> streamlined policies and procedures to create a more reasonable work schedule.

A list of adjectives and adverbs is given below. Review the list and check the ones you think may be useful to you. Try to include them but don't force it. Don't use a word or phrase unless it really fits your personality and strengthens your resume. After writing each draft, go back through the list to see if still another word or two might be useful.

accurate/accurately
active/actively
adept/adeptly
advantageously
aggressive/aggressively
all-inclusive/all-inclusively
ambitious/ambitiously
appreciable/appreciably
astute/astutely
attractive/attractively
authoritative/authoritatively
avid/avidly
aware
beneficial/beneficially
broad/broadly

capable/capably
challenging
cohesive/cohesively
competent/competently
complete/completely
comprehensive/comprehensively
conclusive/conclusively
consistent/consistently
constructive/constructively
contagious
continuous/continuously
contributed toward
decidedly
decisive/decisively
deft/deftly

demonstrably
dependable/dependably
diligent/diligently
diplomatic/diplomatically
distinctive/distinctively
diverse/diversified
driving
easily
effective/effectively
effectually
efficient/efficiently
effortless/effortlessly
enthusiastic/enthusiastically
entire/entirely
especially
exceptional/exceptionally
exciting/excitingly
exhaustive/exhaustively
experienced
expert/expertly
extensive/extensively
extreme/extremely
familiar with
familiarity with
firm/firmly
functional/functionally
handy/handily
high/highly
highest
high-level
honest/honestly
imaginative/imaginatively
immediate/immediately
impressive/impressively
incisive/incisively
in-depth
industrious/industriously
inherent/inherently
innovative/innovatively
instructive/instructively
instrumental/instrumentally
integral
intensive/intensively
intimate/intimately
leading
masterful/masterfully
meaningful/meaningfully

natural/naturally
new and improved
notable/notably
objective/objectively
open-minded
original/originally
outstanding/outstandingly
particularly
penetrating/penetratingly
perceptive/perceptively
pioneering
practical/practically
professional/professionally
proficient/proficiently
profitable/profitably
progressive/progressively
quick/quickly
rare/rarely
readily
relentless/relentlessly
reliability
reliable/reliably
remarkable/remarkably
responsible/responsibly
rigorous/rigorously
routine/routinely
secure/securely
sensitive/sensitively
significant/significantly
skillful/skillfully
solid/solidly
sophisticated/sophisticatedly
strategic/strategically
strong/strongly
substantial/substantially
successful/successfully
tactful/tactfully
thorough/thoroughly
uncommon/uncommonly
unique/uniquely
unusual/unusually
urgent/urgently
varied
vigorous/vigorously
virtual/virtually
vital/vitally
wide/widely

Resume Tips

IN THIS SECTION, many important points are covered to help you make the most out of your resume.

Making It Readable

Since resumes are often scanned the first time through, it must be easy for the reader to pick up key pieces of information quickly. Using long paragraphs of over ten lines or using heavy blocks of text, can cause readers to quickly put your resume aside.

Honesty

Throughout your resume you should be honest and accurate—but positive. Whatever is stated should be true, but you do not need to tell everything. Both in resumes and in interviews you have a right to withhold certain information.

Multiple Resumes

In order to sell you, a resume must demonstrate focus. If you are considering more than one type of job, you may need two or more resumes. In this case you may want to write only one resume, but give it more flexibility by using more than one objective, leaving everything else the same. This is easy to do with a word processor or a memory typewriter.

An example will help. Jim is a very good computer salesperson with no desire to change fields, but we created three different objectives for him to use in three different versions of his resume: "OBJECTIVE: Computer Sales;" "OBJECTIVE: Electronics Sales;" and "OBJECTIVE: Sales." Nothing else in the resume was changed. Computer companies got one resume, electronics companies got another, and if Jim saw something interesting outside those two industries, he sent the one that said "Sales."

Changing the objective, however, may not be adequate if the types of jobs you are seeking are considerably different from each other. Writing a new qualifications section for each objective will often do the trick. Far less frequently, you may need to make small changes in the employment section. Typically that consists of adding an area of experience which was a very small part of your job, but one which will help sell you with that particular objective. You would also look for ways to get the right buzz words in.

Using Cover Letters For Flexibility

A cover letter should accompany each resume you mail out and should be individually typed. The cover letter provides an excellent opportunity to mention points you know are important to that particular employer, but are not mentioned in the resume.

Answering Want Ads

When a want ad provides specific job requirements, there are a number of ways to respond. You can 1) send your resume with a standardized cover letter; 2) send your resume with a custom-written cover letter discussing key points mentioned in the ad; or 3) customize your resume to hit all the important points in the ad *and* write a creative cover letter. Obviously the third approach is likely to provide the best results, and it really doesn't take much more time.

As you customize your resume, you may find that the job descriptions require few if any changes, while the qualifications section might require substantial changes. The entire process of rewriting might take one to two hours. If you are really interested in the position and know you could handle it, consider the time as an investment. Taking time to redo the resume will not guarantee you an interview, but it can *double* your chances. If you lack certain desired skills or experience that were mentioned in the ad, simply ignore those points and really sell what you do have.

What To Call It

It's not necessary to type *Resume, Qualifications Brief, Profile,* or any other such title at the top of your resume. Everyone will know it's a resume just by glancing at it.

Color And Type Of Paper

While paper is available in a variety of colors, textures, weights, and sizes, there are some standard guidelines you should follow. The color of paper you choose can definitely make a difference in the number of interviews you get. White is always a safe color, but my studies reveal that buff or off-white paper provides even better results. The best paper I have found so far is the 20- or 24-pound classic linen made by several paper manufacturers. Many people also like classic laid. Both types of paper have a texture that implies quality without overdoing it. If you prefer a paper without a textured surface, choose one with a "rag" or cotton fiber content of at least 25%. For those seeking management positions a light gray can be effective. Blues and greens have not tested well. Color should have a positive effect; this will nearly always mean you should use light shades. Dark grays and browns or bright colors are not effective. Twenty-pound paper is always a safe standard. A slightly heavier paper is fine, but avoid heavy stocks. Monarch size paper (7" x 10") is fine for thank you notes, but stick with 8½" x 11" for your resume. Good papers have a watermark, so make sure it is right side up if you copy it yourself. Photocopy shops usually check for this, but it's wise to double check this yourself.

Typing Your Resume

My studies show that clean, crisp typing is one of the most important factors in getting your resume read. Most people type their own resumes on portable typewriters and they look home-typed.

Resumes should never be typed on dot matrix printers. As yet, even top-of-the-line dot matrix printers can only approximate the quality of the type produced by letter-quality printers. Using a high quality dot matrix printer for cover letters is acceptable, but not for the resume. If you do print your cover letters on a dot matrix printer, print in the letter quality mode.

Many people have daisy wheel printers in their home. The daisy wheel printer produces true letter quality print and has been the standard for resumes for years. With it you can "bold" your name and the various resume categories such as objective, education, and employment.

A new standard is taking over, however, and that is the laser printer. A laser printer can simply do more things with a resume and make it look sharper. If you have a Macintosh or an IBM clone, you can take your disk to a copy shop or word processing organization which offers the service, and have your resume printed on a laser printer. If you don't have a computer, simply go to a word processing organization and have them type it for you. The $25–50 it will cost will be an excellent investment. Virtually all of them use laser printers.

I do not recommend having resumes typeset. Laser-printed resumes can give you virtually the same look at half the price. With a laser-printed resume it is also faster, easier, and cheaper to make multiple versions or customized versions.

One danger of using laser printers is that people are tempted to overuse such features as different fonts, bolding, underlining, and italics. This produces a resume which looks busy and is overdone. The example following is exaggerated to help you see what I mean; you'll notice your eyes going all over the place, unable to read or concentrate on the job description.

GENERAL MOTORS, Detroit, Michigan 10/87-Present

> **SENIOR ENGINEER** - As part of a team of **Software Quality Assurance Engineers,** evaluate <u>CAD/CAM</u> software and *make* recommendations for improvements before software is made available to users within the company. Review <u>functional specifications</u> to *ensure* all portions are testable and fully meet **user needs.** REDUCED time necessary to fully evaluate software from **45 days** to **18 days**.

As a rule of thumb regarding the use of such features—keep it simple.

Size of Type

There are two sizes of type which are typically used for resumes: 12 point, which is also known as 10 pitch or pica; and 10 point, which is also known as 12 pitch or elite. I generally recommend using 12 point, because is a little larger and more readable than 10 point. If you are using 12 point and your resume just barely goes over a page long, you may want to make minor adjustments to make it all fit on one page. Widening the length of the lines may be all you need, or you could go to a smaller type. With a laser printer, 11 point may do the trick.

Reproduction

Reproduction quality will have a lot to do with the visual impact of your resume. There are a number of advantages to having your resume reproduced at a professional photocopy shop. For one thing, the top-of-the-line copying equipment used in such shops will produce high-quality copies that are crisp, clear, and almost as good as the originals. The quality of photocopiers most have at home or in the office cannot compete with the equipment at a copy shop.

For another thing, copy shops have a variety of high-quality papers to choose from. You can produce your original resume on a plain white bond and have it copied on your choice of paper.

And finally, copy shops are fast—you can usually be in and out in about ten minutes. They are inexpensive as well. Photocopying will cost you five to eight cents per copy plus eight to eleven cents per sheet for special paper. Many people buy extra paper so their cover letter paper will match their resumes.

Mailing

Traditionally resumes are folded in thirds and sent in a standard number ten business envelope. That is still perfectly acceptable, but consider spending a little more and sending the resume in a 9 x 12 envelope so the resume does not need to be folded. It is not a big thing, but if it is not folded it will look nicer in the stack. If it weighs less than one ounce you'll need to add ten cents for a surcharge that the Postal Service charges for oversized envelopes. If it weighs over one ounce, it will cost you the regular price for the first ounce plus the reduced price for the second ounce. In 1993 that cost was 52¢—29¢ + 23¢.

For a really hot job consider having it delivered by an overnight delivery service. For a super hot local job, consider having a messenger service deliver it. The extra effort is one way of saying you want the job.

Photographs

Photographs should rarely be submitted with resumes, although they may be appropriate for models, flight attendants, performers, and media personalities. Many organizations are leery of receiving photographs with resumes because it increases the likelihood of age and race discrimination charges. Employers are nearly unanimous in preferring not to receive photographs.

Confidentiality

Employers who receive your resume will rarely inform your current employer. Even if they know your boss, they understand the importance of confidentiality. I would say that only if your boss or company has a reputation for firing people for "disloyalty," should the steps listed below even be considered. If you are truly concerned about confidentiality, your options include:

1. Write "Confidential" at the top of your resume.

2. At the bottom of the resume type and underline, "Please do not contact employer at this time."

3. Replace the name of your present employer (and possibly your next-to-last employer) with a description such as, "A major manufacturer of automotive parts," "A Fortune 500 Corporation," or "A National Retail Chain."

4. Utilize an executive recruiter (headhunter). A recruiter will sell you to an employer over the phone without revealing your name and will send your resume only if the employer is particularly interested.

If your boss suspects you are looking, but you know you are considered a valuable employee, you have nothing to worry about. You are more likely to get a raise than to get into trouble. In one sense, everyone is looking for another job—some are just more active than others. When headhunters call regarding truly great jobs, I guarantee you, virtually everyone is willing to talk. The World War II saying was "Loose lips sink ships." That's good advice at work also—do not tell even your most trusted friends at work that you're actively looking.

Salary

Salary history and salary requirements should virtually always be omitted from a resume to avoid giving anyone a cause for eliminating you.

Want ads frequently ask for desired salary or salary history. I would recommend ignoring the requested information. In this country what a person earns is one of the most personal and confidential bits of information we possess. Not only are you giving away your bargaining position when you state your current salary or salary requirements, but you are giving private information to people you don't even know.

If you feel compelled to acknowledge the request, you might simply write, "Salary is negotiable."

Relocation

If you are seeking a position with a national company, you'd better be prepared to relocate. Since many people are unwilling to relocate, a statement under "Personal" or "Additional," stating "Willing to Relocate," will make you stand out in a positive way. If you don't have a personal section, merely type it in at the end of the resume.

Reason For Leaving

Everyone has a reason for leaving a job, but the resume is rarely the place for stating it. Invariably an attempt to explain the reason will simply raise more questions than it answers. Save the explanation for an interview where the issue can be handled much more effectively. The only time I ever mention the reason for leaving is if the company or department moved out of state or the company went out of business. Even then it's best to mention it subtly, so that it just seems to be a part of the resume.

Abbreviations

Avoid abbreviations that may cause confusion to readers who are not familiar with them. As a rule of thumb, if you are certain that *everyone*, from the personnel clerk who may screen the resume to the person with power to hire you, will recognize and understand it, then consider using it. Keep in mind, however, that words are more visually attractive when spelled out. For this reason I recommend spelling out the names of states, particularly in the address at the top of a resume. In the employment section I sometimes abbreviate the state, using the Postal Service's two letter abbreviation, if that is the only way the name of the company and city/state will fit on one line. The key is to be consistent throughout the resume. Some exceptions: "B.A.," "M.A.", and "Ph.D." are preferred over spelling them out.

Know The Tradition And Language of Your Field

Learn what is traditional and accepted for resumes in your industry or field. Although I have tried to give you the principles for writing a powerful resume, I can't talk about, nor do I know all the traditions in all fields. While I recommend limiting most resumes to two pages, the four or five page curriculum vitae (the term for resumes used by academics), is perfectly acceptable. There may also be certain formats which are most accepted and expected in particular fields. When you find that is the case, go along with that tradition unless you have a compelling reason not to.

Also, use the language of your field. If this is a new field to you, read the trade journals or books on your field to learn the nomenclature and buzz words. If you weave this language into all of your communications—resumes, cover letters, and interviews—the employer will be more likely think of you as a member of that profession.

Creative License

In some ways my advice about resumes follows tradition, in some ways it does not. A conservative, tried-and-true approach often works best. This, for example, is why I recommend off-white paper. At the same time I also encourage you to be creative. Can you think of something which might just give you an edge over your competition? When you come up with an unusual idea, ask yourself, "Will it work for me; can I pull it off with my personality?" An approach tried by someone with an artistic, flamboyant, personality might be readily accepted, while that same thing attempted by a more conservative, traditional person would not. If you are about to try something rather unusual or "far out," get the opinions of others first, or try it out in a few cases to see what kind of response it gets.

I mention the creative side because over the years clients have suggested trying things which I never would have thought of. Sometimes I caution against the idea, but more frequently I give my full encouragement. When clients use these creative ideas, they've usually worked.

Selecting A Format

The format is essentially the layout of the resume. The sample resumes included in *Resume Power* use the layout that I prefer, after having tested many during the past 15 years. I like the format because it is easy to scan and it makes excellent use of space. Throughout the resume there is a balance of white space and text. There are literally dozens of formats with dozens of variations. If you have seen one that you like, and feel it would do a good job of presenting your background, by all means use it. If you do not have a preferred format, you cannot go wrong if you use the format used in the sample resumes. It is time tested and well accepted.

The Types of Resumes

ESSENTIALLY THERE ARE THREE TYPES of resumes—Chronological, Functional, and Qualifications/Chronological. Chronological and functional resumes have both advantages and disadvantages, while the qualifications/chronological resume offers the advantages of both the chronological and functional resumes, but none of the disadvantages.

Chronological resumes describe a person's work experience in reverse chronological order, with the most recent job appearing first. Traditionally they have emphasized dates, job titles, duties, and names of employers. The primary advantage of the chronological resume is that employers are used to reading it. They know how to scan it quickly and get what they need from it. Its major disadvantage is that it is difficult to show employers the "themes" which run through your experience.

The functional resume, on the other hand, excels at bringing out these themes or functional areas of experience. The job seeker identifies key areas of experience, or "functions," and labels those functional areas with titles such as Management, Design, and Computer Programming. The writer then describes the experience the person has had in those areas. The major drawbacks of the functional resume are that it is more difficult to read, and the employer typically does not know when or where the experience being described took place. For this reason it can sometimes be confusing.

The qualifications/chronological resume is essentially a chronological resume with a qualifications section included at the beginning. It combines the best attributes of both of the other types of resume, but has virtually none of their drawbacks. The qualifications section of a qualifications/chronological resume is usually shorter than the functional portion of a functional resume, but it covers the most crucial areas of experience and provides a quick introduction to the strengths of the individual. The job description section, the other main part of the resume, emphasizes results rather than just duties, making it extremely effective.

On the next two pages you'll see excellent examples of both the qualifications/chronological and the functional resume. Following the examples you will find a complete description of the functional resume, how to write it, how to determine whether you should use it, and samples to give you ideas.

ROBERTA JENNINGS
1121 Peach Drive
Atlanta, Georgia 30601
(404) 574-8769

OBJECTIVE: Airline Management

QUALIFICATIONS

Excellent management and supervisory capabilities. Highly respected by subordinates and able to obtain high performance levels from employees. Created one of the best on-time performance records in the airline industry.

EDUCATION

B.A. - Business, University of Southern California (1979)

EMPLOYMENT

Air Florida 3/85-Present

CUSTOMER/RAMP SERVICE SUPERVISOR, Atlanta, Georgia 6/89-Present. Opened the Atlanta airport facility for Air Florida and have created one of its most efficient and effective operations. Supervise and train 30 Customer Service Agents and Ramp personnel. Responsible for all day-to-day operations decisions and handle all crises related to weather, passenger deaths and illnesses, bomb threats, and hijackings.

Established one of the top records in the industry by successfully loading planes and preparing them for departure in twenty minutes or less, 97% of the time. Effective planning and scheduling permit up to four planes to be serviced simultaneously. Lost time due to illness has been reduced by 68% and industrial accidents by 71%.

CUSTOMER SERVICE AGENT, Atlanta, Georgia 3/85-6/89. Functioned as Ticket Sales Agent, Boarding Agent, and Customer Service Representative. Provided the type of service and concern for customers which made Air Florida one of the fastest growing airlines in the U. S. Became adept at solving problems and satisfying customers' complaints. Consistently maintained monthly sales in the top 10%.

Alaska Airlines, San Francisco, California 1/80-3/85

CUSTOMER SERVICE AGENT - Worked closely with customers to provide the best connecting flights and make each flight an enjoyable experience.

Functional

SUZANNE HALL
18852 52nd S.E.
Bothell, Washington 98011
(206) 481-2756

OBJECTIVE: Personnel Management

QUALIFICATIONS

Personnel Management - Five years experience in Personnel, with three years as Personnel Manager of a store with 230 employees. Supervise and train a staff of four. Significantly increased morale among store personnel and successfully fought off a unionizing effort.

Recruiting, Interviewing, Hiring - Very effective interviewer. Screen and hire all sales, supervisory, clerical, and support personnel. Over 80% of all people hired have remained with the store at least one year. Turnover has been reduced 22% by careful screening and by implementing other improvements throughout the store.

EEO - Perform periodic surveys and ensure all goals are met as required.

Wage and Salary Administration - Identified unfair wage differentials between recent hires and those with longer service. Removed pay scale discrepancies and nearly eliminated turnover among more experienced staff.

Promotions - Work closely with supervisors to determine those ready for promotions. Write all final recommendations for promotions.

Terminations - Arbitrate in all firing situations and participate in all firing interviews. Conduct exit interviews and identify causes for termination. By taking quick action, several terminations have been averted.

Manpower Planning - Predict staffing needs for Christmas and major sales and hire necessary personnel.

Career Counseling - Provide extensive career path counseling to store employees.

Training and Development - Developed and conduct a 16-hour training program emphasizing customer service and job training. Turnover and customer complaints have been reduced substantially after the program was increased from 8 to 16 hours. Supervise additional training during the probationary period.

EMPLOYMENT

Briggins Department Stores, Seattle, Washington (1975 to Present)

Personnel Manager (1987 to Present)
Assistant Personnel Manager (1984 to 1987)
Schedule Coordinator (1981 to 1984)
Credit Manager (1979 to 1981)
Credit Adjustment Processor (1976 to 1979)
Sales Associate (1975 to 1976)

EDUCATION

Attended Bellevue Community College (35 credits)

THE FUNCTIONAL RESUME

The functional resume offers some people the best way to get their story across to employers. If your strengths can readily be put into categories, then you should seriously consider using a functional resume.

In its purest form, a functional resume includes only functions—job titles, dates, and names of employers are omitted. I rarely recommend a pure functional resume because it usually raises more questions than it answers. When dates and employers are omitted, hiring authorities tend to wonder if the applicant is hiding something, such as a long gap in employment. If you have strong reasons for not revealing details of your employment, however, consider a functional resume.

As you will notice in Suzanne's resume, employment was included but job descriptions were not. This is common in functional resumes and helps employers feel more comfortable with the functional format. The functional section in Suzanne's resume is devoted entirely to her duties as personnel manager and assistant personnel manager. Those were the only jobs which were relevant to the position she was seeking. In a chronological resume it would have been difficult to have devoted so much space (24 lines) to just two positions. For Suzanne the functional resume was a perfect choice.

Read the following sample functional resumes to get a feel for how they are constructed and what makes them effective. Although the backgrounds of the people will differ from yours, you should be able to determine whether your experience is better suited to the functional format or the qualifications/chronological format illustrated and discussed throughout the book.

A functional resume worked well for Paul Shupbach and enabled him to go into much more detail about his areas of experience. His job descriptions also add important information.

David Goldman's resume could be labeled a functional resume, but it is really a combination of a functional and chronological resume. It demonstrates that by remaining flexible and creative you can produce something which works best for you and your particular situation. Jason Ryerson's resume enabled an ex-military officer to sell his experience in basically nonmilitary terms.

PAUL SHUPBACH
2917 S. E. 112th
Pittsburgh, Pennsylvania 15203
(412) 579-0002

QUALIFICATIONS

Technical Expertise - Hands-on person. Capable of operating and trouble-shooting virtually any piece of equipment. Understand the problems faced by machine operators and utilize engineering knowledge to effectively solve those problems.

Proposals, Contracts and Negotiations - Have written and developed dozens of proposals and negotiated over 40 major contracts. Heavily experienced in all types of contracts, including DCAS, ASPR and DAR. Consistently negotiate the most favorable terms for Cost Plus, Cost Sharing, Cost Plus Incentive Fixed, and R&D Contracts.

Cost Management, Cost Analysis, Cost Control - Over fifteen years of Cost Management experience with all types of products and components, including processing equipment, fiberglass, and sheet metal parts. Establish Program Financial Controls which pinpoint manufacturing problems and prevent cost overruns. Expert in Value Engineering.

Cost Estimating - Experience covers all facets of manufacturing including machined parts, sheet metal, plastics, fiberglass, and software. Highly experienced in all methods of estimating including Parametric Estimating.

Vendor Selection - Inspect and analyze vendor facilities, equipment, capabilities and quality. Recommendations to use a vendor have virtually always been adopted.

EDUCATION

B.A. Industrial Management, University of Pennsylvania (1971)
B.S. Industrial Engineering, University of Pittsburgh (1969)

EMPLOYMENT HISTORY

Davenport Engineering & Consulting, Pittsburgh, Pennsylvania 1986 to Present

INDUSTRIAL ENGINEERING CONSULTANT - Work on assignments ranging in length from 3 to 12 months in the areas of Bidding, Estimating, Selecting Vendors, Cost Management, and Manufacturing Planning. Enabled one manufacturer to obtain their first ever contract with U. S. Steel and to expand production from $40,000 to $140,000 per month with no increase in personnel. Researched and adapted a new technology which allowed the firm to underbid all competitors.

Pennsylvania Division of Purchasing, Scranton, Pennsylvania 1978 to 1986

SPECIFICATION ANALYST - Developed quality standards, specifications, and test procedures for many raw, semi-processed, and processed materials. The capabilities and sophistication of the Division were substantially increased through these efforts.

U. S. Steel, Pittsburgh, Pennsylvania 1971 to 1978

COST ANALYST - Estimated and analyzed costs of machined parts, hydraulic components, and mechanical systems supplied by vendors. Negotiated prices and engineering changes.

DAVID GOLDMAN
2430 Stoneway North
Little Rock, Arkansas 72202
(501) 254-3242

OBJECTIVE: Project Management

QUALIFICATIONS

<u>Supervising</u>. Took over a district with high turnover and low morale and created one of the top teams in the company. Work closely with individuals to enable both company and personal needs to be satisfied.

<u>Negotiating</u>. Negotiate contracts that are fair, workable, and satisfactory to customer and manufacturer. Work hard to get the best for both.

<u>Coordinating/Planning</u>. Installations have always been completed on schedule. Maintain close contact with customers, manufacturing, and field engineering to deal with all problems as they arise. Able to get commitments and support from those not directly responsible to me.

<u>Computers</u>. Excellent training and broad work experience installing and maintaining computer systems.

EMPLOYMENT

Data Systems, 1973 to Present

<u>SENIOR PROJECT MANAGER</u>, Little Rock, Arkansas, 1986 to Present. Negotiate contracts, schedule deliveries, and troubleshoot all phases of computer installations. Work closely with customers to determine their needs, then gain contractual commitments from manufacturing and field engineering to install systems by specific dates. Monitor factory schedules and software support schedules to ensure delivery schedules are met. Despite many difficulties, all deliveries and installations have been completed on schedule.

<u>DISTRICT MANAGER, FIELD ENGINEERING</u>, Los Angeles, California, 1979 to 1986. Supervised and scheduled the work of 18 field engineers installing and maintaining computer systems. Took over a district with high turnover, low morale, and a poor reputation for customer service. Within one year turnover was reduced from 35% to 8% annually. Response time to down systems was reduced from six hours to two hours. Functioned as Project Manager for the installation of a branch on-line system for Security Western Bank (180 branches). All installations were completed on time.

<u>FIELD ENGINEER</u>, Washington, D. C., 1973 to 1979. Installed and maintained systems for banks, hotels and airlines. Customers were kept very satisfied because of extremely low down-times.

U. S. Air Force, 1967 to 1972

<u>COMPUTER TECH</u> - Maintained and serviced on-board aircraft computer systems. Supervised a five-man team.

EDUCATION

<u>Computers</u>
Field Engineering, Data Systems Manufacturing School - 6 months, 1974
Computer Repair, Computer Learning Institute - 6 months, 1973
Electrical Engineering, Old Dominion University - 1 year, 1972-1973
Computer Tech School, U. S. Air Force - 9 months, 1967

JASON RYERSON
14568 NE 9th Street
Redmond, Washington 98053
(206) 877-7594

OBJECTIVE: Facilities Management

QUALIFICATIONS

Over 20 years of exceptional management experience. Proven ability to successfully complete projects cost effectively and on schedule. Received numerous awards for completion of high quality projects.

Implemented comprehensive programs that dramatically improved productivity and efficiency of personnel.

PROFESSIONAL EXPERIENCE

ENGINEERING MANAGEMENT - Eight years of demanding and successful "hands on" engineering management and plant management responsibilities. Coordinated hundreds of repair jobs conducted by both own work force and outside contractors. In one instance increased overall plant reliability by 300%. While providing repair support for 12 naval ships over a three year period, reduced equipment downtime by 50%.

FACILITIES MANAGEMENT - As Chief Engineer and Material Manager, directly responsible for operation, maintenance, and repair of steam and diesel electric power plants. Associated equipment included heating, ventilation, and air conditioning systems; firefighting and sprinkler systems; and various emergency equipment. Charged also with infrastructure repair and modifications. Supported numerous office and work station relocations in minimal time and without loss of productivity.

CONTRACT ADMINISTRATION - Broad experience in working with prime and subcontractors in overseeing scheduled and emergency repairs. Represented the U.S. Government in the management of an $18 million resupply contract for 76 remote sites in the Pacific.

TROUBLESHOOTING - Volunteered to rebuild a faltering, yet critical department of 95 personnel. Within 45 days identified all major problem areas and initiated a corrective action plan that included a comprehensive training program for 900 people. The revitalized training program improved morale and decreased absenteeism over 60%. Received a special commendation for the project.

EMPLOYMENT

United States Navy 6/69-12/91. Completed Naval service with rank of Commander.

EDUCATION

MA - Political Science, Naval Postgraduate School (1976)
BA - International Studies, University of Washington (1968)

IS A FUNCTIONAL RESUME FOR YOU?

Functional resumes do have drawbacks. While reviewing functional resumes, employers often wonder where the experience occurred since dates, job titles, and employers are not specified for each particular area of experience. Their eyes tend to dart up and down the page looking for the answers. They often become frustrated because the information in the resume is difficult to read and interpret—the applicant is making them work too hard. They may also suspect that something is being hidden.

Keeping these considerations in mind, you may still want to use a functional resume under the following circumstances: if 1) You are changing careers; 2) You are changing industries and you have related experience but no direct experience; 3) You have major gaps in employment; 4) A functional resume seems to be a perfect vehicle to showcase your strengths; 5) The Qualifications/Chronological Employment format seems unsuitable for your background; 6) Your background can easily be listed in categories such as Management, Supervision, Coordinating, Troubleshooter, Motivator, or Training; 7) You've had your current job for many years and you want to highlight different aspects of it.

If you think a functional resume may be good for you, go ahead and write one. Test it out on friends or business associates to determine if it truly sells you and is easy to read. If you get positive feedback, you made the right decision.

Be sure to study the format of the qualifications/chronological resumes. I like the format because it has virtually all of the advantages of the functional resume *and* the chronological resume, with none of their individual drawbacks.

WRITING YOUR FUNCTIONAL RESUME

Once your job sketches have been completed, the first step in writing an effective functional resume is to list the points or experiences that you want to include. Write the points quickly, without being concerned for polished writing. Once you're through listing the points you'll begin to see that some just naturally fit together. At that point begin to select the category titles that you will use. Most functional resumes should contain three to six categories. For your highly specific or technical categories, you'll have to come up with those names on your own, but that should not be difficult. Some of the commonly used categories include: Management, Supervision, Training, Planning, Designing, Research, Coordination, Negotiating, Public Relations, Administration, Marketing, Public Speaking, Organization, Counseling, Writing and Editing, Design, and Teaching.

Next, put the categories on two pages so you'll have plenty of room to write in your points. Initially you wrote those points quickly; now rewrite them in a more polished form as you place them in their appropriate category. Once all the points have been placed in a category, determine the order the points should be in. Usually your strongest points would be listed first within each category. At that point you've done all you should for one day.

After one or two days, review what you've written. By having set the resume aside for some time, it will be fresh and you'll be better able to see ways to improve your writing. In your second draft look for ways to make each point clearer and more concise. Virtually all of the other instructions for writing a resume apply to the functional resume as well.

Writing Your Resume

GETTING STARTED ON YOUR RESUME

Having read through this chapter and having completed your job sketches, it's time to start writing your resume. I can't emphasize enough how valuable you will find your job sketches as you write your resume.

Once you have reviewed your job sketches, you're ready to start. Use a pencil and feel free to erase. If you compose well at a typewriter or computer, by all means use one, but double space so you can write and edit between the lines. I always begin by writing the name, address and phone number at the top. Next, I write the objective. After that I then write in "Qualifications" and skip enough space to complete it after I've written the rest of the resume. Since the qualifications section is often the most difficult section to write, I leave it until last.

At that point I have spent only about three minutes writing, but psychologically I am totally involved with the resume. Three minutes earlier I had been looking for an excuse to postpone the writing, but now I'm *into* it. Next I tackle employment, the section which nearly always requires the most time and thought. Be prepared to spend three or more hours on your first draft. It may be frustrating at times, but keep plugging away. The effort will all be worth it in the end. Once you've completed a first and second draft of your employment section, you'll be ready to work on the qualifications section.

DON'T HESITATE

You should write your first draft relatively quickly without worrying about perfection. Concentrate on getting your thoughts on paper; you can polish the phrasing later. Once you write a phrase, read it out loud to get a feel for how it sounds. When reading, most people subvocalize; while they may not move their lips, their mind is actually saying each word almost audibly. In other words, the way a phrase sounds to you when you say it out loud is the same way it sounds when read by an employer. By the time I finish writing a resume I have read every phrase aloud four to ten times. While I don't worry about perfection on the first draft, I will rewrite some phrases and add or delete words as I go along.

Frequently I will finish the first draft of a resume late in the afternoon. While I may not be satisfied with it, I do know that all the main thoughts and descriptions are there. I will simply set it aside until the next morning. When I pick it up the next day, my thoughts are fresh and I'm able to look at it objectively. Improvements often come spontaneously.

Read over the resume and ask yourself if all the important points have been made. You might think of a point that could be covered in the employment section or an important idea you want to get across in qualifications. Make those changes on the original draft. Go through the draft sentence by sentence and phrase by phrase, rereading them out loud. Cross out extraneous phrases. Ask yourself if you can make the same point with fewer words. Use action words whenever possible. Once you've finished this process, retype or rewrite the resume, incorporating the changes you've made. You have completed your second draft. Set it aside for at least half a day.

SPIT AND POLISH

When you pick up the resume again, take care as you go through it; this may be your last draft. As you read your resume out loud, it should flow. Are there any phrases or words you have used more than twice? If so, look for alternatives. Are all of your sentences very long or all very short? A mixture of short, medium, and long sentences reads best. Too many short sentences makes the resume seem choppy and abrupt. Lots of long sentences cause a reader to forget the main point. Long sentences can often be made into two sentences. This adds clarity and punch.

Look for any troublesome phrases that sound awkward, unclear, or confusing. Your desire is to have employers read your resume completely and thoroughly. You don't want them to stop at any point and wonder what you mean. Just one awkwardly written, hard-to-understand sentence can reduce your perceived value by 10%. Don't let that happen.

Of course *you* know exactly what you mean by everything you've written, so unclear sentences may be hard for you to spot. Have others read your resume and ask if any sentences tripped them up. Ask for their overall impression.

Avoid big, unfamiliar words. The mark of a good writer is the ability to say exactly what is meant by using everyday words.

Spelling must be perfect. It is worth it to make one quick pass through your resume, dictionary in hand, looking up words you "know" are correct. You may be surprised to find that you have been misspelling a word for years. Do not depend solely on computerized spell checkers. If your misspelling is an actual word in the spell checker, it will go undetected. Ask someone to review it to make sure it is grammatically correct and that words are used correctly.

Type the final draft and review it one last time for phrasing, spelling, and punctuation. If you use a word processing service, presenting a typed draft will help reduce your cost and will ensure that everything is readable.

PUTTING IT ALL TOGETHER

Essentially, writing a resume consists of putting all of the pieces together. Most sections, such as education, training, special projects, and employment are independent of each other. So, if each section is well written, the entire resume will be effective when you pull them all together.

PROFESSIONAL EDITING

You may want help in polishing your resume. Career Management Resources offers complete editing to strengthen your work. For more information see page 232.

Sample Resumes To Help You

USE THE FOLLOWING SAMPLE RESUMES to get ideas and to get a sense of how an entire resume fits together. Over 50 sample resumes have been used to help you. Various fonts (typefaces) have been used so you can determine which you like best. The name of the font appears at the bottom of each resume. Times Roman and Helvetica are the typefaces people most commonly use for their resumes.

Because this book presents the basic principles of writing an effective resume, it does not provide examples of resumes for all job titles. The principles given here can be applied or adapted to fit any job title. Feel free to borrow a phrase here and there, but make your resume your own. Instill it with your own flavor and character. Make it personal. And sell yourself.

As you read the resumes, notice that the people being described seem like real, living, highly capable people, a quality rarely found in resumes. Strive to make your resume as interesting as theirs. Do everything possible to bring results into your resume.

Essentially all occupations and people fall into 18 categories, with a miscellaneous category to include those which to not fit well elsewhere. Those 19 categories include:

Recent college graduates 75 – 78	Government employees 112 – 115
Women returning to work 79 – 81	Teachers 116 – 117
Those over 50 82 – 83	Engineers/Scientists 118 – 119
People who use portfolios 84 – 85	Professionals 120 – 122
Military people 86 – 91	Manufacturing/Laboring 123 – 124
Computer specialists 92 – 94	Health Professionals 125 – 128
Salespeople 95 – 100	Retailers 129 – 131
Career changers 101 – 103	Accounting/Finance 132 – 133
Managers/Supervisors 104 – 109	Miscellaneous 134 – 142
Office/Clerical workers 110 – 111	

WAYS TO PERSONALIZE YOUR RESUME

There are dozens of ways you can personalize your resume to make it uniquely yours in appearance. While most of the resumes included in *Resume Power* utilize the same basic format, (or layout) feel free to use a format that presents you in the best way possible. Regardless of the layout you choose, the following ideas will show you some of the ways you can personalize your resume.

1) The job title is bold, underlined, and capitalized - 100
2) The job title is bold, but not underlined - 105
3) The job title is capitalized and underlined, but not bold - 106
4) The job title uses upper and lower case and is underlined - 78
5) The name, address, and phone number are on the left side - 106
6) The entire name, address, and phone number can be bolded - 135
7) The entire resume can be "right justified" - 107, 126, 127

8) The job title and date can be listed on one line, a line skipped, with the job description starting on the following line - 121

9) Different font sizes can be used:

10 point might be used to enable a longer resume to get on one page, or a very long resume to get on two pages. It is harder to read 10 point than 12 point - 83

11 point may be used for the same reasons as 10 point. It is easier to read than 10 point - 77

12 point is the easiest to read - 107

13 point is sometimes used when it is desirable to make a very short resume use up more of a page to make it look better - 124, 130

10) Numerous fonts are available. The most commonly used fonts are Times Roman and Helvetica.

Times Roman is a very easy to read type style - 77

Helvetica does not use a seraph and is often referred to as a very "clean" typestyle - 80

Bookman is similar to Times Roman, but it has some slight differences - 88, 89

Courier is the typeface commonly found on typewriters. If you can print your resume on a laser printer, and have access to other fonts, it would be wise to use Times Roman, Helvetica, or one of the other typefaces found in *Resume Power - 133*

Benguiat - 85

Avant Garde - 97

New Century Schoolbook - 105

11) Headings such as Objective, Qualifications, Education, and Experience can be bolded - 98

12) Sometimes only your name is bolded - 119

13) Some prefer to use no bolding at all - 97, 99

NOTE BEFORE YOU READ THE SAMPLE RESUMES

Many of these resumes were originally two pages. They were reduced in length to enable you to concentrate on key areas.

The resumes in this section were printed on a laser printer and are not typeset as the text of the book is.

Resume Samples

GRADUATING COLLEGE STUDENTS

Although you may not have a lot of work experience, make the most of what you have, especially any experience related to what you want to do. Bookkeeping, for example, is valuable experience for an accounting major. It's not the same as accounting, but it is excellent, practical experience and is recognized as such by employers. A forestry major would emphasize any work with a timber company, even if it was only menial summer work.

As a recent or soon-to-be graduate, you have four things to sell: your education, your personality and character, related work experience, and work experience in general. If you have little or no related work experience, most of your resume will be devoted to revealing your personality, character, and work ethic. Employers need to sense the type of employee you will be. College graduates typically remain with their first employers for less than two years, so it's fair for employers to seek those who will quickly contribute to the organization.

Make the most out of whatever work experience you have. Internships and jobs where you've had a high level of responsibility, are particularly valuable. In John Etter's sample resume on page 77, only one job was actually described because its value was so much greater than the other summer jobs. You, on the other hand, may want to describe each of your summer jobs. Do your best to identify a result in each one. It doesn't have to be big, after all, it was a part-time or temporary job.

Look for ways to reveal your personal qualities. Citing offices held in high school and college reveals leadership and responsibility. Lettering in sports indicates learning the value of teamwork and cooperation. Excellent grades indicate discipline and intellectual capacity. Participation in debate and theater can reveal speaking ability, quick thinking, and willingness to take risks. Participating in school committees and organizations reveals responsibility, willingness to put out a little extra, and loyalty.

The qualifications section of a resume is an excellent place to describe and call attention to some of the qualities you want an employer to know about, as the example below demonstrates.

OBJECTIVE: Mathematics/Statistics

QUALIFICATIONS

Excellent training in math and statistics.

Maintain excellent relations with supervisors. Always a valued employee.
Loyal, cooperative, and easy to work with.

Work well under pressure, learn quickly, hard working.

You may have noticed that none of these statements was backed up with facts. The student who wrote this statement picked qualities which she knows to be true about herself; she is more than ready to give details or examples during an interview. Carefully select the qualities you mention. Be sure they are accurate—don't pick them just because they sound good. You may get an interview as a result, but you'll never get the job unless the "you" in person matches the "you" on paper.

Most graduates should expect to write a one-page resume, but a two page resume is certainly acceptable. Students who earn more than 50% of their total college and living expenses or who are willing to relocate, should consider stating it in the resume. These items may be stated in the following way:

PERSONAL

Earned 60% of college expenses
Willing to relocate

Offices held while in college should nearly always be mentioned. If you're proud of some of your results, describe those results rather than merely listing the offices you held.

Class projects are often worth mentioning in a special projects or education section. Perhaps you were in a group with business students who developed a marketing plan for a small company or in a group of industrial engineering students who solved an actual manufacturing problem. Below is a special projects section by a student who was very active on campus:

Planned and organized the University of Puget Sound 1992 Spring Parents Weekend and set a new record for attendance. Arranged programs and activities, obtained speakers, made hotel arrangements, ordered food, and headed up a four-person committee. Increased attendance 20% over the previous year. Evaluations by parents indicated it was the best organized program since its inception in 1977.

Published the first Parents Association Newsletter which was sent to 3,500 parents of UPS students. The first two editions were well-received and the newsletter has become an official school publication, published three times each year.

JOHN ETTER

Current Address	Permanent Address
426 Harris Hall	1227 Pineway N.W.
Burlington, Vermont 05401	Ascutney, Vermont 05030
(802) 795-2631	(802) 683-2796

OBJECTIVE: Entry-Level Training and Development Position

QUALIFICATIONS

Excellent program development skills. Developed new intramural programs and increased participation by women 220%.

Strong research and writing ability. Published an article in the *Vermont Historical Society Quarterly*.

Speak well before the public. Won numerous debate tournaments and placed fifth in the 1992 national tournament.

Cooperate well with supervisors; reliable and responsible; work hard and complete projects on schedule.

EDUCATION

B.A. - History, University of Vermont, will graduate June 1993 (3.6 GPA)

Business Courses: History of 20th Century Business, Macroeconomics, Microeconomics

PUBLICATIONS

"Effects of the Abolition Movement in Burlington, Vermont 1826 to 1866"
Vermont Historical Society Quarterly, January 1992 edition.

AWARDS

"Outstanding History Senior" selected by the History Faculty (1992)
Fifth place, national debate tournament, extemporaneous speaking (1992)

EMPLOYMENT

University of Vermont, Burlington, Vermont 9/90 to Present

DIRECTOR OF INTRAMURAL SPORTS - Planned, staffed, and organized the intramural sports program. Working with a tight budget, assessed equipment needs, received bids from sporting goods suppliers, and purchased sports equipment. Supervised two assistants and recruited and supervised dozens of volunteers. Developed a new concept in women's athletics and actively promoted the program. Participation by women grew from 20% in previous years to 76%. Maintained the high participation rate in the men's program and organized a successful basketball refereeing clinic.

Summer Employment:

RECORDS CLERK, Stephenson Steel, Ascutney, Vermont 6/91 to 9/91
MAIL SORTER, U.S. Postal Service, Ascutney, Vermont 6/90 to 9/90
LABORER, Isaacson Contracting, Ascutney, Vermont 6/89 to 9/89
FARM WORKER, John Tyler, Ascutney, Vermont 6/88 to 9/88

Typeface: Times Roman

POLLY GLADSON
275 S. Pine Blvd.
Henniker, New Hampshire
(603) 971-2653

OBJECTIVE: Entry level accounting position with a CPA firm.

QUALIFICATIONS

Excellent college training and on-the-job experience. Have worked closely with a CPA firm and helped prepare taxes. Prepared documents for an IRS audit. Have practical business experience handling all bookkeeping functions at a busy restaurant.

EDUCATION

B.A. - Accounting, New England College, 3.21 GPA (June, 1993)

EXPERIENCE

Gulliver's Restaurant, Henniker, New Hampshire (1/87 to Present, full time)

<u>Waitress</u> (2/92 to Present). Provide outstanding service and consistently receive the highest tips among the restaurant staff. Highly professional.

<u>Bookkeeper</u> (4/88 to 2/92). Responsible for accounts receivable, reconciling charge slips, payroll, balancing five registers, recovering on bad checks, reconciling petty cash and inventorying bar supplies monthly. Monitored costs by preparing monthly reports comparing gross sales to labor costs for each department.

Worked closely with accountant and prepared figures as requested. Each year helped auditor track and reconcile all financial transactions. A 1991 IRS audit stated the books were very complete and accurate. Highly respected and trusted - had full access to safe and every part of restaurant.

<u>Podium Hostess</u> (1/87 to 4/88). Redesigned the reservation system which significantly improved service to customers. Developed excellent relations with customers and helped create a loyal clientele. Trained seating hostesses in all facets of the job.

Village Inn, Henniker, New Hampshire (6/86 to 1/87, full time)

<u>Hostess/Waitress</u> - Greeted and seated customers, opened and closed the restaurant, and prepared the registers each day.

ACTIVITIES

Member, American Society of Women Accountants

Active in jazz dancing and dog obedience training

Typeface: Times Roman

WOMEN RETURNING TO THE WORK FORCE

The biggest problems women face when returning to the work force are a lack of self-esteem and a belief that what they have done for the last several years is not valued in the workplace. To overcome these twin problems you must first recognize that you possess numerous transferable skills that are valued in many types of positions.

If you lack confidence in your marketability or your job finding ability, begin looking for a career planning and job finding program at a community college, or consider obtaining help from a career counselor. Also look for a support group made up of women who are returning to work or look for a broader-based support group that the local YWCA or some similar organization may have. If you are divorced or widowed, or must become the primary wage earner, you will probably qualify for a "displaced homemakers" program. Such programs are often available at low cost through community colleges and can really help women get through an emotionally trying period. They typically provide career exploration assistance, job finding guidance, and emotional support.

Even though you have not worked for several years, make the most out of whatever paid work experience you do have. Scour each job to find whatever results and contributions you may have had, even if it was 20 years ago. Establishing the fact that you have been a good employee in the past, even 20 years ago, will effectively convince employers that you have a strong work ethic.

Those who have been out of the work force for many years must often emphasize their volunteer experience. In actuality, volunteer activities are merely jobs you didn't get paid to do. They can be as mundane as licking stamps or as interesting and challenging as organizing a blood donor drive, or handling public relations for a small nonprofit organization. If you consistently spent ten or more hours weekly on a volunteer position, treat it as a job with a job title and a job description, with results included. In the resume there is no need to state the number of hours spent weekly. If an employer is curious you can explain in the interview. If most of your volunteer activities were of short duration, you could treat them as projects (see Special Projects page 43). Concentrate on results, but also describe duties.

Make the most out of each activity. If you held an office, say so. If you obtained excellent results, describe them. *Don't be modest.*

How good a position you get depends on the quality of your resume and how well focused you are. There is probably no need to return to school for a degree, but you may need to study your preferred field on your own or take a few classes at your local community college. Study enough to know the terms, history, and trends in your field.

I've included Sharron's resume because it is so strong in the volunteer area. Don't be intimidated by it. You may not have been as active or may not have had such quantifiable results, but it shows what can be done.

SHARRON COSGRAVE
526 South State Street
Wilmington, Delaware 19803
(302) 543-9161

(objective unstated, but basically looking to become an administrative
assistant to a director of a nonprofit agency)

QUALIFICATIONS

Strong experience in developing effective new programs, motivating and
coordinating large numbers of volunteers, and making office systems more
efficient.

Excellent fund-raiser. Have written three successful grant proposals, one
of which was funded for $20,000. Through PTA fund-raising activities,
increased revenue 18% above the previous record.

EDUCATION

University of Delaware, Liberal Arts, 96 credits, 1966 to 1969

PROJECTS/ACTIVITIES

PTA President, Robert Frost Elementary, 1990/91. Increased attendance
at monthly meetings from 51 to an average of 92. Worked with principal
and teachers to develop five new volunteer programs for parents. Participation in programs increased from 26% of parents to 58%. Because of
active parent involvement, vandalism at the school decreased to almost
zero.

Fund-raising Chairperson, Robert Frost PTA, 1989/90. Coordinated the
efforts of over 400 children and 95 adults in six fund-raising activities.
Exceeded the previous record by 18%.

Board Member, Wilmington Crisis Clinic, 1985 to Present. Analyze and
approve annual budgets, interview and select new directors, and study
proposed program changes. President of the board 1988 and 1989. Wrote
grant proposal which obtained $20,000 in federal funds.

President, Wilmington Chapter, MADD (Mothers Against Drunk Drivers),
1984 to 1987. Organized the local chapter and tripled dues-paying membership each year. Testified as an expert witness before the Delaware Leg-
islature. Coordinated statewide lobbying efforts and helped pass legislation
which significantly strengthened laws against drunk driving.

EMPLOYMENT

McClinton, Brandeis & Nelson, Wilmington, Delaware 7/69 to 9/71

OFFICE MANAGER - Handled bookkeeping, payroll, bank statements,
accounts payable, and accounts receivable. Purchased office equipment
and supplies. Greeted clients, answered phones, scheduled court reporters
for depositions, and developed an improved appointment and court scheduling system for 8 attorneys.

Typeface: Helvetica

The next resume is perhaps more typical of a woman returning to work. She's had two part-time jobs since she got married. In 1992 she decided to return to work on a full-time basis. From her experience at Debbie's Designs (three years, part-time) she knows she would like to own her own shop someday. Her plan is to get a full-time retail sales job at a small but classy store and eventually become the manager or assistant manager. While working there she intends to learn the business inside and out so she'll be ready when she opens her own shop.

JANICE STEVENS
4060 W. Warwick
Chicago, Illinois 60626
(312) 476-2917

OBJECTIVE: Retail sales

QUALIFICATIONS

Excellent retail experience. Work very effectively with customers - able to identify needs, tactfully answer questions, sell products, and solve problems.

EDUCATION

Northeastern Illinois University, Psychology, 20 credits 1979 to 1982

Bates Community College, Liberal Arts, 42 credits 1966 to 1968

WORKSHOPS

Window Dressing, Retail Merchants Association, 12 class hours (1990)
Retail Bookkeeping, Retail Merchants Association, 24 class hours (1989)
Buying for the 80's, Retail Merchants Association, 14 class hours (1988)
Retail Selling/Know Your Customer, Retail Merchants Association,
 20 class hours (1988)

EMPLOYMENT

Debbie's Designs, Chicago, Illinois 2/88 to 4/91

RETAIL SALES - Consulted with customers in the selection and coordination of furniture, fabrics, carpeting, wallpaper, draperies, and gift items. Purchased and priced products and developed attractive displays. Functioned as store manager for extended periods when the store owner was on vacation.

Illinois Arts & Crafts Association, Chicago, Illinois 9/74 to 8/79

GALLERY ASSISTANT - Assisted customers in the purchase of art objects, explained the processes used by each artist, and trained and supervised other volunteers. Handled numerous details for the annual arts and crafts fair, including registering artists, judging art work, and overseeing sales and bookkeeping.

Typeface: Times Roman

THOSE OVER 50

The greatest concern of people over fifty years of age is usually age discrimination. While federal law prohibits discrimination on the basis of age, we know that it persists in both overt and subtle ways. With this in mind, you must decide whether you will reveal your age, since employers by law cannot ask your age or birthdate. Your resume should contain only information you choose to reveal to an employer.

Make the most of your experience and maturity. Some people unnecessarily worry that youth always has the edge. In your resume and during interviews, reveal yourself to be an energetic and youthful person, but one who has the maturity and sound judgment that comes only with age and experience. If you have planned your career carefully, you will probably be at a level where only those with similar age, experience, and results will even be considered as qualified. If that is not your case, then simply recognize that your age is another barrier that must and can be overcome.

Trenton is a 59 year old insurance executive. In his resume education was not included because he does not have a degree. Showing his one year of college was deemed unnecessary because he has so much experience. Two early jobs were left off which accounted for five years. Using a prior employment section was an effective way to concentrate on his higher level jobs.

TRENTON McGRATH
2215 Broadway North
Houston, Texas 77012
(713) 785-2761

OBJECTIVE: Sales/Marketing Management

QUALIFICATIONS

Complete knowledge of Mortgage Lending/Mortgage Finance/Secondary Markets.

Recognized as an outstanding trainer and motivator of sales staffs. Substantially increased market share in each position held.

Broad marketing experience. Developed and marketed new products and services which have consistently been accepted in the financial community.

EMPLOYMENT

Diversified Mortgage Insurance Company, Minneapolis, Minnesota 1/78 to Present

REGIONAL VICE PRESIDENT 1/87 to Present, Houston. Moved into a troubled 16-state zone and have increased market share 61% from 3.2% to 5.2%. Have aggressively marketed new services and became active with the Bond Business, Pension Funds, Swaps, and assisting lenders with Portfolio Sales. Travel extensively and work closely with 4 district sales managers and 20 salespeople.

SENIOR VICE PRESIDENT, SALES AND MARKETING 12/83 to 1/87, Minneapolis. Developed and implemented a reorganization of the national sales force, moving from 12 divisions to 4 zones. Reorganization has been credited with strengthening DMI's national market share. Took part in the development of the Mortgage Finance Unit which has successfully moved DMI into new markets. Developed strategies for participation in Mortgage Revenue Bonds, Pass Through Certificates, Pension Funds Issues, Builder Buy-downs and Pay-through Bonds.

VICE PRESIDENT, NORTHWEST DIVISION MANAGER 9/81 to 12/83, Portland. Covering 9 western states, trained and supervised a staff of 9 account executives, 3 underwriters and 2 secondary market managers. Increased market share in the territory by 88%. Traveled extensively throughout the territory and made calls on CEOs.

PRODUCT MANAGER 1/78 to 9/81, Minneapolis. Developed and implemented marketing plans for specialized insurance products for mortgage lending financial institutions: Error/Omission Coverage, Special Hazard Coverage, and Officers/Employees Liability Coverage. Responsible for national marketing of the products. Sales volume for these products increased an average of 22% per year.

American Insurance Company, Atlanta, Georgia 6/74 to 1/78

DIRECTOR OF FIELD OPERATIONS 6/76 to 1/78, Atlanta. Had total responsibility for sales production of 6 regional and 21 state managers. Introduced new mortgage life and disability insurance programs and created a highly effective sales training program.

REGIONAL MANAGER 6/74 to 6/76, St. Louis. Supervised operations of 4 state managers and personally generated new business in metropolitan St. Louis.

Niagara Home Life Assurance Company, Palo Alto, California 8/68 to 6/74

ASSISTANT VICE PRESIDENT - Negotiated exclusive contracts with S&Ls for the sale of Niagara Home Life's Mortgage Life Plan and Disability Plan. Designed and implemented a specialized Insured Savings Plan for Savings and Loan depositors which had an excellent effect on insurance sales. Recruited and trained sales agents.

Prior Employment

SALES AGENT/TRAINER, Home Owners Security, Inc. 2/64 to 8/68
SALES AGENT, Home Security Associates 2/62 to 2/64

Typeface: Times Roman

PEOPLE WITH PORTFOLIOS

Architects, drafters, artists, designers, photographers, models, and writers, use portfolios to help sell themselves. They often make the mistake of placing too little emphasis on a top-quality resume, assuming the portfolio alone will sell them.

As important as your portfolio is, don't shortchange yourself. There are lots of talented people out there with outstanding portfolios. Taking the time to develop an effective resume will make an important difference to your job hunting success. Your resume can reveal qualities and background that won't come across in your portfolio. A portfolio can express your technical or creative ability, but a resume reveals where you've been and how you developed your ability. In fact, without an effective resume you'll rarely get the opportunity to show that fantastic portfolio you so painstakingly assembled.

Artistic people are stereotyped as temperamental. In your resume do everything possible to demonstrate that you are flexible and easy to work with.

Consider reproducing two or three samples of your work on 8½" x 11" paper. Then, either enclose it with your resume, or give it to employers when you meet them face to face. When reviewing the samples a week or two after meeting you, the employer will be helped to remember both you and your portfolio better. Writers should attach clippings or short pieces for a similar effect.

Graphic artists and designers should feel free to come up with creative formats for their resumes. This is one of the few groups of people who will benefit from having a resume typeset since it is an opportunity to show their graphics ability.

The most important thing to note in Bobbie's resume, is simply that employers will know much more about her than if they only saw a portfolio. Quantifying results is harder for artistic people than for many others, but do your best. In Bobbie's resume, there are no quantifiable results. Still, you get a sense that she is dedicated and very capable. If employers liked her portfolio, the resume will simply help them remember her more easily.

BOBBIE BLANE
1127 Mariposa Drive
Santa Barbara, California 93110
(805) 651-2720

OBJECTIVE: Graphics/Illustration Artist

QUALIFICATIONS

Develop excellent relations with clients and have satisfied even the most demanding. Specialty is personality portraiture used in advertising.

Excellent graphics and illustration training and experience. Skilled in design, layout, paste-up, lettering, story boards, and the use of darkrooms and stat cameras. Knowledgeable of printing procedures and experienced in preparing work for printing. Have operated printing presses and other printing-related equipment. Prepared work for black-and-white and full-color reproduction, as well as two- and three-color.

EDUCATION

Bachelor of Fine Arts, Illustration, Seymour Art Center (1985)

EMPLOYMENT

Freelance Work 1987 to Present

ARTIST - Painted and sold over 45 portraits and scenes using water color, graphite, pen and ink, egg tempura, and oil.

Provided graphics and illustration for numerous projects: notebook cover, Advancetec (1991); brochure cover, Barr & Associates (1991); map and tour guide, Santa Barbara Museum of Natural History (1990); catalog and advertising design, Briton Engineering (1990); work order design, Armor Advertising (1989); logo and menu design, Silk Oyster Restaurant (1989); logo, business card design, Donner Electronics, Inc. (1989); magazine illustration, *Psychology Today* (1988); catalog design, Sunstra Inc. (1987); scratchboard portrait of DeVinci for ad appearing in *Smithsonian* (1987); layout, design, illustration, *Infoworld* (1987).

Jonathan Edwards Galleries, Santa Barbara, California 1984 to Present

ART DEALER - Assist customers in purchasing art works for both personal viewing and as investments. Help customers in understanding the artist and
the art piece. Have developed an excellent reputation with customers for knowledge, helpfulness, and tact.

Redecorate the gallery as new works are shown and touch up damaged pieces. Commissioned through the gallery to do portraits. Currently showing several personal works of children and scenes including "Cool Mist," "High Noon," "Children in the Sun." Help design the monthly newsletter and provide calligraphy and design expertise for gallery signs.

Typeface: Benguiat

MILITARY PERSONNEL

To write a successful resume, the person with 6–30 years in the military needs to have confidence that the abilities he or she possesses are marketable. Without that assurance the resume will probably come out bland and next to useless. Feel good about yourself. Regardless of your function in the military, you developed skills there which are valuable in the civilian job market. If you plan well, analyze your strengths, and are clear on what you want to do in civilian life, you should have no more difficulties than anyone else finding the job you want.

Use Your Strengths

Analyze your background carefully and emphasize the experience that will help sell you into a civilian job. There may be functions you performed in the military that are so unique to the military that they should be mentioned briefly or not at all. You've done plenty of things which civilian managers are looking for so emphasize those things.

If you have been involved in any phase of electronics, computers, mechanics, or other technical fields, you are highly marketable. The U.S. government has invested thousands of dollars training you, and there are employers who seek your expertise and experience.

Many ex-pilots have gone to work for airlines and defense contractors. Don't feel limited to seeking jobs that are directly related to your military functions, however. As an officer you were assigned various command positions. Describe them properly, and you can sell yourself into a midmanagement or executive position. Whatever your background, sell your experience.

Things to Avoid

As you write your resume, scrupulously avoid military jargon, also known as militarese. Let a civilian read your resume to determine if your descriptions are understandable.

Be careful about mentioning the supervision of large numbers of people. In the military, to have responsibility for 500 people is not unusual, but most presidents of companies never have 500 people under their control. Seeing such large numbers can seem threatening. Generally you would only list the number of direct reports.

Avoid phrases like "Responsible for overseeing a $95 million budget." In the military overseeing large budgets is common, but in the private sector, only presidents of the largest companies could make such statements. Again, it can seem threatening.

The same principle would apply if you were a pilot or ship's captain: "Responsible for a $21 million piece of equipment" (pilot) or, "Had total responsibility for operating and maintaining a $260 million piece of equipment" (captain of a destroyer). The statements may sound impressive, but they are actually counterproductive.

Using Evaluations And Letters Of Commendation

As a military person you have undoubtedly saved your fitness reports, evaluations, and letters of commendation. Selected short quotations can be included in your resume to make positive statements about yourself. Praise coming from an objective third party, especially from a superior, will carry more weight than if you made the same statement about yourself. Rarely should anyone include more than one or two quotes in the resume, so choose them wisely. See page 91 for an example of a retired military person who used extensive quotes from evaluations as an addendum to his resume. In places where the evaluation would have said "Captain Handle," it simply states "Handle," in order to remove as much military terminology as possible. These quotes were heavily edited, with only small portions of each evaluation included. When skipping portions of the evaluations there was no attempt to use ellipses (...) to signify a gap. Instead, it was all woven together to make a strong statement about Handle and allowing commanding officers to say things he couldn't say about himself.

Generally you should take your addendum (label it "Portions of Annual Evaluations") with you on interviews so that if it seems appropriate you could give a copy to your interviewer. Occasionally you might include it with your resume when you send it in the mail, but our research indicates that people with professional or technical experience are usually better off not including letters of recommendations or evaluations with their resumes.

For some military people a functional resume works best because no matter how they describe their jobs, those jobs don't sound like anything that goes on in the civilian world. See page 68 for an example.

In the first sample resume, Sanders does an excellent job of convincing the reader that he is totally dedicated to safety. It is clear that the record he set for the most consecutive months without a major accident, came by his dedication and the development of a comprehensive safety program.

In the second and third sample resumes, Tolson and Handle clearly sell their technical ability.

PETE SANDERS
237 Durham Way
Durham, California 95938
(213) 628-9714

OBJECTIVE: Safety Administrator

QUALIFICATIONS

Developed a comprehensive safety program which resulted in six years without a serious accident to any of the 800 personnel.

Proven ability to set up effective, low-cost, industrial safety programs which rely heavily on instilling a safety consciousness in all employees.

Totally familiar with OSHA regulations and compliance procedures and have worked closely with OSHA inspectors.

WORK EXPERIENCE

U. S. Army 1966 to 1992

SAFETY OFFICER - 1971 to 1992
While Safety Officer at Ft. Bradley for ten years, was responsible for the safety of 800 air field personnel ranging from mechanics, machine operators, and vehicle operators to supervisors and management staff. Developed a comprehensive safety program which set a Ft. Bradley record for safety. Awarded a six-year safety award for 72 consecutive months without a major accident (over $5,000 property damage or loss of life).

Directly supervised three safety technicians and coordinated the efforts of 20 officers responsible for safety in their immediate areas. Held monthly safety seminars to promote and enhance safety awareness within each specialized group.

Made daily and weekly inspections of offices, maintenance facilities, and mechanical, paint, electrical, and machine shops, to ensure compliance with safety regulations and performed on-the-spot corrections for minor infractions. Identified potentially hazardous practices and recommended changes.

Formulated and administered safety policies and procedures to ensure compliance with federal and state safety acts. Worked closely with OSHA inspectors and developed excellent knowledge of OSHA regulations.

AIRFIELD SAFETY OFFICER/PILOT, Ft. Bradley, California 1981 to 1992
AIRFIELD SAFETY OFFICER/PILOT, Munsun-ni, Korea 1979 to 1981
AIRFIELD SAFETY OFFICER/PILOT, Ft. Lewis, Washington 1972 to 1979
PILOT/SAFETY OFFICER, Da Nang, Vietnam 1971 to 1972
PILOT, Chu Lai, Vietnam, 1967 to 1971
PILOT, Ft. Benning, Georgia 1966 to 1967

EDUCATION

Business - California State University, 85 credits (1981-1984)

SAFETY EDUCATION

Accident Prevention, U. S. Army Agency for Aviation Safety, 640 class hours (1975).
U. S. Air Force Crash Investigators School, 320 class hours (1975).
Aviation Safety Officers Course, University of Southern California Safety Center, 960 class hours (1974). Course covered reconstructing accidents, investigative procedures, evidence acquisition, analysis of causation factors, methods of accident prevention, and gaining employee cooperation.

Typeface: Bookman

RICK TOLSON
PreComUnit USS Antrim
1102 S W Massachusetts Avenue
Seattle, Washington 98134
(206) 641-2737

QUALIFICATIONS

During seven years in Naval Communications gained broad experience in troubleshooting electronic systems. Specialty is recognizing system or circuit deterioration, isolating the fault, and restoring the system or circuit to normal operation through corrective procedures or by an alternate route. Personally construct, operate, and maintain all types of communication systems.

AREAS OF EXPERTISE

Constructing Communications Systems

Satellite Systems, High Speed Data Systems, Voice Systems, Teletype Systems, Continuous Wave.

Maintaining Communications Systems

Perform quality control and performance monitoring on audio and DC circuits.

Electronic Communications Equipment

Transmitters, transceivers, receivers, modems, multiplexers, demultiplexers, cryptogear, microwave, couplers, antennas, high level black patch panels, high and low level red patch panels, and numerous types of test equipment.

EDUCATION

Graduated Pisgah High School, Pisgah, Iowa (1986)

Navy Schools - Technical Control, Satellite Communications, Management, Communications Supervision, Maintenance and Material Management, High Frequency Transmitters, Antenna Maintenance.

WORK HISTORY

U.S. Navy August 1986 to Present

<u>Tech Controller, 1st Class Radioman</u> Assignments have included Naval Communications Stations, Naval Telecommunications Centers and three Navy ships. Since 1988 have supervised numerous groups of technicians and trained them to use sophisticated communications equipment. While involved with the construction of an FFG-7 class ship, developed an extensive set of lesson plans to explain the construction of the circuits and also diagrammed all of the wiring and block schematics for this new class of ship. These two projects will save hundreds of training hours. Participated in the quality control tests of the USS Antrim.

Top Secret Security Clearance

Typeface: Bookman

PAUL HANDLE
3715 Pearl Ave. N.
Everett, Washington 98206
(206) 954-3721

OBJECTIVE: Electrical, Electronic, Mechanical Maintenance

QUALIFICATIONS

Consistently rated superior in both technical expertise and supervisory ability. Constantly finding more effective methods of making repairs and reducing downtime of equipment.

EDUCATION

Graduated - Sheppton High School, Sheppton, Pennsylvania (1965)

EMPLOYMENT

US Navy, 10/65 to 12/92

ELECTRONICS INSTRUCTOR 2/87 to 12/92. Provided comprehensive instruction to maintenance technicians and pilots covering aircraft electrical and electronic systems. Courses ranged from basic electricity and electronics to advanced solid state theory and repair. Taught 13 separate courses averaging 80 classroom hours each. Course Manager for 5 of the 13 courses. Took difficult courses and made them more practical and easier to understand. Wrote numerous manuals and lesson guides which simplified previous courses. Students consistently outscored the students of other instructors.

SENIOR SUPERVISOR 7/75 to 2/87. Supervised 2 shift supervisors and up to 35 technicians. Developed work schedules for personnel, scheduled maintenance, and provided overall management of a large maintenance shop. Trained new technicians and personally performed many repairs on state of the art aircraft electrical systems, automatic flight control systems, and navigational systems.

Took over one command position where outdated maintenance and record keeping procedures had created serious maintenance problems. Reorganized the reporting and maintenance procedures and streamlined the operation. In 36 months the unit moved from "poor" to "excellent" in readiness reports.

ELECTRONIC MAINTENANCE SUPERVISOR 6/69 to 7/75. Supervised up to 20 technicians in the repair of electrical and electronic aircraft systems.

AVIATION ELECTRICIAN 10/65 to 6/69. Maintenance and service technician on aircraft electrical and navigational systems.

TRAINING - Navy Schools (completed over 75 courses with a total of 2,400 classroom hours)

Advanced Electronics Courses (1970 - 1990)
  Polyphase power and control systems (200 hours)
  Advanced magnetic devices (240 hours)
  Digital, analog, solid-state, and T.T.L. devices (400 hours)
  Advanced syncro/analog/solid state control and indicating systems (400 hours)
  Hybrid solid-state inertial navigation systems (200 hours)
  High resolution hydraulic/electronic T.T.L. control systems (160 hours)
  Component/miniature component repair, including P.C.B (160 hours)

Aviation Electrician Course, 1965 (320 hours)

Typeface: Times Roman

Paul Handle
PORTIONS OF SEMI-ANNUAL EVALUATIONS

Handle's broad qualifications and maintenance know how on A6A electrical systems have enabled him to become a particularly valuable instructor. He is always striving to make difficult courses easier for the students to comprehend by ensuring that proper maintenance procedures are included in his lessons. His willingness to work at any task, no matter how large or small, has contributed materially to the mission of NAMTD. His conduct sets an example worthy of emulation by other officers. He has amply demonstrated a fair and unbiased attitude, readily accepting each and every person as an individual. Handle is industrious, thorough, and accurate in this work and extremely conscientious in all duties and endeavors. He is alert and stable, displaying a creative mind. He shows great ability to develop effective procedural methods and to prepare excellently written and easily understood lesson guides. He secures the attention and respect of his students whom he guides and directs with understanding and tact. He is frequently called upon by other rate groups of this detachment to help solve technical problems in the writing of lesson guides. He attacks these problems with a cheerful and aggressive nature, seeing any problems through to a successful conclusion. Success in his work is shown by the students' final grades and their comment sheets. January 1991

Handle is intelligent, exceptionally quick to learn, with the ability to grasp pertinent details rapidly. Given broad guidelines, he accomplishes assigned tasks in an enthusiastic and exemplary manner. Handle is a conscientious and concerned instructor who demonstrates a sincere feeling of responsibility towards his students and works very hard to ensure they receive maximum benefit from his instruction. He is equally at ease before a group of juniors or seniors. He is very effective in conveying his thoughts clearly and fluently, both in casual conversation or when presenting a formal lesson. During this reporting period, he has been assigned the task of writing the avionics portion of AZF under the individualized instruction format. He willingly assisted other instructors with this new format and readily assumed the responsibility of insuring that uniformity was met by all rate groups. He spent many hours researching instructions. Acting as liaison between rate groups, he arranged and conducted meetings to achieve this goal. January 1989

Handle has been extremely instrumental in the training of the less experienced men assigned to the branch. He can be counted on to do any assigned task correctly, efficiently and safely. January 1987

Handle is a dedicated, knowledgeable First Class Electrician who strives to ensure work is completed safely and that the proper maintenance procedures are utilized. He keeps his superiors informed of all potential trouble areas and draws on his vast experience to propose viable solutions. He leads with an easy-going, unobtrusive manner, never interfering with the personal initiative of those he supervises. He plans the work load efficiently and utilizes a smooth rapport with the men to carry out the work. January 1985

Handle has demonstrated a high proficiency in his field and is very adept at putting his knowledge and experience to good use. He has an ability to quietly evaluate difficult situations and to arrive at practical solutions while working under trying conditions. He is a very thoughtful and sincere person who has the ability to communicate with the younger technicians and to define some of their problems. January 1983

Handle is a calm and reserved supervisor who receives the full support of his subordinates without haranguing or berating them. His assigned tasks are never too insignificant to warrant his total attention. The capable manner in which he plans and assigns work to his technicians is further enhanced by his cheerful and pleasing personality. These traits, coupled with his willingness to work with others, make for a smooth running crew on his shift. January 1981

COMPUTER SPECIALISTS

The computer business is a unique field and requires a special type of resume. This is especially true for programmers. Since the average programmer stays only 18 months with an organization, managers usually look for someone who can step right in and do the job, based on past experience with the computer, language, and operating system used in that organization. This is a source of great frustration for programmers because many feel that in two to three weeks they can master any new system—all they need is an opportunity to prove it. Your task is to make the most out of the experience you have and to demonstrate your adaptability.

It is generally best to list all languages you know, as well as all hardware, operating systems, and applications software you've been exposed to. Usually they would be listed in your order of expertise. The interview is the place to discuss your level of expertise. Listing everything you have exposure to can make the difference in whether you will get an interview because some companies now input your resume into a database via scanning. The computer then spits out the resumes that mentioned all or most of the key items.

The data processing resume is actually fairly simple to write because it consists of several distinct sections that practically write themselves. Start with Areas of Experience. Typically, it will consist of Languages, Systems, Special Programs, Computers, Conversions, and Applications. Applications can be further divided into New Applications and Maintenance. It should be easy, almost like filling in the blanks.

Because programming and other computer jobs are so project-oriented, it is often better to place more emphasis on projects than on job descriptions. A special projects section will work great. Provide just enough information in each project description to give an employer a feel for what you did, then concentrate on results. This section is very important and will probably require three drafts. Start by listing the projects you feel would be most impressive. Since employers usually use resumes as a basis for interviews, be sure to choose projects that you would want to explain and describe in more detail in an interview.

For the first draft of your projects section, don't worry about length, just get your thoughts down on paper. In the second draft look for unnecessary words or phrases. The employer does not require a complete understanding of all the details, just enough information to indicate the degree of complexity and what was required to complete the project. Finish the project by describing the result. Your third draft will simply be a finer tuning of the second.

By emphasizing your areas of experience and special projects sections, your job descriptions will probably be quite short.

KEN WANDER
119 Tri-Cities Way
Richland, Washington 99352
(509) 454-4413

QUALIFICATIONS:

Broad experience in analyzing and solving complex programming and engineering problems. Through systems analysis and applications programming, develop programs that are maintained easily and run quickly. Use structured approach in programming.

EDUCATION:

B.S. - Mechanical Engineering, Ohio State University (1971)

AREAS OF EXPERIENCE:

Languages: COBOL, MVS-XA/JCL, IMS DB/DC, VSAM, TSO/ISPF/CLIST, RPG II, FORTRAN, QUIKJOB, BAL, Macro Assembler.

Special Programs: CRJE, SPF, PANVALET, ICCF, MVS Utilities, SMF/RMF, POWER, ASAP, HASP, JES, ADABAS.

Computers: IBM 370, 30xx, 43xx, and IBM AS/400.

New Applications: Program Inventory Reporting; Budget Updating and Reporting; Cash Flow Reporting; Data Decoding/Translating Systems; Automated Record Updating Systems; Records Management System Updating; Payroll Accounting.

Maintenance: Billing, Inventory Control, Accounts Receivable, and Sales Analysis; Purchase History Reporting; Bill-of-Material Updating and Reporting; Finished Goods Processing and Reporting; Mortgage Loan Reporting.

FUNCTIONAL EXPERIENCE:

Business and Information Applications:

Developed in six weeks a versatile system of RPG II programs for budget revising and reporting to reduce Daytex corporate budget preparation time from 12 man-weeks to 1.

Developed a translator in RPG II to convert System 36 prepared order entry data to fixed format for AS/400 processing. Installed Billing, Inventory Control, Accounts Receivable, and Sales Analysis Systems.

Information Management Applications:

Developed in three weeks a series of COBOL programs to inventory COBOL application programs directly from compressed records in source library.

Developed an ADABAS utility replacement which dynamically formats records and cuts run time from three hours to less than thirty minutes.

Automated record updating using QUIKJOB for 80% of Iowa registered voters from state drivers license tapes and telephone company directory listing tapes.

CHRONOLOGICAL EXPERIENCE:

Consultant, Wander Consulting 1981- Present. Programmer/analyst responsible for new applications and program maintenance in Dayton, OH; Davenport, IA.

Systems Engineer, IBM 1976 - 1981. Responsible for filling SE Services Contracts with sensor-based computer installations; marketing and technical support for customer installations.

Mechanical Engineer, IBM 1971-1976. Worked on various APL analysis applications for test equipment design and had line engineering responsibilities.

Typeface: Helvetica

Aamad Jamaala

250 Templeton   Omaha, Nebraska 68154   (402) 454-0987

QUALIFICATIONS

Strong background in the planning, installation, and maintenance of microcomputer systems, including LANs and WANs. Broad experience in connectivity and group processing. Work effectively as programmer and analyst to customize systems. Strong knowledge of PC-based operating systems including OS/2, MS-DOS, Unix, Xenix, and Novell.

Broad experience in building database, spreadsheet, and desktop publishing systems that enhance and expand current capabilities. Extensive experience with dBase, FoxPro, Clipper, Paradox, Lotus 123, Excel, Pagemaker, and Ventura Publisher. Provide excellent training for users. Experienced with C/C++, Pascal, COBOL, FORTRAN, and Basic.

EDUCATION/CERTIFICATIONS

A.A. - Computer Science/Accounting, Belmont Community College (1985)
Novell Certified Network Engineer (CNE) (1991)
Qualified Instructor, Aldus PageMaker, Xerox Ventura Publisher (1990)

PROFESSIONAL HISTORY

Cyrus Computer, Omaha, Nebraska 1989 to Present

PC SPECIALIST - Install LANs, WANs, and PC systems. Select appropriate software and install on all PCs at each site. Train users and provide support. Create custom software and modify off the shelf software. Special projects include:

Wrote a database listing product in C/C++ for a major bank that works on an intelligent 3270 work station with proprietary BIOS. Developed a dBase file update program giving users ability to update DBF formatted lists using pull-down menus. Product was completed on schedule, exceeds all requirements, and is liked by users.

Complex data conversions include: Large customer data list from a Digital RSX Micro to a DOS / Novell based environment using a DOS A100 emulation. 120M bytes of data from an IBM 34 to Mac by using a DOS 5152 emulation and then DOS to Mac.

Wrote a claims tracking system in FoxPro. System has been in use for two years with no bugs. It has streamlined the claims process and permitted greater accessibility to claims data.

Developed a Lotus spreadsheet interface to the Great Plains Payroll program, permitting a greatly simplified entry process to produce payrolls. Interface was written in Paradox to allow greater flexibility during data entry and better report generation capability.

Micro Accounting Consultants, Omaha, Nebraska 1985-1989

TECHNICAL SUPPORT - Produced a variety of custom programs for small businesses in the greater Omaha area.

Typeface: Times Roman

SALESPEOPLE

Salespeople typically hate to write. That fact is generally quite evident in their resumes, most of which are poorly written, poorly designed, and reveal very little of substance. Taking just four to five hours of your time to write a quality resume could net you an extra $100,000 in your lifetime earnings.

The sales resume is usually one of the easiest to write because it is so results oriented. Sales resumes rarely require extensive details about duties because sales managers already know what you do. What they care about is the bottom line. Don't tell a sales manager how hard you worked or how many phone calls you made or how many sales calls you went on. Did you sell? That's all that counts.

There are a number of ways to show results: sales awards, your ranking within your sales organization, improving the position of your territory compared to other territories in the company, increasing sales, increasing profits on sales, or increasing market share. Use whatever is most appropriate. If you know your market share or can estimate it pretty closely, use that figure. Market share is effective because it provides an excellent means of comparison. During an economic boom with high inflation, the gross sales of even a mediocre salesperson will increase 5-8% annually. To increase market share, however, means you have taken business away from competitors and increased your share of the pie. It means you're doing something right. Employers won't know if you've done it on the basis of your great personality, your outstanding closing techniques, your strong product knowledge, your hard work, or your excellent time management, but it won't matter. Sales managers care only about results.

Showing increases in market share is great, but most companies simply don't do the research to know what those figures are, territory by territory. Use whatever figures will work best for you. During the last recession even many outstanding salespeople were not able to say that they increased sales. In some industries just holding steady was the mark of a great salesperson.

To show yourself in the best light you might use a combination. Let's say from 1979 through 1981 you sold office machines. Those were recession years in some parts of the country. You took over an established territory and only increased gross sales 14% in three years, slightly less than inflation. You obviously won't brag about your sales increases. Out of a sales staff of 18, you were second in sales, since no one else sold well either. That would be the result you would use. In 1982 and 1983 you sold photocopiers. You were in the right place at the right time and sales really took off and increased 20% each year for an actual increase of 44% over two years. Assuming you didn't know what market share was, nor how you did compared to the rest of the sales staff, you would certainly want to use the sales increases.

In 1984 through 1986 you decided to sell cars. You did well and each year won an award from the manufacturer. You were also Salesperson of the Month eight times during your 34 months with the dealership. You were competing with 12 other salespeople. For that job you would mention the awards and the number of times you were Salesperson of the Month. In 1986 you went to work for a tractor manufacturer which paid a research firm to determine the market share in each territory. Between 1986 and the end of 1989 the market share in your territory increased from 15% to 20%, a 33% increase in market share. In 1990 you joined a heavy equipment distributor and moved the territory from seventh to second. Sales were flat due to the recession. The resume might look something like this:

B & N Machinery, Tempe, Arizona 1/90 to Present

MARKETING REPRESENTATIVE - Developed and implemented marketing strategies to increase heavy equipment sales to the construction industry in Arizona. Took the territory from 7th (out of 8) in the company to 2nd during the first 36 months.

John Deere, Phoenix, Arizona 10/86 to 12/89

DISTRICT REPRESENTATIVE - Assisted 26 dealers in Arizona and New Mexico in marketing John Deere products. Set up five new dealers and developed their sales, parts and service departments. Moved seven dealers from near bankruptcy to very strong financial positions. Increased market share 33%.

Gerald Lincoln Mercury, Phoenix, Arizona 1/84 to 10/86

SALESMAN - Each year won the Professional Sales Counselor award for sales excellence. Out of a sales force of 12, was salesperson of the month 8 times in 34 months.

Canon Corporation, Trenton, New Jersey 11/81 to 12/83

SALES REPRESENTATIVE - Sold a full line of photocopiers to end users. In two years increased territorial sales 44%.

Olivetti Corporation, Trenton, New Jersey 1/79 to 11/81

SALES REPRESENTATIVE - Sold typewriters, calculators and dictating equipment to office equipment stores throughout metropolitan Trenton. Worked closely with store managers and sales staffs and provided excellent training in selling Olivetti products. Ranked 2nd in sales in 1981 out of a regional sales force of 18.

If you haven't been doing so up to this time, begin collecting and saving all the sales data you can. Whenever you start a new position, get data on what the territory was doing prior to your taking over. In the absence of cold, hard figures, rely on your memory and your knowledge of the territory. Estimate and guesstimate when you must, but do come up with some figures which you feel are accurate, and be sure you can explain how they were derived.

PAUL KIRSTEN
525 Bates S.W.
Beaverton, Oregon 97006
(503) 962-0013

OBJECTIVE: Sales Representative

EMPLOYMENT

Prescal & Hemsted Wire Rope Company, Beaverton, Oregon 3/85-Present

Sales Representative (2/87-Present). Sell wire rope through 18 distributors and through direct sales to OEM accounts, covering Oregon, Washington, and Alaska. Between 1987 and 1990, built sales from $652,000 to $1,404,000 and have maintained that level despite the logging industry depression. Trained all inside sales staff in effective sales techniques.

Inside Sales Manager/Office Manager (3/85-2/87). Handled all inside sales, purchasing, inventory control, and traffic. Supervised the warehouse and shipping/receiving operations. Reorganized the office and warehousing procedures which increased on-time deliveries and customer satisfaction. Coordinated a switch from a manual to a computerized inventory control and billing system. Regional sales manager attributed most of the 22% sales increase between 1985 and 1987 to the new level of professionalism at the order desk.

Peterson Manufacturing Company, Coos Bay, Oregon 2/79-3/85

Sales Representative (3/83-3/85). Sold replacement parts for the barkers and chippers manufactured by Peterson, covering Oregon, Washington, Idaho, and Montana. Increased sales of replacement parts 16%.

Inside Sales (2/81-3/83). Called on customers of Peterson products and sold replacement parts. Worked closely with purchasers of new machines to ensure an adequate inventory of the parts most likely to need replacing. When replacing 10- to 25-year-old parts, worked with engineering to determine if newer parts could be adapted or required new castings.

Expediter (2/79-2/81). Responsible for expediting, scheduling, and inventory control in the manufacturing of custom-made wood barkers and chippers. Significantly increased total production and on-time deliveries.

EDUCATION

B.S. - History, University of Oregon (1979)

Typeface: Avant Garde

GAIL SHUMWAY
2928 Sunset Blvd.
Phoenix, Arizona 85004
(602) 755-2428

QUALIFICATIONS

As Division Manager and Area Marketing Manager, increased market share each year by effectively identifying new markets, recruiting and developing successful sales teams, and obtaining quantifiable results through Total Quality programs.

EDUCATION

MBA - Marketing, University of Colorado (1978)
BS - Electrical Engineering, California State Polytechnic University (1974)

EMPLOYMENT HISTORY

Dyatech Inc. 11/85 to Present

DIVISION MANAGER - Phoenix Division 7/89 to Present. Responsible for the total operation and profits for this distributor of electronic components and systems, with sales to industrial users, original equipment manufacturers, and federal and state agencies. Supervise 45 employees. Introduced an effective Total Quality program into an organization with low morale and loose controls. As a result, market share has increased from 10% to 14%, while customer retention has been increased 65%.

AREA MARKETING MANAGER - Denver Division 11/85 to 7/89. Managed the 22-employee Colorado Area in the four-state Denver Division. Created and implemented a new concept in technical marketing which doubled sales and increased market share from 12% to 22%.

Insofen Corporation 5/81 to 11/85

FIELD ENGINEER - Denver, Colorado. Covering Colorado and Utah, sold high technology semiconductor products to major manufacturers of electronic equipment. Worked closely with engineers to get proprietary devices designed into new products. Increased sales from $60,000 to $210,000 per month.

Xytex Corporation 7/74 to 5/81

ENGINEER - Boulder, Colorado. Designed power systems and interfaces for data processing peripheral equipment.

Typeface: Bookman

WARREN DRISCOL
927 Honeycut Drive
Atlanta, Georgia 30032
(404) 527-6819

OBJECTIVE: Sales/Marketing Management

QUALIFICATIONS

Strong Sales and Marketing background. Significantly increased territorial market share in each position held, with increases ranging from 45-330%.

EDUCATION

B.S. - Forest Engineering, University of Georgia (1973)

EMPLOYMENT

Ubasco Machinery Company, Atlanta, Georgia 8/90 to Present

FOREST PRODUCTS SALES MANAGER - As Ubasco's first Forest Products Sales Manager, responsible for selling to key accounts and for training the sales staff in methods of increasing sales of earth moving equipment to forestry related companies. Perform extensive market research to target sales and identify sales potential. Gross profit has been increased from 14% to 18% and unit sales have increased an average of 16% per year.

John Deere Tractor Company 7/73 to 8/90

FOREST PRODUCTS SALES REPRESENTATIVE, Atlanta, Georgia 8/85 to 8/90. Developed and implemented marketing strategies to increase sales to the forest industry through 24 Southeastern John Deere dealers. Worked closely with the dealers and trained their sales people to sell earth moving equipment to the forest industry. Created a special training program which covered sales techniques and forestry applications of John Deere equipment. Unit sales were increased 148% and market share was increased from 6% to 26% between 1985 and 1989.

DISTRICT REPRESENTATIVE, Bangkok, Thailand 11/82 to 8/85. Responsible for increasing sales and service levels among all dealers in India, Sri Lanka, Bangladesh, Thailand, Taiwan, South Korea and the Philippines. Identified new market areas, developed marketing strategies for dealers, and trained sales forces in effective sales techniques. Increased John Deere's market share from 14% to 21%.

PRODUCT/MARKET REP, Hong Kong 2/76 to 11/82. Conducted market studies and consulted with dealers on applications and modifications of John Deere equipment. Developed an extensive market study on the uses of wheel loaders in Asia and concluded a huge untapped market existed for wheel loaders to replace track-driven loaders. Made sales calls with dealers throughout Asia as they visited customers. Businesses immediately switched to wheel loaders. Sales of wheel loaders increased an average of 76% each year between 1978 and 1982 and captured over 60% of that market.

MARKET REP, Spokane, Washington 7/73 to 2/76. Acted as machinery application consultant to dealers. Studied mill and mining operations and made recommendations for the most appropriate John Deere equipment.

Typeface: Helvetica

99

PRISCILLA BEACHMAN
2820 232nd Place SE
Renton, Washington 98055
(206) 765-2321

OBJECTIVE: Marketing and Sales

QUALIFICATIONS

Effectively market products and services and substantially increase sales. Create strong working relations with wholesalers and retailers. Excellent reputation and high credibility with buyers from all grocery and drug chains in Washington, Oregon, and Idaho.

Quickly promoted by Modern Circulation because of high sales and increased circulation. Opened up magazine sales in chains that had never before sold magazines. Cultivated excellent relations with those buyers and demonstrated how a carefully monitored magazine sales program could increase profits.

Developed new marketing techniques and tools which are now used throughout the industry.

EDUCATION

Riverside Community College, Business, 72 credits (1980-1982)

EMPLOYMENT

Modern Circulation 6/84 to Present

MARKETING AND PROMOTION MANAGER, Renton, Washington 9/88 to Present. For the largest circulation company in the U.S., responsible for increasing the circulation of 750 magazines within Washington, Oregon, and Idaho. Supervise seven District Managers with a total volume of $40 million. Work closely with buyers from chain stores to obtain rack space for publications and to help increase the chain's profits through magazine sales. Handle publicity and special promotions for various magazines and promote magazines through national and regional trade shows.

Developed a marketing strategy for Pay Less Drugs and introduced a magazine sales checkout program into 148 stores on the West Coast. Rated second in productivity among fifteen Marketing Managers nationwide in 1991 and 1992.

DISTRICT SALES MANAGER, Portland, Oregon 3/87 to 9/88. Worked directly with five magazine wholesalers and dozens of retail accounts to increase circulation of publications. Solved serious problems with one major wholesaler and enabled it to move from 14th largest on the West Coast to 6th. Increased the Modern Circulation line 30% on $6 million of annual sales.

SALES REPRESENTATIVE, Seattle, Washington 6/84 to 3/87. Significantly increased magazine sales to independent retailers and was quickly promoted to District Sales Manager to work with larger accounts.

Colgate Palmolive, Seattle, Washington 10/82 to 6/84

MERCHANDISER. Called on drug and grocery accounts, taking orders, creating displays, and stocking as needed. Opened up Skaggs for the first time to the full line of Colgate Palmolive products.

Typeface: Times Roman

CAREER CHANGERS

And the day came when the risk to remain tight in a bud was more painful than the risk it took to blossom. —Unknown

I applaud people making career changes. Career changers can find greater job satisfaction and a lifestyle more in tune with their current values. Career changers, however, have the most difficult and frustrating experiences with resumes. When they use the traditional approach of mailing out 100 or more resumes, career changers experience very little success. While having an effective resume is still necessary for career changers, the resume *must* be used in a way that takes advantage of the hidden job market.

If you are a career changer, the first thing you must do is determine the type of position you'll be seeking. Then pick out every experience even remotely related to that line of work and insert it in some form into the resume. The qualifications section is often an excellent place to do this.

When you start describing your employment, you have two main goals: 1) show you were successful at what you did; and 2) emphasize any parts of your jobs which are related to your current objective. Your successes are important. Employers are dubious enough about hiring a career changer; they certainly want a person with a proven record of success. Essentially you'll be saying through your resume, "I've been successful in the past, and I'll be successful for you, also." Emphasizing related experience in each job is important. In most cases you should provide an adequate and accurate overview of your entire job, but that can usually be covered in one or two sentences. The remaining space should cover those functions which are related to your objective. In other words, duties which took up only 10% of your time may get 90% of the space.

Career changers tend to have longer qualifications sections than those who have years of experience in the same field. Career changers sometimes do better with a functional resume. Read pages 62 to 69 for a full explanation and several examples. Rosalyn used a lengthy qualifications section very effectively. The points made in qualifications could not have been adequately made in the employment section. Notice how she emphasized everything she had ever done that was related to training and development in any way.

Paula does everything possible to show she is sales oriented and that her efforts have consistently increased revenue. Although she has never held a job labeled "Sales Representative," it is very easy to picture her being successful in sales.

I also recommend that you join appropriate associations and volunteer to head up committees or special projects. Associations are usually begging for people to spend time on projects and you don't need to have been a member for five years. It is an excellent way to get recognized and to meet the top people in your field. Those projects or committee assignments could then go in a special projects section.

ROSALYN RODRIQUEZ
2315 Dixie Avenue
Charleston, South Carolina 29406
(803) 976-4204

OBJECTIVE: Position in Training and Development

QUALIFICATIONS

Broad background in planning and developing programs. Skilled in determining program needs through task analysis. Planned and organized numerous programs, including the Council for Exceptional Children 1989 State Conference.

Extensive knowledge and experience in determining needs, setting behavioral and learning objectives, and developing assessment tools. M.A. in Curriculum and Program Development.

Expertise in selecting appropriate teaching techniques to match the audience. Quickly establish rapport with groups.

Outstanding record in education. Received ratings of excellent to outstanding in all evaluations.

Evaluated and selected speakers and consultants for educational topics and conventions.

Extensive budgetary and purchasing experience with instructional materials.

Excellent writer. Wrote three successful grant proposals and published two articles on curriculum development for the *Journal of Education.*

Extensive knowledge of statistics and research methodologies for determining effectiveness of programs.

Strong abilities in performing and graphics arts. Directed, stage-managed, and designed sets and costumes for numerous theatrical productions.

Designed and produced newsletters, manuals, and brochures using desk top publishing.

Extensive experience writing, producing, and editing video programs.

EDUCATION

M.A. - Curriculum and Instruction, University of South Carolina (1976)
B.A. - Art, Arkansas State Teachers College (1971)

EMPLOYMENT

Teacher, Charleston Public Schools, Charleston, South Carolina 9/78 to Present
Teacher, Greenville Public Schools, Greenville, South Carolina 9/71 to 9/78

ASSOCIATIONS

Member - American Society for Training and Development
Member - Council for Exceptional Children; State Bylaws Chairperson 1986 to Present;
Chapter President 1985; Chapter Vice President 1984

Typeface: Times Roman

PAULA PROJASKA
2531 Sealdan Avenue #26
Danbury, Connecticut 06816
(203) 752-9628

JOB OBJECTIVE: Sales

QUALIFICATIONS

Proven ability to sell products and services. Quickly develop product knowledge and relate very well to people at all levels.

Strong track record. The Four Winds Hotel increased its revenue 70% in six years without remodeling or advertising more heavily—the staff simply cared more and gave more.

EDUCATION

B.A. - Public Relations, Wesleyan University (1985)

EMPLOYMENT

Four Winds Hotel, Danbury, Connecticut 1986-Present

EXECUTIVE ASSISTANT (1991-Present). Implemented numerous training and staff development programs which have raised guest service to the highest level found in Danbury. Increased communication and cooperation between departments and implemented an effective cross training program. Since 1991 hotel revenue has increased an average of 14% per year. Work closely with the Chamber of Commerce and perform PR functions with other local businesses and organizations.

FOOD SERVICES COORDINATOR (1988 to 1991). Introduced new food and room services which increased room revenue 11% per year and food/beverage revenue 12% per year. Supervised a staff of sixty.

ASSISTANT FOOD SERVICES COORDINATOR (1986-1988). Coordinated all food services including room service, coffee shop, dining room, lounge, and meeting rooms. Supervised a staff of 20. Designed a new training program which instilled more professionalism in the staff. Annual turnover was cut from 20% to 5%. As service improved, room revenue and food and beverage revenue each increased 40% in two years.

Typeface: Times Roman

MANAGERS/SUPERVISORS

Providing results in a resume is important for everyone, but is especially critical for managers. Being a manager is unique in that most of the work you accomplish is through the efforts of others. As a manager, however, you get to take credit for any results of your department or work unit. While others did most of the actual work, you guided and oversaw the efforts, approved the actions taken, and of course, had responsibility for the success of your department as well as any projects or programs.

The resume is the place to describe your results and the interview is the place to provide the details as to how those results were achieved, who they were achieved through, and what your role was. The resume is definitely not the place to try to give credit to your staff, and it is unnecessary since everyone reading your resume will know that others assisted you.

In the resume and in interviews get rid of any tendencies toward false modesty. You must come across as confident, dynamic, and decisive.

If you have not done so already, start a habit of quantifying your results at the time they occur. As you begin a project do your best to quantify what the current situation is. If you are trying to decrease rejects you need to know the current level of rejects and the level of rejects after you have implemented your new process. If you are trying to improve customer satisfaction, you need to know the current level, probably through some type of a survey. In this way the numbers you report in your resume will be "harder" and thus more impressive. For results from the past, you'll have to be satisfied with your best estimates and whatever figures you have.

It often helps to indicate the size of your department, the number of direct reports, and the dollar value of your department's budget, but include it only if you feel it will help sell you.

See pages 27 to 32 for more on results. Sometimes it is best to show the before and after raw figures, other times it is preferable to use percentages or dollar figures. Do not get caught in the trap that your results must be super impressive. If rejects are reduced from 6.5% to 6%, that is still an 8% decrease and is very significant. Use your results to show that wherever you are, you constantly looking for ways to improve your operations.

DOROTHY MICKULIN
9103 Union
Kansas City, Missouri 64133
(816) 276-4217

OBJECTIVE: Operations Management

QUALIFICATIONS

Strong background in branch operations management. As a branch operations troubleshooter, have turned around operations at eleven branches. At each branch have strengthened training, and reduced operations charge-offs, absenteeism, and turnover. Through extensive cross-training, have increased productivity and reduced overtime. Very effective in training staff to sell banking services and maintain customer loyalty.

EMPLOYMENT

Kansas City Trust & Savings 10/69-Present

BRANCH OPERATIONS MANAGER 9/85-Present. Responsible for the smooth functioning of branch operations, while supervising 20 employees. Produce many weekly, monthly and annual reports, including Charge-off, Dormant Control, Expense Accounts, Full Time Equivalent, Methods and Analysis Branch Study, Suspense, Internal Certification on Branch Accounts, and Budget and Profit Plan.

As Branch Operations Manager of two branches, have overcome morale problems and increased productivity. Worked closely with each staff and significantly improved morale through better training and supervision. At each branch absenteeism, turnover and operations charge-offs have been significantly reduced. The customer service rating has been increased at each branch at least 35%.

RELIEF SUPERVISOR 9/79-9/85. Functioned as temporary Branch Operations Manager at nine branches. Supervised 8 to 20 employees. Given a mandate at each branch to resolve operational, procedural, and employee problems. Turned around the situation at each branch to the satisfaction of the Executive V.P. of Operations.

Prior positions with Kansas City Trust & Savings:

Operations Supervisor 8/72-9/79
Management Trainee 8/71-8/72
Note Teller 10/69-8/71

Typeface: New Century Schoolbook

DON ABRAHMS
6317 Avery Road
Fairfax, Virginia 22033
(703) 282-1971

QUALIFICATIONS

Broad experience in all phases of Property Management and Building Management. Able to keep occupancy rates high and tenants satisfied.

Strong ability in negotiating new and renewal leases.

Creative problem solver. Able to negotiate solutions to the satisfaction of all parties.

Able to identify new methods for cutting operating costs while increasing tenant services.

EDUCATION

A.A. - General Studies, Whipple Community College (1979)

EMPLOYMENT

Bridgeport Property Management, Fairfax, Virginia 6/80 to Present

PROPERTY MANAGER 8/88 to Present. Property Manager for Southfield Office Park and other commercial/industrial properties in Fairfax County. Negotiate new and renewal leases, resolve tenant problems, and oversee the maintenance of the buildings and grounds. As General Contractor, completed a major renovation of 10,560 square feet of office space at 18% under the estimated cost. Increased square footage rates 22% during the last year and a half and increased the occupancy rate from 92% to 97%. Using a long term, no interest federal government loan, initiated an energy management system which reduced energy costs 20%. Actively involved with budget planning and instituting cost controls.

BUILDING MANAGER 5/82 to 8/88. Managed all maintenance functions at Southfield Office Park and acted as General Contractor for tenant alterations and improvements. Worked effectively with subcontractors and consistently completed projects on schedule and within the budget. Planned and initiated an in-house HVAC mechanical department which reduced maintenance costs and increased tenant satisfaction. Obtained excellent results from janitorial and security services. Personally performed many repairs.

FIELD SUPERVISOR 6/80 to 5/82. Supervised grounds crews of up to 22 employees while constructing the Southfield Office Park. Operated cranes, cats, and other heavy equipment while supervising the land reclamation, and the construction of building sites, streets, parking lots, and utility systems.

Typeface: Helvetica

JON ARNETT
19112 Edgecliff Drive
Cleveland, Ohio 44119
(216) 726-3982

OBJECTIVE: Manufacturing Management

QUALIFICATIONS

Strong background in all aspects of production supervision in the electronics industry including job scheduling, quality assurance, inventory control, purchasing, and customer relations. Consistently increase quality, productivity, and on-time deliveries.

EDUCATION

Business, Dennison Community College, 66 credits (1976-1979)

EMPLOYMENT

Advanced Circuits, Cleveland, Ohio 7/89-Present

PRODUCTION MANAGER - Supervise 16 shop personnel in the production of prototype circuit boards. Handle cost estimating, job scheduling, production control, and inventory control. Reduced turnaround time on orders from three weeks to one without adding staff or increasing overtime. Established a Total Quality program which has reduced rejects 65%. Significantly reduced purchasing costs through a more effective inventory control program.

Digital Systems, Ashtabula, Ohio 5/85-7/89.

DRILLING AND FABRICATION SUPERVISOR - Supervised 12 production workers operating computer numerically controlled drilling and fabrication machines. Developed a new job scheduling system which reduced late deliveries by 30%. Researched inventory needs for raw materials and supplies and determined lead times. Data enabled company to reduce inventory on numerous items and also reduced work stoppages due to lack of parts approximately 40%. Increased production of printed circuit boards 22% with no additional employees.

Hudson Manufacturing, Akron, Ohio 3/78-5/85

LEAD PRODUCTION SUPERVISOR - 6/82-5/85. Supervised 2 supervisors, 4 leads, and 35 production personnel. Implemented a job scheduling system which increased on time deliveries 44% with an average of 150 shipments monthly. Heavily involved in the design of a new facility and planned the actual move.

SHOP LEAD - 4/79-6/82. Assigned jobs to 18 production workers in drilling, screening, plating, fabricating, and camera work. Developed a maintenance program which reduced production losses due to breakdowns 70%.

SILKSCREENER - 3/78-4/79. Hand screened circuitry, bakeable and UV curable solder mask, and sheet metal front panels.

Typeface: Times Roman

KYLE BAUMGARTNER
814 Horgen Avenue
Orlando, Florida 32807
(305) 981-4660

OBJECTIVE: Physical Distribution/Traffic Management

QUALIFICATIONS

Experienced in all phases of traffic management. Developed two traffic departments into smooth functioning, money saving organizations.

EDUCATION

A.A. - Transportation Management, Saltwater Community College (1984)

WORK HISTORY

Webber Industries, Orlando, Florida 8/89 to Present

TRAFFIC MANAGER - Manage the Traffic Department of this $25 million appliance parts manufacturer. Annual freight costs total $2.3 million. Set policies for freight handling, route all orders, negotiate rates and contracts with carriers, maintain compliance with transportation laws, file freight claims, mediate customer problems and complaints, and audit freight bills for payment.

Negotiated freight rates with a major carrier, cutting the rate by 20% and saving $75,000 per year.

Introduced a routing and consolidation program, saving $80,000 per year through multi-bill consolidations, utilizing carrier discounts, consolidating orders, and carrier selection.

Negotiated a product classification change for California freight, saving $12,000 annually.

Custer Distributors, Orlando, Florida 6/84 to 8/89

TRAFFIC AND DISTRIBUTION MANAGER - Managed the Shipping and Receiving and Distribution departments for this $28 million distributor of retail products. Annual freight costs totaled $1.9 million. Set up and managed a private trucking operation, saving $65,000 annually and significantly improving customer service. Introduced new procedures which increased productivity and created annual cost savings of over $85,000.

Typeface: Helvetica

MARSHALL TREVES
924 Durhamtree Place
Louisville, Kentucky 40229
(502) 666-2413

QUALIFICATIONS

Coordinate well with contractors and subcontractors. Resolve problems effectively and maintain excellent relations.

Extremely analytical and inventive. Develop unique solutions to construction problems.

Proven ability to get projects completed ahead of schedule and under budget. Produce highly accurate estimates.

Experienced in all phases of construction.

EMPLOYMENT

Blouton Ceiling Installation, Louisville, Kentucky 7/90 to Present

JOB SUPERINTENDENT - Manage projects for this ceiling subcontractor. Projects have included the First National Building, the remodeling of eighteen Louisville schools, and the Westgate Mall.

As Job Superintendent for the First National office building, supervised a crew of four and coordinated with the contractor and subcontractors to handle the many changes in the smoothest way possible.

While functioning as foreman of a crew remodeling schools in Louisville, developed a system which speeded up the work and allowed the project to be completed under budget and ahead of schedule.

As Job Superintendent on the sixty-five shop Westgate Mall, took a project that was over budget and ten weeks behind schedule and turned it around. Developed an excellent working relationship with the general contractor, organized the work more effectively, and created a highly motivated crew. Project was completed under budget and ahead of schedule.

Treves Construction, Louisville, Kentucky 2/81 to 7/90

OWNER/MANAGER - Provided subcontracting work in framing, finishing, dry wall, insulation, metal stud framing, aluminum siding, and soffits. Gained expertise in estimating, bidding, and purchasing. Developed a reputation for high quality work.

Prior Experience: Carpenter 6/72 to 2/81

EDUCATION

Electrical Engineering, Kentucky State University (1970-1972) 105 Credits

Typeface: Times Roman

OFFICE/CLERICAL WORKERS

As an office worker your primary responsibility is to demonstrate that you possess strong office skills, that you are hard working and efficient, that you are easy to work with, that you are reliable and resourceful, that you can take on greater responsibility, and that you look for ways to improve office operations.

Either in the qualifications section of the resume or in a section called Office Skills, you can list the types of computers you have used, knowledge of operating systems such as MS DOS and MS Windows, and experience with various applications software such as MS Word, Word Perfect, Lotus 1-2-3, and others. If you are really an expert in one or more applications, you can state that in qualifications, or you can divide the applications software into two categories under office skills, and label them "Expert In" and "Experienced In." If a term like "expert in" is a little too strong, try "Highly Experienced In."

Demonstrating that you are a hard worker, that you are very efficient, and that you are easy to work with, is usually best covered in the qualifications section and in the cover letter. If you really feel you have these qualities, simply tell the reader through the resume and cover letter. Another excellent way to sell these qualities is to show that you are a results oriented person. By selling your results you will sell the fact that you are efficient and easy to work with.

Do not feel that you must list every single duty that you had on each job. I've seen clerical resumes that were virtually unreadable because they simply consisted of a long list of duties. You may have had a duty which you carried out in each of your last six jobs, but in the resume you may choose to include that duty only in your first three jobs just to show that you have experience in that area. Of course with a key skill, you would list it in any job where you used it.

Some duties do not need to be mentioned at all. Since virtually every office person types and answers the phone, those two duties do not need to be mentioned unless you want to.

Sometimes a person is responsible for producing 10-15 different reports each month. Generally the names of those reports will have no meaning to a reader. If you are going to mention them at all, give them generic names such as "expense report" or "inventory report." You could say, "Produced 15 reports each month including the expense report, inventory report, and sales report."

As with any resume, your key task is to show your results. Initially many office workers tell me they don't have any results, but invariably we come up with several. The main question to ask yourself is whether you have improved processes or created systems which made something better, easier, or faster.

People frequently believe their improvement is not big enough to mention in a resume. Nearly any improvement is worthy of putting on a resume, but of course you would emphasize the most important ones. If a process saved you or your organization over ten hours per year, or if a system saved over $300 in expense or time, it may be worth mentioning. Even if you decide not to include some of your smaller results in the resume, you may still want to mention them in interviews.

Remember, to mention a result, it does not have to be big or to have saved thousands of dollars. Look at it this way, if *everyone* found ways to save a few hours here and a few hours there, organization would be much more profitable.

JANICE TENSLEY
12733 169th Place N.E.
Issaquah, Washington 98056
(206) 885-8872

OBJECTIVE: Office Administration position utilizing computer skills

QUALIFICATIONS

Strong office administration background. Implement systems that significantly increase office productivity. Quickly learn word processing, data base, and spreadsheet software. Excellent supervisor. Flexible, creative, and work well under pressure.

EMPLOYMENT HISTORY

BTC Computers, Issaquah, Washington 5/91-Present

OPERATIONS SUPPORT - For this manufacturer and distributor of computers, created and implemented a computerized inventory control system. Introduced the system throughout the company and within three company-owned retail stores. System has enabled BTC to continue its rapid expansion with excellent control of its growing inventory. Instructed all staff in the use of the system and act as troubleshooter when problems or questions occur. System provides excellent controls and saves over 20 hours per week in staff research time.

Introduced a computerized accounting system utilizing Great Plains and a Novell network. Oversee computer data maintenance of inventory, purchase orders, posting, and order entry modules. Also involved with the input and maintenance of the accounts payable and general ledger modules. Provide technical software support and problem solving within the organization.

L & M Investing, Seattle, Washington 4/83-5/91

OFFICE MANAGER - Supervised and trained five employees and coordinated all work flow in the office of this investment counselor and financial planner. Maintained all office information systems. Maintained files and computer data bases on several hundred clients, as well as documentation dealing with securities, mutual funds, limited partnerships, and insurance. Tracked all purchases by clients and calculated commissions. Handled accounts receivable and processed buy or sell orders by clients. Produced and edited a monthly newsletter and created all graphics. Developed data bases and spreadsheets which owner stated increased office productivity by 30%. Considered a key person in the growth of the firm.

COMPUTER KNOWLEDGE

Excellent knowledge of Wordperfect 4.2/5.1, dBase III+, Lotus 1-2-3, Great Plains Accounting, MS DOS 5.0, Windows 3.1, Q&A, Client Manager, Newsroom, PC Paint, Personal Publisher, Novell networking.

EDUCATION

A.A. - General Studies, Bellevue Community College (1990)

Typeface: Helvetica

GOVERNMENT EMPLOYEES

As with any resume, demonstrating results will help you get more interviews and more job offers. Your goal should be to demonstrate that you design and implement successful, cost-effective programs, or that you are highly skilled at your work. Quantify your results whenever possible. Do your best to show the before and after. If you were head of a program to improve air quality in a metropolitan region you should be able to provide accurate figures. If you worked with a summer youth program you might be able to indicate that you obtained more private sector jobs for youths than in previous years.

In addition to specific results, you should look for ways to demonstrate that you work well with the public. Show that you have a real feel for public relations, that you can sense in advance when there will be a public outcry over a new policy, and that you can defuse tense situations.

If your job will involve you with elected officials or citizen boards, demonstrate that you know how to deal with them. Show that you make persuasive recommendations and that your recommendations are usually approved. Show that you work well with community groups to gain their support for your programs, but that you are not afraid to stand up to them when necessary.

If your work is more in the planning area, describe your overall responsibilities and then mention key projects you were involved with. Provide the names of the projects or programs since some of your readers may be familiar with them, and in any case, it makes the project or program something they can better identify with. Also, provide key information so the reader will understand the size and scope of the project/program, as well as the complexity.

If you or your department has been particularly effective in obtaining grants, mention that. You may want to list the number of grants and their average amount, or you may want to merely list the amount for the largest grant obtained.

LAURA DONOHUE

401 Eastman West   Arlington Heights, Illinois 60015   (312) 871-2652

QUALIFICATIONS

Excellent organizational ability. Successfully developed new systems which have increased productivity and quality of work.

Broad speaking experience. Frequently speak to groups of 100-500 people. Received a standing ovation at an annual convention for making a difficult subject easily understood.

Excellent public relations ability. Work effectively with organizations and individuals while solving problems and explaining policies. Quickly gain the respect of all parties.

EDUCATION

Graduated - Colville High School, Colville, Washington (1975)

EMPLOYMENT

United States Railroad Retirement Board, Chicago, Illinois 11/81-Present

CONTRACT REPRESENTATIVE - 11/87-Present. Explain and interpret complex laws and regulations related to retirement, disability, and unemployment benefits. Interview claimants and obtain necessary documents. Substantiate evidence and determine eligibility and amount of benefits. Provide training sessions for union and management groups to explain changes in regulations. Successfully introduced a group interview procedure for explaining unemployment compensation when claims rose from 250 to 2,100 per month. Developed numerous systems which decreased backlog and increased staff morale.

UNEMPLOYMENT CLAIMS EXAMINER - 11/81-11/87. Interviewed claimants and former employers to determine eligibility for benefits. Monitored job finding efforts of claimants and assisted in their obtaining new positions. Developed a new system for coding claims and won the Region Accuracy Award in 1986.

Social Security Administration, Chicago, Illinois 6/76-11/81

SERVICE REPRESENTATIVE - 4/79-11/81. Provided assistance and technical information about Social Security, Medicare, and Supplemental Security Income to beneficiaries and the general public. Resolved problems, untangled red tape, and helped make the system work. Received a cash bonus award for suggesting improvements in Social Security forms.

SECRETARY - 6/76-4/79. Ran the office efficiently, answered correspondence, and compiled statistical reports.

Typeface: Helvetica

CHARLES PARSONS
1226 3rd Avenue N.W.
Minnetonka, Minnesota 55343
(612) 378-5162

QUALIFICATIONS

Over twenty-two years of progressively responsible experience in all areas of Human Resources Management. Highly successful in planning, organizing, and coordinating a wide variety of Human Resources Development programs.

EDUCATION

M.P.A. - Public Administration, Tufts University (1970)
B.A. - History, Western Kentucky University (1968)

EMPLOYMENT HISTORY

U.S. Office of Personnel Management, Minneapolis, Minnesota 7/87 to Present

PERSONNEL MANAGEMENT ADVISOR - Responsible for promoting Human Resources Management practices with State and Local governmental organizations in Minnesota, Iowa, and Wisconsin. Plan, design, and implement Human Resources systems including policies, procedures, job evaluation, compensation, benefits, recruitment, selection, employee relations, employee development, management information systems, organizational development, and safety. As project manager, develop and adhere to budgets, supervise and train staff, and coordinate activities with client agencies. Most recommendations have been adopted, with agencies experiencing improved quality of service, increased morale, and greater productivity.

Hennepin County, Minneapolis, Minnesota 9/81 to 7/87

CLASSIFICATION AND PAY MANAGER - Developed, implemented, and directed the classification and pay function for a totally new, comprehensive personnel management system. Unit became a highly respected part of the County Office of Personnel. Designed and developed the County's first uniform pay system. Promoted, planned, and coordinated a Personnel Management Information System which significantly increased the amount of personnel data available for management decisions. Improved service delivery 35% by instituting a personnel generalist approach.

State of Minnesota Merit Employment, St. Paul, Minnesota 7/77 to 9/81

SUPERVISOR OF CLASSIFICATION AND PAY - Selected, trained, and supervised the professional staff which maintained and improved the State classification and pay systems. Developed improved classification and pay policies.

Public Administration Service, Chicago, Illinois 8/70 to 7/77

ADMINISTRATIVE CONSULTANT - Provided administrative, organizational, and personnel management consultative services to state and local governments nationwide for this highly respected, non profit consulting organization established in 1933.

Typeface: Times Roman

DOREEN CAFFEY
13206 127th N.E.
Kirkland, Washington 98033
(206) 821-4454

OBJECTIVE: Contract Administrator

QUALIFICATIONS

Broad Contract Administration experience, covering solicitation preparation and advertisement, contract awards, claim settlements, negotiation of changes, and terminations.

Strong ability to recognize potential problems, research the problem, and propose solutions or alternatives.

EDUCATION

B.S. - Sociology, Oral Roberts University (1983)

EMPLOYMENT

U.S. Forest Service, Seattle, Washington, 7/83 to Present

CONTRACT ADMINISTRATOR - 6/87 to Present. Responsible for preparation of solicitations for bid, advertising solicitation, and opening and awarding contracts. Handle complete contract administration including negotiation of changes, settlement of claims, suspension of contracts, ensuring timely contract completion, and termination of contracts for default and convenience of the Government. Developed procedures which have reduced the time necessary to let a contract from 90 to 72 days.

Work with corporate sureties in take-over agreements and claims against bid, performance, and payment bonds. Research previous contract law interpretations and work closely with the Office of General Counsel when contract appears or bid protests have been docketed.

VOUCHER EXAMINER - 7/83 to 6/87. Made payment to vendors for supplies and services. Prepared monthly report of obligations (accounts payable). As Property Accounting Clerk for the forest, converted a massive manual property accounting system to a computer system thereby increasing accuracy and substantially reducing maintenance costs. Worked with accountant and budget analyst in preparation of the General Administration budget for the forest.

Typeface: Times Roman

TEACHERS

Teachers have a problem with their resumes because teachers all tend to look alike, after all, they all have the same duties. Using your nonclassroom activities can be one good way to set you apart from your competitors. Mention it if you were department chair, heavily involved in advising, active in after-school activities, or actively involved in school committees. Mention any awards you've received or any improvements in standardized test scores in your classroom. Your cover letter could be the place to quote a few snippets from your reviews, or perhaps even from parents who have made comments to you or sent letters to you.

It is critical that the reader realize that you are an energetic, enthusiastic, effective teacher. Your resume and cover letter are your tools to accomplish that. Your cover letter can be an excellent place to state a concise version of your teaching philosophy. Also, use your cover letter to express what it is that makes you a highly effective educator. Typically cover letters are fairly short documents, but you may want to write an expanded cover letter in order to reveal things about you which are difficult to get across in the resume alone.

BRENDA BERKELEY
5693 Smugglers Cove Road
Portland, Maine 04017
(207) 876-3562

OBJECTIVE: Educator

QUALIFICATIONS

Strong teaching background. During ten years of teaching have obtained excellent results with children and have instilled a desire to learn. Thoroughly enjoy working with kids and seeing their personal growth.

EDUCATION

MA - Curriculum Development, Boston College (1985)
BA - Education/Speech Therapy, University of Maine, Farmington (1982)

PROFESSIONAL EXPERIENCE

Portland School District, Portland, Maine 1982-Present

<u>EDUCATOR</u> - 1987-Present. Teach first through third grade to high risk students. As chairperson of the Staff Training and Development Committee, completed a needs assessment and identified numerous training needs among teachers and teacher's aides. Sold the teaching staff on the need for training and developed a training program which has met all of its objectives.

<u>PROGRAM COORDINATOR/EDUCATOR</u> - 1984-1987. Coordinated all aspects of the Early Childhood Special Education Program, including hiring and training of staff and support professionals, and the design and implementation of curriculum. Marketed the program throughout the community and in six months tripled the size of the program to 190. Persuaded parents to participate in special events with their children, resulting in a 70% increase in parent involvement. Spoke to business, community, and physician groups which gained community support for the program and enabled professionals to make appropriate referrals.

<u>COMMUNICATION DISORDERS SPECIALIST</u> - 1982-1984. Provided therapy to students with communication disorders. Participated in all aspects of Project Redi, a screening program for kindergartners, including the selection of assessment procedures, training staff, and analyzing statistical reports. Presented information on the process to other schools which resulted in their adopting similar procedures.

Typeface: Times Roman

ENGINEERS/SCIENTISTS

By all means keep your resume interesting. Although it is perfectly acceptable, and often necessary, to have a resume filled with technical terms and jargon, be careful of overdoing the technical terminology. Listing key buzz words, however, will certainly help because human resources people and hiring managers will be looking for evidence of experience in certain areas.

When you write your resume, use both broad terms and specific terms. If you have spent your last two years working in a highly specialized area, it is unlikely that another employer will hire you to do *only* that type of work, unless it just happens to be a very hot specialty. In qualifications, for example, you might say, "Ten years experience in _____, with specialties in ____, _____, _____, and _____. In the job description portion of the resume you might say "Responsible for all areas of _____, including _____, _____, _____, and _____. In this way the broad term gets embedded in the mind of the employer, as well as the specific areas.

Although experience with certain technologies is important, it is just as important to reveal that you are good at what you do. When you can truly claim it, indicate that you virtually always complete projects on schedule and within budget. If you design a product that becomes a hot seller, mention it. Do not worry that people will think you are claiming you did it all by yourself. Everyone will know that you did it as part of a team. Do your best to bring results into your resume.

Organizations today are looking for team players who can also work well independently. Show that you have worked as a team member on projects. Then take credit for your individual achievements as well as for the team achievements.

Quantify results whenever you can. In your job sketches list the objectives or specifications of the product, or research project. Then determine if you met the specifications or goals. Once you've determined that you met the specifications, try to quantify some aspect. If you've got hard figures, by all means use them, but don't hesitate to use numbers even if you have to do some estimating.

Engineering and scientific fields are typically very project oriented. Therefore, in the first paragraph of your job description you would typically begin with an overall description of your duties. Often the remainder of that job description will consist of describing three or four key projects. Most projects will require 2-4 lines to adequately describe them. Don't try to give all the details of the project. Instead, give just enough information so that the reader will have a reasonably good idea of what the project was about, and then concentrate on results.

JOHN MYERSBY
1487 Laurel Hill Road
Ann Arbor, Michigan 48103
(313) 576-2191

OBJECTIVE: Electronics Engineer

QUALIFICATIONS

Excellent engineering background including experience with microprocessing design.

EDUCATION

B.S. - Electrical and Computer Engineering, University of Michigan (1982)

EMPLOYMENT

Ransey Systems, Ann Arbor, Michigan 6/88 to Present

SENIOR ENGINEER - As part of a team of Software Quality Assurance Engineers, evaluate CAD/CAM software and make recommendations for improvements before software is made available to users within the company. Review functional specifications to ensure all portions are testable and fully meet user needs. Analyze test results, identify problem areas, and make final recommendations.

Performed a cost improvement study which documented savings through the Software Quality Assurance Program of $400,000 annually. Program has eliminated duplication of testing, produced a more organized software development process, and resolved problems at earlier stages.

Mutual Signals, Ann Arbor, Michigan 7/82 to 6/88

MANAGER OF ENGINEERING SERVICES - 4/84 to 6/88. For this firm which designs, sells, and installs industrial and municipal signaling and alarm systems, designed systems and oversaw installations. Analyzed job specifications to determine necessary equipment, did takeoffs from blueprints for bids, modified or designed/built equipment, and provided technical support on sales calls. Oversaw installations and tested large systems upon completion. Played a key role in enabling the firm to grow an average of 18% per year.

ELECTRONICS TECHNICIAN 7/82 to 4/84. Installed and tested systems and did takeoffs from blueprints, as well as supervised technicians at installation sites.

Typeface: Palatino

PROFESSIONALS

With this category I am referring to those in the "professions" such as medical doctor, attorney, professor, accountant, psychologist, and counselor, as well as all other professions, those occupations in the sciences and liberal arts which typically require degrees.

Professionals often find resumes hard to write because it can be difficult to quantify results. Despite the difficulty, virtually everyone can come up with results and find ways to sell them in the resume.

Before beginning your resume, first determine how you know you are good at what you do. You can certainly include that your boss, your colleagues, and your clients all tell you that you are good, but don't stop there. Ask yourself why they feel you are good. Write down those points regardless of whether you can quantify any of them. When you are through, determine which of them you can use in your resume, and which would be best used in your cover letter. Some points will be best left for an interview. Remember that your goal is to cause people to want to meet you.

Although you may have done many things in your career, emphasize those things that you would like to do more of in the future. Devote more space and detail to those things.

Use your nomenclature where appropriate but don't overdo it. You will want to include key buzz words and hot terms, but only when appropriate.

Professionals often do well by including special projects in their job descriptions, or even having a separate "projects" section if many of the projects have occurred off the job or as part of a professional society.

MARIAN OSTEGAARD
4006 Walton Avenue
Ypsilanti, Michigan 48197
(313) 264-2372

OBJECTIVE: Director of a Social Service Agency

QUALIFICATIONS

Strong social service administration background gained during 21 years with one of the most respected agencies in Michigan.

EDUCATION

M.A. - Social Work, University of Michigan (1971)
B.A. - Sociology, Psychology, University of Michigan (1968)

PROFESSIONAL EXPERIENCE

Counseling Services of Detroit, Detroit Michigan 7/71 to Present

ASSISTANT EXECUTIVE DIRECTOR 6/88 to Present

Direct the agency's counseling program, including ten branch offices and 30 employees. Manage the salary budget which represents 85% of the total budget. Created and implemented a new middle-management structure which has increased accountability of branch operations. Counseling productivity has been increased 24% through improved training and time management.

UNIT ADMINISTRATOR 9/84 to 6/88

Managed five branch offices, and supervised 15 professional employees and eight volunteers. Taught Family Life Education classes, and acted as Field Instruction Supervisor for counseling interns. Provided consultation and training to other organizations, and spoke before numerous business and public groups. Organized a Citizen's Advisory Committee.

SENIOR COUNSELOR/BRANCH MANAGER 7/78 to 9/84

Opened and managed several branch offices. Responsible for counseling services, Family Life Education, Field Instruction, volunteer supervision, and public speaking.

COUNSELOR 7/71 to 7/78

Provided counseling services to a wide variety of clients on individual, family, and marital issues.

Typeface: Times Roman

DEBRA SLAWSON
1503 Adrian
Minneapolis, Minnesota 55102
(612) 281-6964

QUALIFICATIONS

Broad experience in designing, teaching, and supervising training programs in a large training department.

Develop effective teams and establish a strong sense of commitment.

EDUCATION

M.S. - Curriculum Design Administration, University of Minnesota (1971)
B.S. - Education, Moorhead State University, Minneapolis, Minnesota (1968)

EMPLOYMENT HISTORY

Prodigital, Inc., Minneapolis, Minnesota 10/84 to Present

Medical Training Administrator 10/89 to Present. Responsible for designing and implementing workshops nationwide which train medical professionals in the uses and benefits of digital radiography. Consult with Prodigital subsidiaries to assess training needs and help them establish training departments.

Developed a comprehensive program to train the fifteen member technical training staff in effective teaching techniques. Ratings from customers after equipment installations have improved 40% since the program was implemented.

Clinical Application Training Supervisor 6/86 to 10/89. Administered and monitored week-long training workshops for domestic and international customers. These workshops have firmly established Prodigital's reputation for providing excellent service and training after the sale. Developed programs for introducing new product lines to the national sales force. Hired, trained, and supervised a staff of three medical trainers.

Training Specialist 10/84 to 6/86. Designed and created one week product orientation courses for customers. Due to the success of the courses, the format and procedures were adopted for all training courses.

Thompson Manufacturing Co., St. Paul, Minnesota 9/78 to 10/84

Training Support Manager 8/82 to 10/84. Developed sales training courses and materials for new and experienced sales people. Took highly technical data and constructed practical, understandable courses.

Technical Training Specialist 5/80 to 8/82. Identified needs and designed a five week technical training program for domestic and international specialists. The program became the model for other workshops within Thompson.

Administrative Assistant To Product Planning Manager 9/78 to 5/80. Researched market trends and studied products and marketing plans of competitors.

Prior Employment: Teacher 9/68 to 6/78

Typeface: Times Roman

MANUFACTURING/LABORING

This category includes machine operators, assemblers, machinists, tool and die makers, technicians, laborers, warehouse workers, and carpenters, as well as any people who work with their hands.

The main goals for your resume should be to show the breadth of your experience, the tools and equipment you can use, and the fact that you are very good at what you do.

It may be appropriate for you to use a section called "Tools," "Equipment," or "Processes." In other words, if you have special knowledge or experience, you may want to use a special category to showcase it. You'll need to come up with the most appropriate term.

As with all resumes, identifying results will help set you apart from the competition. Try to recall any improvements you have brought about. Perhaps you discovered ways to produce a product with fewer steps. For example, perhaps you found a way to produce a part using only three different machines instead of four. Perhaps you discovered that a hole was specified at plus or minus .001, but you determined that for the product's purpose, .005 was actually quite acceptable, and as a result fewer parts were rejected. Perhaps you discovered a faster way to assemble a component and thus increased productivity by 15%. Perhaps you found a way to maintain equipment more effectively and thereby reduced downtime. The possibilities are nearly endless.

Use your cover letter and resume to demonstrate that you learn new pieces of equipment easily and that you are the type of person who is always looking for a better way to do things.

PAUL YOKIHANA
13097 Mona N.E.
Honolulu, Hawaii 96821
(808) 292-3724

OBJECTIVE: Machine Operator

QUALIFICATIONS

Strong mechanical, tool, and woodworking ability.

Excellent knowledge of the working characteristics of a variety of hardwoods.

Easy to get along with. Cooperative. Flexible.

EDUCATION

Wood working, Kauai Community College, 60 credits (1991)

EMPLOYMENT

Exotic Woods Inc., Honolulu, Hawaii 6/91 to Present

<u>MACHINE OPERATOR</u> - Responsible for production of domestic and exotic hardwood molding for this small picture frame manufacturer. Handle all operations including selecting wood, ripping, rabbeting, shaping, rough sanding, finish sanding, staining and oiling. Set up and operate jointer, table saws, wide belt sander, molder-planer, radial arm saw, and wood shaper.

Duties include operation of hand sanders and chopsaws. Occasionally finish and assemble frames. Train new employees and ensure smooth operations in the shop. Produce a very high quality product which has enabled the firm to double its business since 1991.

Previous Employment

Maintenance, CST Inc., Honolulu, Hawaii 5/87-6/91
Waiter, Spring Winds Resort Hotel, Kapaa, Hawaii 4/85-5/87

Typeface: Times Roman

HEALTH PROFESSIONALS

In your resume you will want to make the most out of your experience, demonstrate that you seek opportunities to further your knowledge, show that you are good at what you do, and prove that you are a dedicated professional.

Health professionals often have a hard time because it can be difficult to quantify results. You should, however, look for every opportunity to identify your results, and if possible, quantify them.

Results will most often be found in a special project you worked on. Perhaps you were part of a committee that examined a process and recommended that it be done differently. If the new procedure was found to be superior, you could mention the result on your resume and would make every effort to quantify it.

List any awards you may have received such as employee of the month or of the year. You would mention the award whether it was for the whole facility or just your department. Awards demonstrate that people think highly of you. Indicate on the resume the reasons for receiving the award rather than merely listing it.

You will likely want to mention seminars you have attended, as well as significant in-services. The information would probably be listed under "Special Training." If you intend to list more than ten, the category should appear at the end of the resume on the second page, or you should consider an addendum page which would be labeled "Training" or "Special Training."

You may want to showcase your areas of experience. That can easily be done by using a paragraph under qualifications which would read, "Broad experience in _____, _____, _____, _____, and _____." If you have numerous items you want to mention you could have a separate category below the qualifications section which would be called "Areas of Experience."

If you know yourself to be a highly qualified health professional, please do not be satisfied with merely listing your duties and showing your years of experience.

ELEANOR SIEVERS
3116 Indale Avenue
Athens, Georgia 30606
(404) 643-8014

OBJECTIVE: Director of Nursing/Administrator for Nursing Services

EDUCATION

M.A. - Hospital Administration, University of Houston (1977)
B.S. - Nursing, University of Texas (1971)

PROFESSIONAL EXPERIENCE

University Hospital, Athens, Georgia 4/85 to Present

Associate Administrator For Nursing Services 4/91 to Present. Direct the activities of a 520 FTE nursing staff with a $30 million budget in a 380 bed medical center. Responsible for all inpatient units including medical, surgical, and cardiac intensive care units, an eight room operating suite, and a level one trauma/emergency department. Work directly with four Division Directors and twelve Nursing Supervisors.

Developed new standards for care and set up daily mechanisms which ensure compliance. Established more effective budgetary and staffing monitoring systems which save over $400,000 per year. Opened six critical care beds and added a head nurse.

Division Director, Acute Care 1/89 to 4/91. Responsible for this eight unit division with a 205 FTE nursing staff — 190 beds, $12 million budget. Established workable and effective budgetary controls. Installed and coordinated a capital equipment purchasing system which saved $85,000. Implemented two medical services. Established, trained, and supported a service for ventilator dependent quadriplegics in the Rehabilitation unit. Trained staff in troubleshooting ventilators and working with patients.

Nursing Administrative Supervisor, Medical/Surgical 4/85 to 1/89. Had responsibility for two 24-bed units with a 69 FTE staff. Established a six bed telemetry unit and a cardiac patient teaching program. Developed a primary nursing care model and upgraded the staff from mostly aides to mostly RNs. Increased the role of head nurses by giving them greater budgetary and administrative responsibilities. Established preoperative standards.

The Methodist Hospital, Houston, Texas 5/71 to 4/85

Nursing Administrative Supervisor, Acute Medicine 3/81 to 4/85. Administered two medical units with 62 beds and a 65 FTE staff. Trained new staff as the units moved from mostly aides to a staff of RNs. Worked with head nurses as they were given more managerial responsibility.

Inservice Instructor 3/77 to 3/81. Provided orientation and continuing education of RN staff and skills training for nurses assistants.

Head Nurse, Cardiac Unit 2/75 to 3/77

Staff Nurse, Intensive Care, Intensive Care Unit, Cardiac Unit 5/71 to 2/75

Typeface: Times Roman

PETER SIMMONS
1527 Broadway #217
Irvine, California 92713
(714) 523-7615

OBJECTIVE: Emergency Room Nursing

QUALIFICATIONS

Highly trained and experienced. Considered by supervisors to be an excellent emergency room nurse. Strongly motivated, provide quick, accurate assessments, and work effectively with doctors and other ER staff. Develop excellent rapport with patients.

EDUCATION

Diploma, School of Professional Nursing, St. Lukes Methodist Hospital, Cedar Rapids, Iowa (1984)

Certificate - Emergency Medical Technician (1984)

EMPLOYMENT

University of California, Irvine Medical Center, Orange, California 10/81-Present

STAFF R.N. - EMERGENCY ROOM - In this busy, twenty-two bed emergency room, work with up to sixty patients per shift. As the triage nurse on the seven nurse staff, stabilize patients, make critical decisions, and handle the flow of patients. Receive a high number of trauma patients.

Scripps Memorial Hospital, San Diego, California 6/89-10/91

STAFF R.N. - EMERGENCY ROOM - Night shift charge nurse for this eight bed emergency room. Worked with many cardiac, respiratory, and psychiatric emergencies. Independently assessed patients and initiated diagnostic procedures. Ordered x-rays and lab tests. Consulted with patients by telephone and determined appropriate actions.

Las Cruces Memorial Hospital, Las Cruces, New Mexico 5/87 to 4/89

STAFF R.N. - EMERGENCY ROOM - Performed all emergency room functions at this sixteen bed emergency facility. Trained nursing students and supervised the outpatient methadone treatment program. Also assisted in the minor surgery department and the bronchoscopy department.

Mercy Medical Center, Roseburg, Oregon 6/85 to 4/87

STAFF R.N.- EMERGENCY ROOM - Treated many motor vehicle and sawmill accident trauma patients at this twelve bed emergency room. Charge nurse last ten months. Also functioned as mobile intensive care nurse working by ambulance with an EMT and respiratory therapist. Taught IV therapy, CPR, and assessment skills to EMT's as part of an extensive training program.

Typeface: Helvetica

BARRY KOCH
1706 5th N.E.
Ryersly, Pennsylvania 18512
(412) 562-3216

OBJECTIVE: Director of Pharmacy

QUALIFICATIONS

Strong pharmacy management experience. Proven ability to introduce cost saving measures while increasing quality and productivity standards. Work effectively with all levels of hospital administration and have significantly improved relations with other departments.

EDUCATION

B.S. - Pharmaceutical Science, Northwestern University (1979)

PROFESSIONAL EXPERIENCE

Ryersly General Hospital, Ryersly, Pennsylvania 6/79 to Present

ASSISTANT DIRECTOR OF PHARMACY & IV THERAPY 3/89 to Present. Maintain overall responsibility for ordering medications and supervising and scheduling fifteen staff pharmacists and technicians. Implemented a mobile cart system with pharmacists making rounds and dispensing medications at nurses stations. System has increased quality control and improved relations between Nursing and Pharmacy staff. Developed a centralized piggyback program which relieved nurses of the duty of mixing solutions and turned it over to pharmacy technicians. Program has given techs greater responsibility and has significantly reduced errors and increased quality standards.

Responsible for keeping Pharmacy, Medical and Nursing staffs current on effects and uses of new medications and developing policies regarding their use. Consult extensively with doctors on difficult cases. Currently developing a Clinical Program to provide more inservice training for doctors and nurses and completing development of a kinetic counseling program to better serve doctors. Represent the Pharmacy Department on the Pharmacy and Therapeutic Committee. Actively involved in helping the committee produce a complete formulary.

STAFF PHARMACIST 6/79 to 3/89. As staff pharmacist monitored and recorded patients' medications and IV therapy. Provided consultations with doctors, nurses and patients to ensure proper therapy. Ordered all medications and kept the department well supplied. Designed a diabetic program which reaches 100 diabetics annually and helps them maintain more effective therapy.

Typeface: Times Roman

RETAILERS

In your resume do everything possible to demonstrate that you are good at what you do. Just by your job title most employers will know your basic duties, so stressing your duties is not recommended. Instead, make the most out of your results. Retailing is one of the most statistics filled industries, therefore, make use of the data available to you.

When I say don't stress duties, I do not mean that you should not list them. Listing them, however will probably be all that is required. You will rarely need to provide detailed descriptions.

If you had duties not typically associated with your job title, and you want employers to know about those duties, by all means mention them.

If your job entailed special projects, provide descriptions of the projects and emphasize the results achieved.

If you are primarily in sales, emphasize your sales success. You could indicate increases in sales, your rank among your colleagues in your department, or your rank within the region.

If you are a buyer, do everything you can to show that you have a good sense of trends and that you can sense what will become the next hot item or style.

If you are a department or store manager, you would emphasize increases in sales, your department's or store's ranking within the chain, increases in profits, or increases in market share. You might also mention such things as inventory turns, sales per square foot, or sales per employee work hours.

Make mention of any involvement in planning or coordinating an opening of a store or of a major remodel. Show that you make effective use of co-op advertising and that you work well with manufacturers for special promotions. If you introduced a special new line of products or opened a new department, you could mention the increase in sales.

As a manager you can mention such things as your ability to train staff and your ability to decrease turnover and increase productivity.

PERRY CARLTON
13922 Navajo Court
New Bedford, Massachusetts 02740
(617) 823-7947

QUALIFICATIONS

Strong store management background. Rapidly promoted based on exceeding sales and profit goals. Increased sales an average of 24% per year.

EDUCATION

B.A. - English Literature, Massachusetts State University (1984)

Graduate Gemologist, Gemological Institute of America (1986)

EMPLOYMENT

Werner Jewelers, New Bedford, Massachusetts 8/84-Present

MANAGER - 8/89-Present. Maintain profitable store operations and supervise nine employees. Control all special ordering, oversee mark-up on special orders and shop repairs, and perform all accounting functions. Increased sales an average of 24% per year and have taken the store from #8 to #3 in sales for this chain of 12 stores.

ASSISTANT MANAGER - 7/86-8/89. Sold jewelry to customers and assumed responsibility of sales training and scheduling. Promoted to store manager for improving customer service in each of three stores served.

SALES - 8/84-7/86. Rose to the top 5 in sales among 150 salespeople. Became a Graduate Gemologist and was recognized as one of the most knowledgeable in gemstones within the chain.

Typeface: Bookman

MEGAN HATHAWAY
2401 Belle Haven Road N.W.
Roanoke, Virginia 24019
(703) 829-7913

OBJECTIVE: Retail Management

QUALIFICATIONS

Experienced in all phases of retail marketing, merchandising, and sales.

Quickly promoted from sales to Department Manager.

Receive frequent compliments for creative displays and effective layout of merchandise.

Supervise employees very effectively. Have obtained excellent results from a young sales staff.

EDUCATION

AA - Merchandising, Fashion and Design Institute of Los Angeles (1984)

EMPLOYMENT

Brodericks, Roanoke, Virginia 7/84-Present

DEPARTMENT MANAGER - 3/89-Present. Managed the luggage and young men's departments with a staff of twelve. Responsible for displays, merchandising, scheduling, price changes, merchandise transfers, and twice yearly inventories. Interview, hire, and train new employees and write performance reviews.

Work closely with store buyers and manufacturer's representatives to maintain high quality merchandise. Took the luggage department from #6 in the chain to #2 in sales in the first three years. Significantly improved the look of the young men's department through creative displays and new merchandising techniques, and have increased sales an average of 15% per year.

ASSISTANT DEPARTMENT MANAGER - 6/86-3/89. Sold handbags, accessories, and designer ready-to-wear clothing. Supervised and trained a staff of ten salespeople.

SALESPERSON - 7/84-6/86. Sold handbags, accessories, and young ladies' clothing. Received Salesperson of the Month in recognition for strong sales over the previous six months. Over a twelve month period, took over the duties of assistant department manager.

Typeface: Times Roman

ACCOUNTING/FINANCE

There are four ways you can excite an employer: demonstrate you can make money for the organization, save money, solve problems, and reduce the stress and pressure the boss is under. Those in accounting and finance are typically able to demonstrate all four when they succeed in quantifying their results. In your job sketches, concentrate on recalling past projects you worked on and determine what the results of those projects were.

With so much financial and accounting information computerized these days, it should be relatively easy to review past reports and demonstrate what your successes have been.

Although you will certainly want to let employers know what your duties were, devote the greatest amount of time to determining what your results have been.

Although more and more accountants now have experience in converting from manual to computerized systems, and from one computerized system to another, make the most of your experience. If a firm anticipates a conversion in the next 2-3 years, your conversion experience could make you very valuable. Don't just indicate that you were involved in conversions, but also indicate the level of success. If the conversion was smooth, if the consultant indicated you had done a good job of preparing for the conversion, or if it was completed on schedule, say so. No conversion takes place without a hitch, so to say that it was a smooth conversion merely means that bugs were quickly fixed and that it was completed on schedule or close to schedule.

Look for various types of results. Did you produce new management reports or modify existing reports to make them more useful and timely? Many reports are extremely time sensitive, so if you reduced the time needed to produce a report from 14 days after quarter-end, to ten days after, that would make a strong statement.

Did you computerize an operation which had been done manually? Then calculate the number of man-hours saved. If it eliminated the need for a position, indicate that as well.

Perhaps you improved the accounting operation so well that your audits were much improved. Perhaps you could say that exceptions were reduced by a certain percentage or from ten the previous year to only one, or perhaps none.

If you were involved in accounts receivable perhaps you could state that 90-day and over receivables were reduced by a certain percent or that days outstanding were reduced from 40 to 30.

I've worked with several accountants who started making use of previously unutilized short-term cash. By creating a system for investing excess cash for a few days, I've seen controllers of small companies earn the equivalent of their salary just by doing so.

Other accounting people have found ways to reduce the transaction time on billings or reduce invoicing errors. Others have developed systems to avoid double paying invoices on their accounts payable.

Finance people have found ways to reduce interest expense on loans, have taken companies public and raised new monies, negotiated larger lines of credit, and found ways to reduce taxes.

PAUL HUSTED
406 Ash
Boise, Idaho 83702
(208) 361-2918

OBJECTIVE: Senior Accountant/Controller

QUALIFICATIONS

Strong accounting experience with a broad background in auditing, business and individual taxes, and cost control programs. Effectively implement computerized accounting systems.

Excellent manager. Consistently obtain high productivity from employees.

LICENSES

CPA, Idaho State Certification (1976)

EDUCATION

B.A. - Accounting, University of Idaho (1975)

EMPLOYMENT

Brandon Refrigerated Service Inc., Boise, Idaho 3/88 to Present

CONTROLLER - For this refrigerated freight hauler, prepare financial statements and supervise 12 payroll, rate, billing, and AP/AR personnel. Extensively involved in customer relations, establishing credit ratings, approving credit, reviewing and approving customer claims, and making collections. Manage the cash flow of the company. Developed a major cost control program which has cut overhead 15%. Maintain the smooth functioning of a sophisticated computerized accounting system.

Bestway Freight Lines, Boise, Idaho 8/84 to 3/88

CONTROLLER - Responsible for financial statements and tax preparation. Supervised ten employees handling rates, billing, payroll, claims, and AP/AR. Oversaw the payroll system covering six separate union agreements. Developed the company's first cost studies and identified areas for substantial savings. Cut the shop force from 21 to 14 with no reduction in work completed.

Worked closely with vendor and contract programmer while converting to a new computerized accounting and payroll system. Implemented a computerized system to track commodity transactions which reduced required staff time each month from 180 to 6 hours.

Robert Perkins, CPA, Boise, Idaho 6/75 to 8/84

STAFF ACCOUNTANT - Performed audits and developed financial statements for a wide variety of clients. Handled state and federal taxes for individuals, trusts, estates, partnerships, and corporations. Provided management services and designed cost control programs.

Typeface: Courier

MISCELLANEOUS

The following resumes do not fit well in any of the previous categories yet they provide excellent examples of well written resumes from from key job categories.

As with any resume, concentrate on including your results. Study the resumes to see how each person inserted results whenever possible.

WILLIAM SAXTON
641 Arastradero
Palo Alto, California 94306
(415) 881-9595

OBJECTIVE: Purchasing Management

QUALIFICATIONS

Strong background in purchasing management. Consistently develop systems which cut costs and provide the timely delivery of products.

EDUCATION

B.A. - Geography, San Jose State University (1972)

EMPLOYMENT

Rapsody Clothing, Palo Alto, California 7/85-Present

DIRECTOR OF PURCHASING - For this $20 million clothing manufacturer, supervise a staff of four and have responsibility for the purchasing of all nontextile items. Developed an inventory control system which has eliminated duplication of supplies. Increased the level of buying with key suppliers and developed stronger relationships as well as larger discounts, resulting in a reduced cost of 15-35% on items purchased. Save $20,000 annually on continuous data processing forms and have increased copying efficiency 50%. Developed and implemented a departmental charge back system for supplies. System has increased accuracy and equity in calculating actual departmental costs.

Administer all aspects of national and local trade shows, including planning, purchasing new exhibits, contracting with trade people, obtaining sites and floor spaces, purchasing materials, and handling transportation. Trade show costs have been reduced $75,000 annually over the last three years.

Ryans Department Stores, Los Angeles, California 7/72-7/85

DIRECTOR OF PURCHASING - 9/81-7/85. Negotiated, awarded, and administered contracts with vendors for the procurement of over 500 items. Personally redesigned gift boxes and saved $150,000 annually in production and storage costs. Developed a unique automated packing material system which reduced labor and handling costs and saved $20,000 annually. Planned and managed an increased volume of purchasing from $1.1 million to $3.2 million as the chain increased from 6 to 14 stores in four years. Managed the paper stock warehouse and in-plant print shop.

Prior positions within Ryans: Assistant Director of Purchasing 3/78-9/81; Purchasing Agent 10/75-3/78; Purchasing Assistant 7/72-10/75.

Typeface: Times Roman

TERRY PROHASKA
4047 Westavia Drive
Raleigh, North Carolina 27612
(919) 971-3242

QUALIFICATIONS

Strong experience in implementing cost saving purchasing programs. Extensive background in developing and introducing data processing systems to aid in cost reductions. Established reputation as an excellent negotiator.

EDUCATION

B.A. - Business Administration, Oakwood College, Huntsville, Alabama (1976)

EMPLOYMENT

Conway Inc., Raleigh, North Carolina 10/84 to Present

MANAGER, FACILITIES PURCHASING - 6/89 to Present. Manage a staff of twelve buyers and four clerical personnel. Department annually purchases $80 million dollars of supplies, parts, and equipment for the maintenance, repair, and operation of Conway facilities. Review and approve all purchases over $40,000 and resolve discrepancy reports. Developed and implemented a major program to reduce inventory and operating costs. Since 1991 inventory has been reduced from $5.4 million to $2.9 million, with documented savings of $1.1 million. Continuing to implement additional cost savings measures.

SUPERVISOR, CORPORATE PROCUREMENT - 10/84 to 6/89. Negotiated, awarded, and administered contracts with vendors for the procurement of over 20,000 different standard parts. Worked closely with company plants throughout the country to calculate future needs for stocked parts. Improved coordination led to larger orders and decreased costs. Aggressively sought out new vendors desiring Conway business in order to take advantage of innovative equipment and methods they possessed. Full procurement program led to $15 million in documented savings in four years on purchases of $70 million.

Nova Co., Valdez, Alaska 8/81 to 10/84

PROCUREMENT ADMINISTRATOR - Installed a catalog list purchasing system and purchased all electrical equipment and hardware for this electrical contractor on the Hunt Oil Refinery. Developed procurement policies and procedures which led to significant savings and introduced volume procurement. The previous small order system resulted in parts delays and higher prices. Worked closely with the architect on this design-build project to predict future needs, then purchased the materials necessary to complete entire sections of the project.

Bronka Industries, Birmingham, Alabama 8/76 to 8/81

MATERIEL ADMINISTRATOR - Developed a solid foundation in the principles of purchasing. In 1977, with a task force of four people, designed and implemented a Stockless Purchasing System which is still used throughout Bronka. System reduced PO's by 75%, enabled the reduction of the buying group from sixty to twenty-five, and reduced administration costs 22%. Oversaw the system and continued to handle purchasing duties.

Typeface: Times Roman

TED INGALLS
1887 Hamlin Drive
Dayton, Ohio 45414
(513) 623-7122

OBJECTIVE: Manufacturing Management

QUALIFICATIONS

Strong knowledge of manufacturing practices and procedures.

Develop Quality Control and Material Control procedures which significantly reduce rejects and improve procurement and flow of materials.

Able to strengthen working relations between departments and with vendors.

EDUCATION

B.A. - Business Administration, University of Notre Dame (1986)

EMPLOYMENT

Embarco Manufacturing, Dayton, Ohio 6/86 to Present

QUALITY ENGINEER 4/89 to Present. For this machinery manufacturer, responsible for quality and material control. Developed QC policies and procedures, including heat treatment requirements, storage procedures, methods to reduce product liability exposure, and raw material and casting specifications. Have significantly increased consistency in design specifications of like parts. Handle Process Review and Process Control duties. Review all discrepant work orders and identify sources of problems in-house and with vendors. Analyze all rejected parts and determined the most cost effective means of disposition.

Developed material control policies and procedures and helped redesign the inventory control system. New procedures have significantly reduced delays due to out of stock parts. Developed new procedures for procurement of raw materials and castings which have reduced discrepant work orders. Analyze data processing requirements for material control.

EXPEDITER/SCHEDULER 6/86 to 4/89. Expedited parts through machine shops, vendors, and assembly. Issued work orders, scheduled machine shop operations, and participated in the fiscal inventory.

Typeface: Bookman

RACHEL HUANG
4215 West Pinegrove Drive
Madison, Wisconsin 54709
(608) 272-1945

OBJECTIVE: Flight Attendant

QUALIFICATIONS

Excellent experience gained as a Waitress, Salesperson and Assistant Store Manager. Deal very tactfully and effectively with difficult customers. Handle emergencies and crises smoothly and efficiently. Develop rapport and respect among customers and fellow employees.

Service oriented person. Received many compliments from store and restaurant customers for going far beyond the norm.

EDUCATION

A.A. Brunswick Community College (1986-1988)

TRAINING

Customer Service, Daytons, 16 hours (1991)
Achieving Your Potential, The Pacific Institute, 12 hours (1992)

WORK EXPERIENCE

Daytons, Madison, Wisconsin 1/91 to Present

RETAIL SALES - Sell women's clothing and shoes in an environment where the customer and service to the customer is first and foremost. Obtained outstanding training in customer service with an emphasis on professionalism. Have received many letters and words of thanks from satisfied and appreciative customers.

Silver Shell, Madison, Wisconsin 2/89 to 1/91

ASSISTANT STORE MANAGER - In ten months moved from Salesperson, to Head Cashier, to Assistant Manager for this women's fashions store. Handled payroll, developed weekly and monthly sales reports, scheduled staff, and trained new personnel. Created store and window displays and helped coordinate fashion shows.

Satin Turtle Restaurant, Milwaukee, Wisconsin 1/88 to 2/89

WAITRESS - Became an excellent waitress and received many compliments for my service, helpfulness, and friendliness. Developed a knack for sensing when additional help was needed at a table.

Typeface: New Century Schoolbook

MARVIN GALUSKA
7212 Lundy Drive
Florissant, Missouri 63031
(314) 682-3098

OBJECTIVE: Field Engineer

QUALIFICATIONS

Strong technical ability in troubleshooting and repairing computer systems including peripherals and mechanical devices.

Heavily involved in critical customer responsibility. As an on-call field engineer have developed excellent relations with customers by showing genuine concern for their problems and by keeping downtime to an absolute minimum.

EDUCATION

Certificate - Electronics Technician, Gresham Vocational Technical Institute (9/86 - 3/88)

EMPLOYMENT

Control Data Corporation, St. Louis, Missouri 2/90 to Present

FIELD ENGINEER - Provide on-site maintenance of many types of computer equipment including minicomputers, disk drives, magnetic tapes, printers, and communications devices. Perform preventive maintenance and diagnosis/fault isolation at the component and board level. Responsible for repairing all mechanical devices and peripherals. Personally installed several small minicomputer systems. Was lead over two to three other field engineers on larger installations. Involved with installing several mainframes. Frequently relocate systems.

As Site Engineer for McDonnel Douglas (6/90-9/92) drastically reduced response time and downtime. Analyzed inventory needs and significantly reduced inventory, saving Control Data over $10,000 per year, while also reducing out-of-stock situations by 20%.

For the Midwest branch, responsible for monitoring factory change orders and ensuring changes are made at all customer sites. Assist Inventory Control Manager in keeping branch inventory and site inventories at proper levels.

N.C.R. Corporation, Indianapolis, Indiana 5/89 to 2/90

FIELD ENGINEER - Maintained financial processing equipment on-site, including check processors and c.o.m. units. Worked closely with customers to solve their problems.

L.F.N. Electronics, Inc., Indianapolis, Indiana 3/88 to 3/89

ELECTRONICS TECHNICIAN - Performed bench repair and calibration of all varieties of mechanical and electronic UHF/VHF tuners used in televisions. Handled inventory control duties.

Typeface: Times Roman

JOSE LEANDRO
13224 Caroline Avenue
Syracuse, New York 13209
(315) 454-2906

OBJECTIVE: Project Manager, Field Service Manager

QUALIFICATIONS

Strong experience in installing and maintaining computer systems and have created an excellent record for smooth deliveries and installations. Noted for ability to solve hardware and software problems before installation.

Develop effective working relations with customers, software engineers, hardware engineers, and field service engineers.

Provide excellent training for technicians and field service engineers.

EDUCATION

Certificate - Electronics, Big Sky Community College (1982)

EMPLOYMENT

Distol Engineering Corporation, Syracuse, New York 9/87 to Present

SYSTEMS APPLICATION ENGINEER - Prepare, install, and maintain real time process control computers. Using system specifications and functional descriptions, integrate hardware into proper system configurations. Construct system block diagrams, system cabling diagrams, and design cables necessary for final installation. Compile proper documentation packages for each system.

Check out individual items and prepare computer systems for in-house acceptance. Supervise the installation of power and signal cables and peripherals. Train mill personnel in the operation and maintenance of the systems. Assist in debugging application software and write programs used in the check out of all systems. Troubleshoot and repair systems after installation.

Interface between customers, project managers, software engineers, and hardware engineers during all phases of system development and installation. Highly successful in identifying potential problems and resolving them before installation. Consistently receive the most complex and difficult assignments.

Compudata, Inc., Long Beach, California 6/82 to 9/87

FIELD SERVICE ENGINEER - Repaired and serviced computer systems at customer sites. Assembled, checked out, and installed computer systems and peripherals.

Typeface: Helvetica

RITA SAWYER
1202 Guthrie Avenue South
Tulsa, Oklahoma 74119
(918) 693-4217

OBJECTIVE: Quality Control Inspection

QUALIFICATIONS

Excellent training and experience in all phases of quality control inspection. Work hard and produce excellent results. Work well with engineers, production supervisors, production workers, and vendors.

Broad experience with many measuring devices, including Vernier calipers and scales, micrometers, sineplates, air gauging equipment, durometer and Rockwell hardness testing, XYZ coordinate measuring machines, optical comparators, roughness measurement equipment, and height gauges. Experienced in surface plate inspection.

EDUCATION

Graduated - Keota High School, Keota, Oklahoma (1984)

TRAINING

Advancetech, Certificates in: D.C. Electronics, A.C. Electronics, Semiconductor Devices, Digital Technology, Geometric Tolerancing

EMPLOYMENT

Advancetech, Inc., Tulsa, Oklahoma 10/89-Present

QUALITY CONTROL INSPECTOR - Responsible for all first article inspections and final inspections for this sheet metal fabricator. Using blueprints, calculate dimensions and bend factors to check and approve flat pattern layouts. Verify proper sequencing of production plans. Receive and log incoming sheet metal and other products. When parts do not meet customer's specifications, work closely with engineers to discover if the fault was in the original design or in the fabrication process. With discovery of fault, work with engineers to correct it. Through improved processes reduced rejects by customers by over 20%.

Electrotech Laboratories, Oklahoma City, Oklahoma 3/86-10/89

QUALITY CONTROL INSPECTOR - Inspected incoming vendor supplied sheet metal and small precision parts. Used hand measuring devices as well as XYZ measuring machines and optical comparators. Inspected for conformance to geometric tolerances. Inspected and tested electrical components and electrical subassemblies.

K & I Industries, Muskogee, Oklahoma 8/84-3/86

MACHINE OPERATOR - Set up, operated, and maintained six Brown & Sharp and two Traub single spindle screw machines. Inspected manufactured parts. Recorded set-up procedures for ease of manufacturing the part in the future, saving approximately 100 hours per year among five machine operators.

Typeface: Times Roman

BRAD PIERSON
219 Diehl Street
Raleigh, North Carolina 27608
(919) 688-4216

OBJECTIVE: Law Enforcement/Investigation/Internal Security

EDUCATION

B.A. - Business Administration, North Carolina State University, 3.5 GPA (1986)
Graduated - North Carolina State Training Commission Police Academy (1978)

LAW ENFORCEMENT TRAINING

Accident Investigation, Northwestern University Traffic Institute, two weeks (1981)
SWAT School, FBI, two weeks (1980)
Drug Enforcement, Drug Enforcement Administration, two weeks (1980)
Homicide Investigation, North Carolina State Training Commission, one week (1979)
Advanced Law Enforcement, North Carolina State Training Commission, one week (1978)

EMPLOYMENT

Wake County Prosecuting Attorney, Raleigh, North Carolina 4/87 to Present

INVESTIGATOR 4/87 to Present. Assist deputy prosecutors in case preparation, research, and courtroom preparation. Involved in most major cases and homicides. Was chief investigator for the office in the recent Chet Thurston triple homicide trial. As illustrator, draw crime scene diagrams, sketches, and illustrations for use in trials.

As part of this very aggressive prosecuting team, have increased conviction rate from 56% in 1986 to 84% in 1992. From 10/88 to 5/92, member of the experimental Career Criminal Unit. Met and exceeded goals of keeping repeat offenders incarcerated until trial, bringing cases to trial quickly, and obtaining maximum sentences. Unit had a 98% conviction rate.

As Police Liaison Officer since 1989, maintain open communications with Federal, State, and Local law enforcement agencies. Keep individual officers informed of progress in cases they investigated and made arrests in. Have developed excellent relations with all departments.

Raleigh Police Department, Raleigh, North Carolina 4/78 to 5/87

PATROL OFFICER (6 years) Handled all types of cases including shop lifting, burglaries, robberies, con artists, and traffic accidents. Worked closely with several retail chains to break up a four-state shoplifting ring. Handled numerous internal fraud and theft cases with large companies. One of three officers on-call to investigate traffic fatalities. Received very high interdepartmental ratings and received many letters of commendation from individuals, businesses, and agencies. Member of SWAT team.

SPECIAL INVESTIGATIONS (3 years) Specialized in narcotics investigations including undercover assignments. Involved in several major narcotics arrests including breaking up a large heroin distribution ring. Investigated homicides, burglaries and frauds as well.

Typeface: Times Roman

SAMPLES OF RESUMES

The following section contains portions from many resumes and many job titles. The job titles are arranged alphabetically. You can also check the list on page 74 to see if any job titles that are of interest to you are included as full resumes or in this section as portions. The full sample resumes contained in *Resume Power* should be adequate to enable you to determine what formats you will want to use. These portions have been selected to give you ideas, especially ideas on how to include results.

ACCOUNTING

QUALIFICATIONS

Strong finance and accounting background with excellent management experience. Develop effective financial management and accounting systems which have enabled firms to grow rapidly and maintain solid financial positions.

❖

Strong background in accounting and finance. Work effectively with top management and produce cost saving systems and procedures.

❖

Broad experience in all areas of accounting. Recognized by CPA firms for ability to create accounting systems with extremely clean audit trails. Consistently able to reduce receivables, improve cash flow, and develop effective cash management programs.

EMPLOYMENT

Developed a standard collection letter that saves 3-4 hours each month.

❖

Created a manual system for tracking the monthly expenses of 50 agents which provides virtually immediate answers for top management.

❖

Prepared a standardized bank reconciliation form that simplifies the process, saving several hours each month.

❖

Work closely with auditors and compile data for internal audit requests. Work closely with auditors during physical audits from the parent company.

❖

Controller - For this electrical construction contractor, responsible for the complete financial management of the company. Maintain the general ledger, prepare financial statements, reconcile bank statements and the general ledger, and prepare all tax and union reports.

❖

Took over all collection work and reduced ninety day and over receivables by 50%.

❖

Established a cash management program which has doubled the earnings of the previous system. Set up a bank investment account for short-term deposits and utilize money market accounts and CDs for longer deposits.

❖

Set up a simplified accounts payable system which is more effective and requires only half the time as the old system.

❖

Began managing the profit sharing program which had serious accounting problems and put it on sound footing.

❖

Implemented the company's first cash management program which earned an extra $10,000 per year.

❖

Negotiated the loan for the purchase of a business which has added substantial profit to the company.

❖

Negotiated a highly favorable revolving working capital line of credit with a major bank, equal to 30% of net worth.

❖

Manage risk and insurance administration, keeping premium increases significantly below the industry average. Renegotiated a new employee benefit plan which increased coverage with little negative impact on employees or the company.

❖

Planned and oversaw a 30% staff cutback while still increasing sales and production.

❖

Effectively manage corporate cash and investments, preserving equity capital and the financial strength of the company.

❖

Work closely with all levels of corporate management.

❖

Oversee all areas of finance and accounting for this mechanical construction company and produce financial statements including income statements, balance sheets, sales reports, AR/AP listings, and cash management reports.

Developed and implemented a job costing program which has saved thousands of dollars. Program has enabled the company to determine the profit or loss of each job, allowed project managers to review current spending and revise plans, and increased the accuracy of cost estimates. Company now concentrates on the types of projects it can complete most profitably.

❖

Prepared financial statements and cash flow analysis reports. Handled intercompany fund transfers, scheduled payables and receivables, and scheduled debt service.

❖

Worked closely with customers and reduced receivables from 20% being 90 days or over, to less than 10% over 90 days.

❖

Recognized by CPA firm for creating an accounting system with records so clean and organized that audit trails were extremely easy to follow.

❖

Introduced solid accounting and internal procedures for this financial planning company and became instrumental in enabling it to expand from four agencies in one state to twelve agencies in five states.

ATTORNEY

QUALIFICATIONS

Fifteen years outstanding experience in all aspects of commercial law. Excellent litigator with a track record of affirmative results. Effective administrator and personnel manager.

❖

Sixteen years experience as a trial attorney with a strong background in handling complex criminal litigation at the federal level. Highly regarded for thorough preparation and effective delivery of client defenses with an excellent reputation for negotiating favorable dispositions.

❖

Excellent legal background with strong emphasis on preventative law. Work closely with clients to identify potential contractual and other legal problems and minimize exposure. Highly regarded by clients for legal knowledge, thoroughness, and dedication to their concerns.

EMPLOYMENT

As head of the commercial litigation department, represent a diverse clientele including commercial finance and leasing companies, local and national organizations, investors, lenders, municipalities, insurance companies, and brokers. Have successfully directed the efforts of partners and associates in cases totaling over $65 million.

❖

<u>Associate</u> - Handled all phases of defense preparation and delivery for this prominent law firm. Practice included civil and criminal cases. Duties included bail arrangements, technical pre-trial motions, investigations, jury selection, witness preparation, litigation, appeals, and extraordinary writs. Assumed full responsibility for felony cases and achieved excellent results, becoming one of the firm's leading trial lawyers.

❖

Established case management procedures for the growing practice as well as billing and collection procedures. Implementation of a computerized docket system with the case management system significantly increased efficiency in handling cases and improved client relations.

❖

Handle trial practice primarily involving the areas of insurance defense, personal injury, and commercial and real estate litigation. Heavily involved in corporate practice, municipal law, and the representation of developers. Major clients include Lincoln County Public Utility District, First National Bank, and State Farm Insurance.

> For the Lincoln County PUD, handle condemnation proceedings, environmental litigation, competitive bid and construction law litigation, and water system rates litigation. Advise the PUD regarding Public Disclosure Act matters and bid specifications. For State Farm Insurance defend insureds in personal injury actions, evaluate claims, and negotiate litigation.

> For developers, negotiate and draft real estate contracts, loan agreements, agreements with municipalities, and handle construction litigation and hearings before public agencies.

(This attorney also used an addendum entitled "Significant Litigation Handled." Examples include:)

> Represented a developer on a 654 unit project in Sanderford. Handled hearings with the City, and in the face of heavy citizen opposition, negotiated approval of 548 units.

> Successfully defended a closely held corporation with $18 million in annual sales against a minority shareholder's suit for dissolution. Trial court decision affirmed by the State Court of Appeals.

> Successfully defended in federal court against a claim of a disappointed bidder for a dam contract, resulting in a savings of over $14 million.

❖

BANKING

QUALIFICATIONS

Strong background in the mortgage lending industry. Broad experience in loan processing, underwriting, closing, and new accounts sales. Key person in the rapid growth of two branches of a savings and loan. Highly knowledgeable of conventional type processing and experienced with FHA and VA financing. (loan processor)

❖

Established an excellent reputation for providing outstanding service for home buyers and agents alike. Quick and accurate processing, leading to timely closings, has resulted in strong repeat business with real estate companies. (loan processor)

❖

Thirteen years of increasingly responsible managerial positions in the banking industry. In each position held, consistently introduced new methods and equipment which produced substantial savings and increased revenue.

❖

Broad background in commercial lending with strong business development experience. Extremely thorough in analyzing loan applications.

EMPLOYMENT

Process all loans for this rapidly growing branch. Review each file for necessary documentation, clear the title, confirm accuracy of all credit and personal data supplied in the application, and handle questions from customers and real estate agents. (loan processor)

❖

Developed and directed a team of high achievers to success in market penetration, profitable growth, and development of new ventures. Expanded National Accounts' new business efforts four-fold and developed targeted marketing strategies in five new market segments.

❖

Fostered the creation of a Cash Management Division which formalized product delivery and expanded the market position. Managed the 33% average annual increase in earning assets, including a five-fold increase in Trade Finance assets, while controlling portfolio quality and diversity. Improvements in branch relations produced 20% annual increases in international service volume and fee income.

❖

Developed the MICR Quality Control Unit which produced documented savings of $1.9 million by reducing prime pass check processing rejections 19%.

❖

As a savings representative/investment counselor, work closely with customers to evaluate needs and required liquidity. Explain features of each type of account and help customers select the best one for personal needs. Opened a $1 million twelve-month account and numerous $100,000 CDs. Have successfully demonstrated the benefits of longer deposits and have convinced many to select accounts with deposit periods longer than originally planned.

❖

Solicit, establish, and service commercial accounts and handle all types of lending including SBA loans, term loans, unsecured lending, contractor financing, A/R financing, and commercial real estate loans. Solicit and obtain loans ranging from $250,000 to $30 million and carry each loan through all steps of the lending process. Work closely with accounts to determine the most suitable type of loan and to work out conditions acceptable to both the bank and the customer. Consistently meet or exceed all quarterly quotas.

❖

Accepted loan requests and made credit evaluations. Approved or declined loan requests and maintained a record of less than 1.5% delinquencies on an installment loan portfolio of $16.8 million. Collected on past due accounts, and through highly effective collection procedures, kept collection costs 87% below budget.

❖

As branch manager, responsible for all internal branch operations including loan development, credit approval, supervising delinquency adjustment and litigation, and staff hiring and training. Increased loans outstanding from $1.5 to $2.8 million in 14 months and created the first profits for the branch in five years. Delinquencies were reduced from 4.7% to less than 1%.

❖

Direct all activities of the marketing department and have played a key role in creating income growth averaging 12% annually since 1988. Oversee all daily department functions including market research, internal communications, advertising agency relationship, new product development, media advertising, public relations, and sales training. Manage an annual budget of $750,000. Marketing and sales programs developed in the first year resulted in a 16% increase in deposits (4% industry average) and growth in annuities sales from $4.5 million to $8.9 million.

BOOKKEEPING

QUALIFICATIONS

Excellent accounting and computer operations experience. Learn new systems quickly and have a record of producing fast, accurate work. Coordinate effectively with customers, coworkers, and intercompany departments.

❖

Broad experience in all aspects of office management with strong bookkeeping experience. Develop systems that enable offices to run smoothly and efficiently.

EMPLOYMENT

Produced twelve financial statements monthly using a computerized journal entry system. Reviewed all purchases made by the branches and researched any discrepancies in expenses and kept them in line with the budget.

❖

On an annual basis, completed all work schedules for the yearly audit and worked closely with five Coopers & Lybrand auditors throughout the audit. Told by those auditors that the books were some of the best documented and complete they had ever worked with. Through improved documentation, and effective troubleshooting during the audit, played a key role in significantly reducing the time required to complete the audit.

❖

Researched and cleared problem accounts and handled payables and receivables between IBM entities. Produced corporate tax reports. Coordinated with the purchasing department to reconcile billing discrepancies. Recommended and helped implement a change in work assignments that significantly increased productivity.

❖

For this geotechnical engineering firm, handled all bookkeeping as well as detailed cost accounting. Designed new time sheets for the cost accounting program that reduced paperwork for the engineers and saved time in preparing payroll and billings. Designed a new system for collecting receivables which reduced the number of overdue accounts by 65%.

BROADCASTING

EMPLOYMENT

Editor - Edit daily news stories and supervise the production of one of the evening news broadcasts. Assign stories to other editors and remain in constant communication with production staff during the broadcast of the news program. Personally edit late stories and revise production schedules to accommodate late-breaking news reports. As the first editor assigned to the legislative news team, developed procedures which have significantly improved the quality of legislative stories.

COMPUTER OPERATIONS

EMPLOYMENT

For this food distributor, supervise three computer operators and have responsibility for completing all computer runs on schedule. Produce an average of 30 reports and 40 customer orders daily. Personally run all period end reports and all special reports for managers and customers. Established an effective training program which has been key in reducing turnover from 80% to 15% and has increased productivity substantially. In 1990, 1991, and 1992 had the highest operations productivity among eight branches.

❖

Solely responsible for the third shift operation of three large mainframe computer systems. Troubleshoot all phases of computer operations and coordinate with vendors concerning equipment malfunctions. Designed and implemented production job standards and operations documentation procedures, enabling systems analysts to produce more effective new software systems. Work closely with system analysts concerning the operation of software and user documentation. Responsible for maintenance and control of production schedules and system documentation. Recognized for maintaining an excellent on-time delivery record.

CONSTRUCTION MANAGEMENT

QUALIFICATIONS

Outstanding record for completing projects on schedule and within budget.

❖

Extensive experience with fast track and value engineered projects. Consistently save large sums of money through innovative designs and construction techniques.

❖

Excellent background in marketing. Work effectively with government and corporate leaders to promote projects and gain approval.

❖

Effective negotiator. Consistently negotiate highly favorable contracts and agreements.

❖

Strong background in all aspects of Project Management. Broad experience in accounting, detailing and drawing, estimating, negotiating contracts, purchasing, and critical path scheduling.

❖

Broad experience in light commercial and residential construction. Strong background in onsite preparation, installing roads and utilities, framing, and rough carpentry. Experienced in cement work, sheetrocking, insulation, painting, landscaping, plumbing, and roofing.

❖

Proven ability to complete projects on schedule and within budget. Able to get high production rate and high quality standards out of subs. Work well with building departments and inspectors. Strong ability to foresee and resolve construction problems.

EMPLOYMENT

Supervised 11 Superintendents and 300 Portuguese and Israeli laborers and craftsmen in the construction of hardened, reinforced concrete structures on the Telve Air Base. Constructed one million square feet of forms and poured 80,000 cubic yards of concrete in 20 months. The project, originally estimated to take five years, was completed in three years. Accumulated 1.4 million man-hours without a death or serious injury. Provided strong technical assistance in expediting critically needed foreign vendor materials. Received a strong letter of commendation from the US Army Corps of Engineers.

❖

As project manager, involved in the early development of architectural designs, estimating, budget preparation, and negotiations. Responsible for the overall success of each project. Handled all purchasing, met daily with site superintendents and architects, and monitored progress. Completed projects include:

> Columbia View: A 15 story office building in downtown Portland. Completed this fast track, value engineered, $16 million project ahead of schedule and saved $800,000 through value engineering.

> Motorola Corporation: Developed the 32 acre site and completed the $12 million accelerated construction project in only twelve months. Brought it in ahead of schedule and within budget. Project required highly sophisticated heating and mechanical systems for the acid waste treatment facility and the plant for manufacturing electronic parts.

❖

As project manager, responsible for overseeing each project, scheduling the project, and keeping costs within the original estimate. Work closely with each site superintendent to ensure construction is progressing and to resolve problems as they occur. Negotiate contractual changes with owners and architects. Hire subcontractors and write the contracts. Typically manage two to three projects at a time. All projects have been completed on schedule. Projects have included:

> Westgate Plaza, Denver, $9.5 million. Five story office building, 127,000 square feet, post tension ductile frame, concrete structure. Due to the critical schedule of the project, designed a flying form system which speeded up construction and resulted in substantial savings. Because of attention to buyouts and scheduling, project has been the most profitable in the history of the company.

❖

CONSTRUCTION SUPERINTENDENT - Highlands Estates. For this sub-division, built twenty-eight custom homes ranging from $290,000 to $380,000. Prepare sites and put in streets and underground utilities. Obtain bids, hire subs, and maintain production schedules. Personally handle grading, sewer work, framing, insulation, painting, landscaping, cement, and form work. Each house has been completed in under ninety working days.

COUNSELING

QUALIFICATIONS

Consistently enable clients to function more effectively.

❖

Effectively research and develop courses and programs relating to human growth and development. Always receive high ratings from students for knowledge and enthusiasm.

EMPLOYMENT

Art Therapist/Program Coordinator - Work with chronic schizophrenics aged 27-80. Act as coordinator of a new program, as well as art therapist/case manager. Lead twelve therapy groups weekly and maintain an active load of individual clients using both psychotherapy and art therapy. Participate in team meetings and have responsibility for case load treatment plans and progress notes.

As program coordinator, developed a program to bridge the gap between two already established resocialization programs with patients functioning at widely divergent levels. Produced a full client load through extensive outreach to local agencies and social workers. With each intake evaluated client needs and produced patient plans. Referred patients to psychologists, social workers, and group programs. Program has been considered highly successful by Center administrators.

DRAFTER

EMPLOYMENT

<u>Project Lead</u> - Supervise eight drafters and coordinate closely with the engineering department. Produce weekly status reports and attend project meetings to answer questions and provide reports concerning progress and problem areas. Work effectively with engineering and production to resolve problems as they occur. Quickly established a reputation for handling difficult assignments and completing them ahead of schedule.

<u>Mechanical Drafter</u> - Draft details, assemblies, and injection molded parts for cardio-vascular monitoring equipment. Frequently use true positional tolerancing and dimensioning. Due to problems with drafting consistency, developed and introduced drafting standards. The new standards have significantly increased drawing quality and staff efficiency.

EDUCATION

QUALIFICATIONS

Supervise student organizations and activities which have consistently been among the most successful in the school district.

Highly effective with parents. Able to actively involve parents in Individual Education Plans and provide valuable counseling to them.

Strong background in coordinating support personnel to enhance education for the profoundly retarded.

Perceptive and sensitive to the special needs student.

❖

Effectively plan, implement, and evaluate educational programs.

❖

Broad assessment and observational experience.

EMPLOYMENT

As chairperson of a department with fourteen instructors, maintained a high quality department in the face of budgetary cutbacks. Evaluated all new programs, developed class schedules, oriented new teachers, assisted substitute teachers, purchased all supplies for the department, and served on the principal's advisory board.

❖

Instituted and maintained the Russian language program at a new high school and created individualized instruction packages for advanced-level German students. Chairman of the foreign language department for the past five years at this high school with 1200 students. Member of the district foreign language curriculum committee for formulating and writing district goals.

❖

Effectively plan and implement functional, individualized educational programs for the profoundly retarded student. Informally assess their progress and adapt their programs accordingly. Emphasize the skill areas of self-help, socialization, communication, pre-vocation, and home living. Develop thorough Individual Education Plans. Highly involved with the coordination of support personnel in program development.

ELECTRONICS TECHNICIAN/FIELD ENGINEER

QUALIFICATIONS

Excellent supervisory experience. Department has maintained the lowest rework and rejection rate in the company for the past five years and has completed all production on schedule.

❖

Broad experience in analyzing and solving complex computer hardware problems. Effectively handle all aspects of customer relations from courtesy calls to handling irate customers. Experienced in the supervision and training of field service personnel. Strong reputation as a highly effective troubleshooter.

EMPLOYMENT

<u>Wiring Department Supervisor</u> - Supervise eight solderers and assemblers. Responsible for production scheduling of avionics and related products. Wrote and continually update a training manual which has reduced errors and has enabled more cross-training than had previously been done. Maintain a complete parts inventory and developed a simple yet effective system for inventory control. Interface with the engineering department in the design or redesign of procedures used in wiring projects. Department has received management recognition for being the most efficient of the six production departments in the company and has for the past five years maintained the lowest rework and rejection rate.

❖

<u>Senior Hardware Support</u> - For this company which packages a hardware/software system for the mortgage banking industry, test and repair hardware and provide customer support. Test all PCs, hard drives, printers, and modems prior to shipment, and repair as necessary. Troubleshoot units returned from the field and repair to the board level. Initiated a failure analysis program to track and isolate hardware and software problems. Provide all customer support for customers with problems in the field. Oversee work orders to ensure on schedule deliveries. Largely responsible for increasing on time deliveries from 60% to 95%.

❖

<u>Test Technician</u> - For this manufacturer of heart monitoring equipment, troubleshoot units returned from the field and repair to the component level. Analyze circuits using various test methods and repair luminance boards, system control boards, audio boards, and servo boards. Received the Presidential Award in 1991 for developing an alignment procedure for technical service reps in the field. By periodically adjusting the alignment the failure rate due to misalignments has been reduced from 14% of all failures to less than 1%.

❖

<u>Installation Manager</u> - Supervise production and shipping schedules to ensure timely delivery of orders to customers. Negotiate with freight companies to secure the best price and delivery schedule for clients, and arrange for local installation of units. Handle customer service calls regarding shipping, delivery, installation, and warranty repairs. Developed and implemented quality control procedures and wrote the quality control manual to ensure compliance with regulations governing government subcontractors. Instituted in-process and final inspection procedures which have cut warranty calls 70% and have significantly increased gross profit margins.

❖

<u>Mechanical Technician</u> - Maintain and repair mechanical systems on automated industrial machines, including riveting machines, milling machines, and high speed wire coding machines. Have maintained a record of extremely low downtime on equipment valued at up to $900 per hour. Won a Ford "Excellence" award for designing an inexpensive component for a wire making machine which reduced downtime and saved over $32,000 annually.

❖

<u>Field Engineering Manager</u> - Supervise and schedule the work of 18 field engineers installing and maintaining computer systems. Took over a district with high turnover, low morale, and a poor reputation for customer service. Within one year turnover was reduced from 40% to less than 10% annually. Response time was reduced from six hours to two hours.

ENGINEERING

EMPLOYMENT

Responsible for administration, PS&E, and construction engineering for the 600 foot, $9 million apron construction just completed at terminal 21, Port of San Francisco. Directed six engineers and two drafters to completion within budget. Instituted an innovative structural concept using ductile vertical concrete piles to resist lateral loads with reduced construction and maintenance costs. Terminal 21 has been described as "the prototype for future port expansions" by port authorities.

❖

<u>Chief Structural Engineer</u> - U.S. Navy drydock construction covers for nuclear frigates. Directed the structural design of two 100' x 120' self-propelled, track mounted, steel truss enclosures. Developed the structural system to minimize spread between tracks due to live loads and arch rib tiedowns for 95' x 75' closure curtains. This one-of-a-kind project received the Grand Award in the CECW 1988 competition.

❖

<u>Senior Cost and Scheduling Engineer</u> - As Control Team Leader for a $58 million, 280,000 tons-per-year iron ore plant, provide cost and scheduling analyses for Fluor and client. Assess client requests for changes and determine impact on construction cost and schedule. Monitor subcontract awards and procurement activities to ensure work will proceed according to the master schedule and budget.

❖

<u>Senior Construction Engineer</u> - Reviewed all design changes for the retrofitting of the Edison Electric nuclear power plant. Determined design feasibility and identified potential design problems. Resolved construction problems as they occurred. Recommended design changes as necessary. Verified quality and completion of work performed per each design change request. Monitored material status and the construction schedule and completed the project ahead of schedule. In 1992 received a cash bonus that was awarded to less than one percent of all engineers in the grade 25 and above category. Bonus was based on quantity and quality of work performed.

❖

<u>Utility Engineering Manager</u> - With a staff of 10-12 engineers and technicians, managed the design and construction of all water and sewer capital improvement projects for the City of San Jose, as well as the design and construction of water and sewer expansion facilities initiated by private developers. Developed new procedures which enabled projects to move from inception to completion in 18 months versus over two years in the past.

❖

<u>Structural Design Engineer</u> - Design landing gear detail parts and assemblies for a large classified aircraft. Integrate landing gear part designs into CAD/CAM format for use in manufacturing. Coordinate with systems groups and adapt design to incorporate additional equipment. Assist outside vendors with review and discussion of technical specifications and help resolve manufacturing problems. Design engineering phase was completed on schedule and within budget.

FINANCE

QUALIFICATIONS

Broad experience in financial analysis including valuation, investment analysis, and determining the best sources for external capital.

❖

Strong management, finance, and operations background. Experienced in taking companies through rapid expansionary periods while remaining solid financially.

EMPLOYMENT

For this engineering firm, develop large, complex computer models using Lotus 1-2-3 and BASIC to compute pro forma financial statements for proposed projects, generate graphics, perform sensitivity analyses, and evaluate and compare alternate sources of financing.

❖

Perform simulation studies to develop frequency distributions and other statistical information pertaining to measures of investment merit such as IRR and NPV. Use various analytical techniques to estimate cash flows and appraise risks.

❖

As chief financial officer for one of the largest ComputerTech franchises in the country, played a key role in enabling the firm to expand from four stores to fifteen in four years. Responsible for the financial, administrative, and development related activities of the company.

❖

Obtain financing for growth, oversee purchasing and inventory control, negotiate leases, and work closely with contractors during the construction of new stores.

❖

Successfully recovered the prior year's tax payments and eliminated the current year's liability of over $500,000 through several tax avoidance programs.

❖

Renegotiated the bank line rate from prime plus two points to prime plus one point, saving $30,000 annually. Doubled the line of credit to $6 million.

❖

Joined this start up company during its second year and played a key role in strengthening its financial base during a period of rapid growth. Assumed responsibility for obtaining and controlling capital resources, setting up and refining accounting systems, and dealing with all aspects of administration. Negotiated two stock purchase and option agreements totaling $2.3 million and obtained a $1.9 million line of credit for vehicles.

❖

Worked with attorney on the preparation of two private placement memoranda and one rights offering.

FLIGHT ATTENDANT (Seeking first position)

QUALIFICATIONS

Excellent sales and customer service background. During six years of retail sales experience, always create strong customer loyalty and receive very high ratings from supervisors.

❖

Recognized by supervisors and coworkers as easy to work with, friendly, reliable, conscientious, and poised. Highly energetic. Work well under stress.

❖

Excellent sales and customer service experience. Work hard to satisfy customers and always develop strong customer loyalty. Enjoy serving and helping people. Handle stress and pressure effectively.

❖

Strong customer service experience. Recognized as cooperative, friendly, self-confident, poised, and effective in high stress situations. Quickly develop rapport with people from all ethnic backgrounds, and as a waitress have built a highly loyal clientele.

EMPLOYMENT

(Emphasize sales experience and customer service experience. Restaurant and retail experience is excellent. Throughout your job descriptions do everything possible to demonstrate that you relate well to people from different cultures, that you are customer oriented, that you work well under pressure, and that you establish rapport quickly with people.)

❖

Waitress - Take lunch and dinner orders from customers and serve food and drinks. Quickly developed a loyal clientele, with many customers regularly requesting my tables. Frequently handle the entire cocktail lounge single-handedly. Received several commendations from the manager and owner for the ability to work effectively under pressure and create excellent customer relations.

FORESTRY

QUALIFICATIONS

Strong background in all phases of timber sale administration and log purchasing. Maintain an excellent record for keeping mills supplied with logs purchased at the best price possible. Recognized for ability to accurately estimate the value of a stand and judge the quality of logs.

EMPLOYMENT

Forester - Responsible for maintaining an adequate supply of logs for the stud mill and for obtaining them at a profitable price. Appraise timber stands placed on sale by the US Forest Service, Department of Natural Resources, Corps of Engineers, and private owners. Assess the value of the logs on the open market and determine the amount of timber usable by the stud mill. Have appraised over one hundred timber sales. Develop excellent working relations with other sawmills and purchase logs from those mills as well as independent loggers. Purchase approximately 10 million board feet per year.

❖

Forestry Technician - For preparation of timber sales, tag boundaries, cruise stands for volume, identify trees for cutting, and assist in putting in road locations. Develop environmental impact statements for proposed timber sales after reconning designated areas. Make recommendations regarding road development, silviculture, logging techniques, and post harvest activity.

GOVERNMENT

EMPLOYMENT

Claims Representative - As a claims representative for the Consumer Protection Division, interview consumers regarding unfair or deceptive business practices and make recommendations for appropriate action. Determine jurisdiction of the issue and refer to other agencies for assistance when appropriate. Investigate complaints and mediate cases in order to arrive at solution satisfactory to both parties. Have maintained an excellent success rate.

❖

Administrative Coordinator - As Administrative Coordinator of Grant County, report to the county council and have responsibility for all administrative functions. Developed and implemented new systems that have reduced operating costs and increased efficiency. Annually prepare and administer a $90-110 million county budget. Developed and implemented an effective purchasing system and instituted cost saving measures such as bulk purchasing and competitive bidding. Write and administer policies concerning personnel, safety, vehicle use, and ethics. Negotiate labor agreements. Simplified the administration of the contracts by consolidating five agreements into two master contracts covering 300 employees. Act as liaison with Federal, State, non-profit, and private agencies. Heavily involved in grant writing, grant management, and public speaking.

❖

Responsible for promoting and achieving code and ordinance compliance through construction inspections. Work closely with developers, builders, and architects to enable them to produce innovative projects which comply with both the spirit and letter of the law. Recognized as fair but tough in the interpretation of codes. Coordinate with architects and builders on major projects to discuss difficulties in achieving code compliance and work out solutions which benefit both the City and the builder.

Resolve disputes over code interpretation between inspectors and construction personnel. Review and approve the use of new materials by researching lab test results. Recommend code changes and ordinances for adoption by the City Council as needed. Played a key role in developing and implementing a computerized system which effectively handles all building department functions and has been adopted by several cities nationally.

HUMAN RESOURCES

QUALIFICATIONS

Seasoned executive with twenty years experience in all facets of human resources and labor relations. Proven problem solver dedicated to higher levels of profitability through increased efficiency, planning, and employer/employee harmony.

EMPLOYMENT

Employee Relations Manager - Responsible for the employee relations function for this farm implements manufacturer with 1200 employees. With a staff of 15, oversaw all hiring and recruiting, compensation, benefits administration, promotions, job evaluations, security, printing, company cafeteria, and the infirmary. Have developed and implemented numerous labor and cost saving practices including a Quality of Worklife program which has improved productivity 26%. Also instituted an effective employee assistance program.

Enhanced the existing safety program and reduced industrial accidents 45%. Represent the company in all OSHA, FEPC, and EEOC administrative hearings. Work closely with four labor unions to maintain harmonious working relations. Grievances have been reduced from over 40 per month to less than 15.

<u>Manager of Corporate Industrial Relations</u> - For this 11,000 employee manufacturer, responsible for labor negotiations, contract administration, arbitrations, labor board appearances, and the development and implementation of labor relations programs. Work with numerous unions including Steelworkers, UAW, Machinists, Teamsters, and craft unions.

Successfully directed union avoidance efforts at nine locations, and have negotiated over 32 labor contracts. Developed methods for determining true costs of a union contract and created a prenegotiation research methodology which has become the corporate standard. Created an on-going union/management communications forum which has largely been responsible for reducing grievances 34%. Through a foreman training program, the absentee rate has been reduced from 12% to 4%.

INSURANCE CLAIMS

EMPLOYMENT

<u>Senior Claims Adjuster</u> - Review medical, dental, vision, and time loss claims, and assist in training new personnel. Handle all claims for two major client companies and ensure that each claim is legitimate and in line with standard medical practices. Have developed close working relations with policyholder reps and frequently answer questions of individual employees. Maintain an excellent record in loss control and in identifying discrepancies that frequently lead to denial of claims or reductions in amount paid. Among the staff of 45, one of two to be named on the "high production" plaque six consecutive quarters.

As branch manager review and assign each claim and supervise a staff of 10. Recognized within the company as the best training branch and typically receive employees who have had difficulty at other branches. Highly successful in turning them into effective claims people. Among eight regional offices, consistently maintain the highest production per person, and for the last four years the office has been among the three lowest in cost per claim.

<u>Claims Examiner</u> - Assigned claims with serious injuries and handled cases through settlement or litigation. Examined all facts and details of a case and determined liability and the worth of each claim. Set the reserves, obtained recorded statements, police reports, and medical reports, and negotiated with individual claimants or their attorneys. Consistently assigned the most difficult cases, which often involved deaths or paralysis. For cases being prepared for trial, introduced the case to the attorney and made recommendations for defense strategies. Right up to trial day continued to negotiate with claimant attorneys and usually settled cases to the satisfaction of both parties.

INTERIOR DESIGNER

QUALIFICATIONS

Broad experience in institutional, commercial, and residential design applications. Perform extensive research to ensure proper application of products, to maintain affordability, and to achieve a unique quality.

Strong background in designing and implementing commercial interior space plans. Thoroughly research individual and group needs and develop designs that are aesthetically pleasing and ergonomically efficient.

EMPLOYMENT

Design interiors for nursing homes, hospitals, and clinics. Work primarily from blueprints and travel to each job site to direct the installation of furnishings. Completed five 100 bed nursing homes in one year with each one receiving excellent reviews from staff and patients.

❖

Design and furnish residential and commercial interiors. Select and purchase stock for showroom displays and schedule installations. Have established an excellent reputation for quality and uniqueness. Lobby of the Torrance building in St. Louis was featured in *Professional Builders* magazine.

❖

Space Planner - Worked closely with architects and designers to develop space plans for the company's new corporate headquarters building. Gathered and analyzed data from department managers and employees on equipment, space, and communications requirements, departmental functions, and planned growth.

Created a space plan based on user needs, space allocation formulas, requirements for shared equipment, and the distribution of environmental support systems. Developed a furniture standard for all operational levels which improved the visual quality of the work environment, achieved a unified design throughout the building, and significantly reduced furniture expenditures.

LANDSCAPE ARCHITECT

QUALIFICATIONS

Broad knowledge of environmental issues as well as local, state, and federal regulations.

❖

Strong background in organizing and conducting public involvement programs. Experienced at making presentations to clients, citizen groups, and agency personnel.

❖

Solid experience in Landscape Architecture, Land Use Planning, Urban Design, and Environmental Research.

EMPLOYMENT

Provide design and construction services for developments and private residences. Instituted an interactive design and construction process for a private school which involved parent groups, teachers, and school administrators. Developed a site plan for an athletic club which included solving circulation problems, a planting plan, and design alternatives for an outdoor courtyard.

❖

Provide support in the technical areas of visual resource management, aesthetics, recreation, and land use planning. Managed a visual/aesthetic resource assessment of effects generated by the construction and operation of a major skiing and recreational facility in the Canadian Rockies. Contributed to the landscape restoration and recreation elements of the project.

LAW ENFORCEMENT

QUALIFICATIONS

Nineteen years experience in law enforcement for a major metropolitan police department. Fourteen years as a detective with a reputation for utilizing innovative procedures in preventing as well as solving crimes. Work effectively with federal, state, and local law enforcement agencies throughout the western United States.

❖

Strong management experience with a broad background in all phases of investigation. Planned and established numerous programs which have met objectives and have been widely adopted within the Drug Enforcement Administration.

EMPLOYMENT

<u>Detective, Portland Police</u> - Develop sources of information on criminal activity in the Portland area through a variety of means including the use of confidential informants, electronic surveillance, and such innovative techniques as Phone Toll Analysis. Initiated contacts that resulted in the largest sting operation in the state and resulted in breaking up a nine-state cocaine ring. The operation, consisting of officers from four federal agencies and three states, netted $3 million in cash and contraband and the arrest of 15 dealers. Received a "Recognition Award" from the Drug Enforcement Agency.

❖

<u>Special Agent, DEA</u> - As an undercover agent infiltrated crime groups and played a key role in breaking up the operations. Undercover work in one case resulted in one of the largest confiscations of heroin in DEA history and also resulted in the conviction of high ranking organized crime figures. Upon completion of the investigation in St. Louis, reassigned to Washington D.C. for nine months to develop a program to follow up the case and obtain arrests in foreign countries. Further investigation led to high government officials in a Middle East country. Methodology for the probe continues to be used.

❖

<u>Police Officer</u> - As Patrol Officer, handle traffic control duties, aid in emergencies, and investigate crimes. Initiate and maintain cooperative relations with local businesses and the general public. Have exceeded department standards on all reviews.

MACHINE OPERATION

EMPLOYMENT

<u>Mixer</u> - Operate all mixing equipment and have established records for both quantity and quality. Weigh and mix ingredients with extreme accuracy and ensure that all ingredients are mixed properly. Hold mixing records for ten of the twenty primary products, with production of up to 2800 cases in an eight hour shift. Maintain a rejection rate one-fifth the plant average. Train new employees and have helped produce some of the top mixers. Frequently make recommendations that have enabled other mixers to increase speed and accuracy.

❖

<u>Millwright</u> - Install, move, repair, and maintain equipment as needed at the Aurora power plant. Repair air compressors, vacuum compressors, vacuum pumps, electric motors, conveyor systems, valves, gear boxes, fork lift trucks, and overhead cranes. Developed a preventive maintenance system for ash hopper pumps which was adopted throughout the plant and saves over $18,000 annually. Developed a system for exchanging filters on motors which run forced draft fans. The new exchange system does not necessitate shutting down the boilers and saves approximately $1 million each year in production time.

MEDICAL

EMPLOYMENT

<u>Medical Clinic Manager</u> - Oversee the day to day operations of this three doctor medical practice and supervise a staff of seven. Purchase supplies and equipment, handle all accounts payable and accounts receivable, make collections, and develop quarterly financial statements. Have resolved serious personnel problems with a significant increase in productivity and a substantial reduction in absenteeism and turnover.

❖

Nursing Home Administrator - Manage this 54-bed nursing home and supervise 85 full-time and part-time employees. Have built a well motivated and stable staff which provides high quality patient care. As a result, each year the State has increased allowable costs. Staff turnover has been reduced over 30%. New programs for patients and their families have been implemented which have significantly increased visitations by family members. During the first two years increased patient count from 40 to 54, and have since built a large waiting list.

❖

Clinical Supervisor - Supervise the Orthopedics department with 45 FTEs and a $2.2 million budget. Work closely with one head nurse and three assistant head nurses and have developed a very strong department. Recommended and then implemented a program to enhance staff professionalism. Staff mix went from 60% aides to 85% RNs as the department moved into primary nursing. Have established a highly competent staff which demonstrates great concern for patients, leading to a significant reduction in patient complaints. In 1989 merged spinal cord injury patients into Orthopedics.

❖

Director of Health Records Department - Supervised a staff of three and trained them in methods of assembling and analyzing charts. Developed and wrote a policies and procedures manual, improved filing of medical records through a new color coded system, and set up a medical library. Developed a new analysis sheet which resulted in more complete and better documented charts. Revised rules for charting for nursing staff which improved documentation, reduced legal risks, and increased revenue from insurance carriers. Worked with insurance companies to supply necessary records while maintaining confidentiality of patients. Significantly improved relations between Health Records and other departments of the hospital.

❖

Dental Hygienist - As an Expanded Hygienist, provide complete adult and child prophylaxis including charting, reviewing health history, blood pressure, and oral exam. Perform perio scale, soft tissue curettage, and root planing. Administer local anesthetic and nitrous oxide as needed. Also condense and carve single surface amalgams on children as well as apply pit and fissure sealants. Take full-mouth, bite wing, and periapical radiographs. Provide complete demonstrations and instructions for home health care. Order all supplies related to dental hygiene. Assist with sterilization of instruments. Developed a highly effective recall system.

❖

Radiology Technologist - As a staff technologist in this 285 bed hospital, produce radiographs in routine and specialized procedures. Rotate weekly through surgery, emergency room, and special procedures. In special procedures produce venograms, meleograms, IVP, voiding cystograms, facet blocks, lymph angiograms, fluorscopy, arthograms, and neo-natal radiographs. Have received many compliments from patients, radiologists, and physicians for providing excellent care and producing high quality radiographs.

❖

Admissions Coordinator - Established and defined the position of Admissions Coordinator in order to improve patient services and improve community perceptions of the quality of care provided. Developed procedures for physicians to specify admission dates, necessary tests, and other details about patients. Make arrangements with all appropriate departments. Upon arrival, meet with patients to perform physical and mental assessments. Through improved procedures, average patient waiting time for initial nursing contact has been reduce from one hour to less than fifteen minutes. Program has received favorable response from physicians and is helping to lead to more physician referrals.

❖

Assistant Director of Nursing - Provide overall direction for nursing services and develop new programs and systems. Developed a system for monitoring nursing hours per patient day. Through better utilization of staff and increased productivity, have decreased the nursing hours per patient 12% while maintaining the same high quality care. Program saves $180,000 per year. Established a program which has significantly improved communications between staff and nursing administration.

MILITARY

QUALIFICATIONS

Six years of management and supervisory experience. Departments have always received higher ratings as a result of new systems and better organization.

❖

Consistently received annual evaluations rated top 5%.

❖

Trained and experienced in Human Resource Management. Able to isolate personnel problems and implement solutions.

EMPLOYMENT

Legal Officer - Investigated crimes, gathered evidence, and made recommendations for prosecution. Resolved claims for and against the government. Investigated accidents and other claims and negotiated settlements. Provided financial counseling for those with debt problems. Developed strong working relations with Naval Investigative Service, County Prosecutor, and US Secret Service.

❖

Scheduler/Flight Leader - Oversaw the training of student officers, making sure all phases of training were completed in the least time possible.

❖

Quality Assurance/Maintenance Safety Officer - Developed the squadron into a top rated unit. Won the Battle Efficiency Award (1988) and the Chief of Naval Operations Safety Award (1987, 1989) for being the highest rated among 13 squadrons.

❖

Human Resources Officer - Developed Command Action Plans using input from the squadron to deal with problems such as drug and alcohol abuse, poor morale and communications, and racial conflicts. Received the highest Human Resource Management rating within the wing (six squadrons). The Action Plan became the model used throughout the wing. Drug and alcohol use were substantially reduced and reenlistments among minorities increased over 40%.

❖

Electrical Instruments Officer - Managed the base shop which repaired gyros, inertials, and other instruments. Operation readiness rose from one of the lowest ratings to the highest.

❖

Procurement Officer - Responsible for providing supplies, procuring equipment, and planning logistics for an agency of 700. Each year develop a proposed budget based on the needs of the agency and establish justification for all expenditures. As needs or problems occur throughout the year, request funds to procure nonbudgeted items. For nonstandard products work with vendors to obtain the best product available while remaining within budget. Items have included portable investigation laboratories, computers, police radios, and emergency equipment. Also maintain property accountability including real estate, buildings, desks, equipment, and arms. Perform or supervise investigations when property is lost or stolen. Developed a system which reduced procurement time for major equipment from an average of 96 days to 69.

❖

<u>Military Police Supervisor</u> - Supervised 25 MPs and the handling of police work and investigations at Fort Lewis. At different times coordinated investigations with the FBI, Pierce County Sheriff's Department, and the Criminal Investigation Department of the Army. Cases Investigated included homicides, rapes, thefts, illegal use of drugs, and destruction of equipment.

NONPROFIT

EMPLOYMENT

<u>Program Director</u> - Have complete responsibility for fundraising, publicity, and promotion of athletic programs for the Boys and Girls Club. Supervise a staff of four in addition to 24 part-time officials. Through new recruiting procedures, have increased participation in athletic programs over 15%. Played a key role in fundraising solicitations and sports team sponsorship, which produced 48% more revenue than originally budgeted. Recruit volunteer coaches and train and supervise large numbers of part-time staff. Through close coordination, have vastly improved relations with agencies and organizations which the Club depends on for use of their facilities. Plan, organize, and schedule leagues and special events.

OFFICE/CLERICAL

QUALIFICATIONS

Strong administrative and office experience in the areas of inside sales, customer relations, customer troubleshooting, accounting, purchasing, collections, and supervision. Establish office procedures which increase efficiency and productivity.

❖

Excellent supervisory and administrative background. Develop procedures that increase departmental productivity and establish excellent customer relations. Highly regarded for ability to handle difficult assignments.

EMPLOYMENT

<u>Lead, Order Entry Department</u> - Responsible for scheduling, training, and supervising four employees. Delegate work load, resolve internal and customer problems, and coordinate with other departments. Handle customer maintenance and the updating of computerized information. Developed procedures which have increased order entry accuracy 40%. Played a key role in a computer conversion and recommended program changes which save an average of ten hours per day.

❖

<u>Administrative Supervisor</u> - For this firm which markets computer systems to pharmacies, handled numerous administrative functions including purchasing, billing, accounts payable, accounts receivable, and inventory control.

Hired to resolve numerous problems which developed over the previous year due to rapid growth. Delinquencies of 60 days and older were reduced from 40% to less than 5% and outstandings were reduced from $380,000 to $80,000 in just six months. Established an effective billing system which ensures that all accounts are paid on schedule.

Twenty-five percent of all price quotes were seriously underbid prior to 1990, forcing the company to absorb large losses. Developed a system to keep prices updated and reduced losses due to underbidding to zero.

❖

<u>Sales Assistant</u> - As sales assistant in agriculture chemicals, handle traffic management and work closely with customers while taking orders. Provide total follow-up for customers by answering questions, tracing shipments, and handling damage and

shortage claims. Schedule deliveries for the company-owned truck, and work with freight companies to deliver products. Track inventory at eight stocking points through monthly physical inventories. Successfully reduced inventory 40% while providing better delivery times than before.

❖

Office Manager -Administered all business functions of a three chair dental practice. Set up a computerized patient information and billing system and trained office personnel in its use. Instituted an incentive program and trained staff in sales techniques, resulting in increased monthly production from $18,000 to $32,000 in eight months. Introduced new bookkeeping procedures and collection policies which enabled the office to collect 102% of actual production for two consecutive years, including over $30,000 in outstanding and delinquent accounts. Significantly increased staff productivity by reorganizing and simplifying office systems.

❖

Agency Secretary - Supervise seven office people and act as main contact person and troubleshooter for the company's insurance agents. Research records and resolve agents' problems regarding new or existing policies. Deal directly with clients and answer questions concerning payments or policy issues. Supervise the processing of new applications and cancellations. By reorganizing office procedures overall efficiency has been increased and the turnaround time for correspondence with agents has been decreased from four days to two days. In appreciation of contributions, received recognition at three regional sales meetings and air fare for two to England.

❖

Executive Secretary - Assisted the Western Regional Manager in secretarial and administrative functions. Typed, transcribed dictated material, maintained office files, composed correspondence letters, scheduled appointments, planned itineraries, and arranged meetings. Purchased supplies and equipment and prepared expense reports for the Regional Manager and other sales staff. Highly trusted to carry out various special assignments.

PROGRAMMERS

EMPLOYMENT

Had total responsibility for the entire accounts receivable system on a 24-hour basis. Supervised three computer operators and worked directly with the Accounts Receivable Department. Did all troubleshooting and resolution of system errors. Implemented program changes that significantly reduced run time and increased program efficiency.

❖

Maintained financial applications and rewrote existing RPG II programs to COBOL to improve their maintainability. Wrote all programs to the automated system and completed testing of the system. Wrote interface programs with general ledger packages. Developed entry screens and reports for users. Wrote complete and easy to use documentation.

❖

As a systems analyst, work on state of the art projects in system design. In charge of the design and implementation of a software product which will monitor the construction of the NASA Space Station. Normalized and logically designed data, prototyped logic design into P.C. - Oracle database and uploaded finished prototype to ORACLE IBM-4341/MVS.

❖

In charge of all phases of development of a data security system. Gathered requirements, conducted system analysis, wrote functional specifications, and tested the access and security portion of System Wide Features, an IMS shell that manages screens and transactions. Also wrote user documentation and conducted a three day training seminar. Received letter of commendation in recognition of design efforts and outstanding performance in creating a highly efficient and effective system.

PROPERTY MANAGEMENT

QUALIFICATIONS

Nine years experience managing all aspects of a diversified real estate portfolio of over one million square feet. Consistently improve profitability of all properties by improving occupancy rates, customer satisfaction, and implementing cost-saving procedures.

EMPLOYMENT

Property Manager - Direct operations of four shopping centers, eight office buildings, and seven multi-family projects. Coordinate all leasing activities including tenant recruitment, qualifying, and negotiating. Regularly inspect all properties and maintain close contact with tenants. Act immediately on complaints or concerns. Coordinate and schedule maintenance and monitor all work. Provide status and financial reports to owners. Develop annual budgets and monitor adherence. Through a remodeling project, took one building from a 71% to a 96% occupancy rate. At one 80-unit luxury apartment complex, increased rents 45% over four years, while maintaining a 98% occupancy rate.

PUBLIC RELATIONS

QUALIFICATIONS

Excellent background in researching, planning, and coordinating public relations projects. Establish strong working relations with clients, editors, and vendors. Excellent writer, able to quickly assess clients' needs, and produce creative promotional material. Proven track record for completing complex projects on schedule.

EMPLOYMENT

Public Relations Director - Perform market analysis for business-to-business advertising and conduct extensive research to assess clients' current and future position in the marketplace. Use analyses to implement advertising campaigns and PR programs, and develop new markets. Write and distribute articles, press releases, and new product information sheets. Contact editors of trade journals regarding product reviews and follow up to ensure publication. Write brochure copy for industrial and manufacturing accounts, and occasionally place media. Wrote a series of direct mail letters utilized in national advertising campaigns which achieved extremely high returns.

PURCHASING

QUALIFICATIONS

Strong background in material control and purchasing. Broad experience in setting up automated systems that have significantly increased productivity. Consistently able to decrease purchasing cost and increase on-time deliveries through effective expediting.

EMPLOYMENT

Purchasing Manager - Directed the expenditure of $80-100 million for material, equipment, and supplies to attain price, quality, and delivery schedule objectives. Established purchasing policies, formulated department procedures, and guided personnel actions to achieve goals. Supervised up to 24 employees responsible for supplier selection and negotiations, cost/price maintenance, resolution of discrepant shipment reports, resolution of receiving problems, and expediting. Implemented a cost reduction program which produced $800,000 in confirmed savings in the first 12 months of the program. Designed new procedures which ensure on-time, errorless cost/price updates.

❖

Purchasing Manager - (business forms printing company). Responsible for all areas of purchasing, inventory control, shipping, receiving, stock handling, and deliveries. Procure all inventory products, equipment, and MRO supplies. Negotiate with vendors and expedite orders. On-time delivery of orders has increased from 65% to 96%. Lead time needed for orders has been reduced from 28 working days to 10. Redesign of the warehouse layout has reduced inventory loss and damage from 4% to less than 1%, and picking time on orders has been reduced 45%. Buy virtually exclusively from mills and have reduced warehouse buying of roll paper stock 95%, saving $58,000 per year.

❖

Procurement Specialist - Purchase computers, terminals, and peripherals. Negotiate noncompetitive contracts with vendors and write contracts from scratch. Monitor vendors to ensure total compliance with contracts, particularly in the area of maintenance and repair. Instituted a money-saving purchase order system which saves over $20,000 annually. Won six cost-saving awards for negotiations and new methods which saved a total of $1.6 million.

❖

Buyer - Purchase over 5,000 different machine shop tools based on specs. Make on-site visits to vendors to inspect their facilities and to identify prospective vendors. Obtained several new vendors which have produced numerous parts at 25-50% less than previous vendors. Heavily involved in competitive bidding and writing of contracts.

QUALITY CONTROL

QUALIFICATIONS

Broad experience in all phases of the production and inspection of hybrids and micro-electronics, gained through 13 years in the industry. Extensive experience in hiring, training, certifying, and supervising inspectors and technicians. Work effectively with engineers to resolve production and vendor problems. Extensive experience using military standards.

EMPLOYMENT

Inspect microprocessor hybrids at the diebond, wirebond, internal visual, and external visual stages. Recognized for fast and accurate inspecting. Certify and train inspectors. Work effectively with government source inspectors to gain approval of completed hybrids. Provide technical advice to buyers, procurement engineers, and manufacturing engineers to resolve production and vendor problems. Work with laboratory personnel in failure analysis to determine causes of component failures. Developed a failure trend analysis record log which has enabled the firm to trace failures back to vendors by quality lot number.

❖

Quality Assurance Supervisor - At the salmon processing plant, supervised a staff of four and ensured all product met Castle and Cook's high standards. Decreased wastage and internal losses through better monitoring of production. Had close contact with food brokers and quickly dealt with any quality problems. Established new production procedures which resulted in a 40% drop in quality complaints and saved $230,000 in returned product. Gained the cooperation of production and sales management and brought the QA department to its highest level of respect ever.

RESTAURANT MANAGEMENT

EMPLOYMENT

<u>District Training Supervisor</u> - Train and develop new Assistant Managers. Provide training seminars and supervise the floor training during the four month program. Work closely with the District Manager and have played a key role in taking the district from the lowest rated to the second highest rated in the region.

❖

<u>Division Manager</u> - Oversee the operations of three full service restaurants and have responsibility for sales, yearly profit and loss budgets, marketing and special promotions, menu development, hiring entertainment, and management training. Visit restaurants weekly and work closely with managers to develop their staffs and create ways to improve service to the customer. Developed and introduced numerous promotions that have been popular among customers and have helped establish a more loyal clientele. During the past three years increased profits an average of 18% per year.

❖

<u>General Manager</u> - Supervise a staff of 30 at this full service dinner house and have full profit and loss responsibility. Established new procedures which cut food and labor costs by over 25%. Introduced incentives among wait staff that have decreased turnover 75%. Built an entirely new menu and wine list that better matched the changing clientele and established a strong repeat business. Promotion of community events and contests has significantly increased customer loyalty. Annual sales have increased an average of 38% per year and gross profit margins have increased from 56% of sales to 71%.

❖

<u>Opening Supervisor</u> - Had major responsibilities in the opening of fifteen restaurants in Texas, California, and Hawaii. Interviewed, hired, and trained new staff, and oversaw publicity efforts. Provided thorough training for each position and worked closely with the staff during the first two weeks of operations. Instilled in staff the Denny's way and the Denny's concern for quality and service. Generated an excitement among staff for opening day that resulted in some of the most successful openings Denny's has ever had. Established staff schedules, contracted with vendors, and set up inventory and ordering procedures. Quickly became on of the top trainers in the corporation and received special assignments for the most important openings.

RETAIL/RETAIL MANAGEMENT

EMPLOYMENT

<u>Store Manager</u> - Manage this AT&T PhoneCenter and supervise a staff of eight. Came in with a mandate to increase sales and bring the store to a position of profitability. Brought in four new people and completely retrained the staff. Remerchandised the store and implemented incentive programs. Performed a market research study and identified new markets that were not being fully tapped, especially small business systems. Through improvements in training, staff productivity, merchandising, and marketing, have taken the store from 34th in sales out of 46 stores in the region, to 5th.

❖

<u>Store Manager</u> - Opened this specialty sporting goods store and immediately had an impact on the community. Hired 12 salespeople and have developed them into a strong sales team. Attend four trade shows each year and handle all preseason buying. Developed a sophisticated inventory control system which provides accurate sales data and demonstrates excellent predictive ability. As a result, maintain a high merchandise turnover rate. Have established a store which is known for it high quality merchandise and its outstanding service orientation. Sales have increased an average of 48% for each of the last three years.

❖

<u>Buyer</u> - Oversee purchasing of lumber and building supplies for sales totaling $169 million annually at 110 retail outlets. Determine appropriate wholesale prices to be paid, specific terms of agreements, and appropriate differential pricing for individual products at the retail level. Played a key role in developing lumber and related building materials as major profit-making lines for the organization. Conduct training sessions for both managers and members of their sales forces to guarantee effective purchasing, pricing, and selling procedures at the store level.

Set in place all elements of a new program to import a laminated oak door to be manufactured in Taiwan. Selected the manufacturer and obtained very favorable terms. Product line produced sales of $5 million in its first year and has grown over 30% per year for each of the last four years.

❖

<u>Buyer, Paint & Furniture</u> - Responsible for buying, merchandising, and sales activities for 45 stores. Designed and implemented a private label paint strategy for increased profitability, using an in-store and multi-media advertising campaign combined with personnel training and incentives. Increased private label share from 20% to 40% of total sales, and increased department profits by 35%. Designed and developed a private label paint brush program that increased sales of top line products from 22% to 32% of total through packaging design and off-shelf merchandising. Developed a new furniture program that took furniture sales from $400,000 to $3 million.

❖

<u>Clothing Sales</u> - Assisted in opening the Redondo Beach men's sportswear department and merchandising it for opening day. Named "All-star" in 1991 in recognition of strong customer service over the previous months. Exceeded 1992 sales goal by 35% and achieved the #2 sales position in the store for 1992 with sales of $443,000.

SALES

QUALIFICATIONS

Strong sales track record. In each of three territories managed, increased sales significantly. Salesperson of the Year in 1991 for a major manufacturer of medical equipment. Obtain excellent sales through direct calls on users and by motivating and training distributors.

❖

Strong sales and management background. As Branch Manager of a store fixture distributor, implemented effective marketing strategies which led to an 88% increase in sales in three years. Set a sales record in 1991 and have the company in its strongest position in 20 years.

❖

Strong sales track record. Increased market share 45% in three years. Work effectively with dealers and distributors.

❖

Strong background in sales management. Experienced in setting up effective regional and national sales forces, and marketing products both regionally and nationally. Outstanding sales trainer. Use trade shows effectively to reach new markets.

EMPLOYMENT

<u>Sales Representatives</u> - For this manufacturer of clinical diagnostic laboratory equipment and reagents, turned around a neglected territory in less than twelve months. Sell to hospitals, physicians, and veterinarians in six western states through seven distributors. Worked closely with five existing distributors to reestablish confidence in Smercon, and added two highly productive distributors. Increased sales in the territory 300% in the

first year. As a designated Training Manager, developed a new sales training program which has been adopted throughout the corporation.

❖

<u>Sales Representative</u> - For the second largest supplier of school awards, class rings, and graduation items, call on 85 high schools throughout Maine. Developed excellent relations with school officials and in six years took a territory with 24% market penetration and built it to a 45% level, ranking fifth in the country among 435 territories.

❖

<u>Sales Representative</u> - Opened up a four-state territory to market an entirely new line of state of the art, high-end quartz watches. During the first year of these newly developed products, created strong market penetration and established excellent accounts with mass merchandisers and high-end jewelry stores. Called on headquarter accounts, set up effective co-op advertising programs, and developed strategies for penetrating major accounts. Out of 34 territories nationally, built the Midwest territory to 8th in 1990, 5th in 1991, and 3rd in 1992.

❖

<u>Account Manager</u> - For the Beauty Care Division, call on key accounts and manage a territory through five account reps, two merchandisers, and one food broker. Work with buyers and store management to increase distribution and introduce new products. Develop promotions and contests and coordinate advertising throughout the territory. In 1989 added Nordstrom and Macy's as key accounts and have increased market share 46% since 1988. From among twelve managers in the Central Region, selected as District Account Manager of the Year for 1990 and 1991.

❖

<u>Sales Representative</u> - For this wholesaler of variety items geared for grocery and drug stores, call on established customers and develop new accounts. Train and supervise merchandisers to service accounts. In the first twelve months opened 56 new accounts and have increased sales 90% in two years. Took the territory from #15 in 1989 to #4 in 1990 and #2 in 1991.

❖

<u>Account Executive</u> - For this Fortune 100 company, sell electronic key telephone systems in a highly competitive market. Meet with customers and identify the cost savings that can be achieved through the most advanced telephone systems available. Design systems to meet customer needs and negotiate contracts. Coordinate the installation as well as the training of users. Follow up after each sale to ensure the system is working as expected. Since 1986 have ranked in the top 10% each quarter in the fourteen-state region.

❖

<u>Vice President, Sales and Marketing</u> - Performed all marketing research and obtained the North American rights to a unique commercial roofing product. Established marketing strategies and built a strong distribution network through a group of wholesalers. Sell the product through retail home centers, agricultural co-ops with over 3,000 retail stores, and OEM accounts. Sales have increased an average of 26% annually for the past six years.

❖

<u>District Sales Manager</u> - For this manufacturer of data communications equipment, manage a two-state district and have total responsibility for maximizing sales and profits. Supervise 12 sales representatives and four systems engineers. Administer the sales compensation package and annually establish sales objectives for individuals and sales teams. Provide technical and managerial resources for the sales staff and work closely with them to establish marketing and closing strategies. In three years have averaged 24% annual sales growth and in 1991 led the six-district region in adding new accounts, with 94. In 1992 inducted into the "Marathon Club" for exceeding revenue quota five consecutive years.

SCIENTISTS

EMPLOYMENT

<u>Research Scientist</u> - Have participated in research projects and surveys funded by EPA, NOAA, and other agencies. On one EPA project, identified over one hundred organic and inorganic pollutants found in 26 sewage systems. Made recommendations for the detection and removal of trace elements in sewage and sludge.

Managed an EPA Superfund hazardous waste investigation using laboratory techniques. Received and tested samples from landfills, leachate, and industrial water discharge from all over the country to detect heavy metals. At the completion of the project, received an EPA performance evaluation rating of 96%, the highest among five other laboratories.

❖

<u>Corporate Industrial Hygienist</u> - Responsible for material toxicological research, personnel exposure monitoring, evaluating laboratory results, determining Company compliance status with occupational safety and health standards, and analyzing potential or existing hazards for a wide variety of manufacturing processes. Specify engineering, administrative, or protective equipment exposure controls where needed. Carry out extensive on-site communication with shop workers, supervisors, and division safety offices to solve and prevent health and safety problems. Authored the company standard on PCBs.

❖

<u>Researcher</u> - Perform applied research and develop design criteria in studies for the development of fish hatchery water treatment systems, reconditioning filter systems, solid waste disposal methods, fish hatchery water quality requirements, and metabolite production in the aquatic environment.

In two major studies for the Corps of Engineers, demonstrated the effectiveness of buffering water systems chemically in solution. The new process saves over $65,000 per year for most water systems by eliminating construction and operating costs of expensive equipment.

TOOL AND DIE MAKING

EMPLOYMENT

Build mill fixtures, checking fixtures, blanking dies, form dies, joggle dies, draw dies, injection molds, and rubber molds. Consistently given the most difficult and complex assignments with the smallest tolerances. Have produced many cost saving measures by reducing the number of steps needed in the production of various parts.

❖

Make form, blank, and multistage dies. Build replacement dies, die blocks, and punches. Fabricate hydraulic parts, high speed machinery component parts, and x-ray equipment.

❖

Responsible for the fabrication and maintenance of blanking, parting, draw, multistage, and form dies. Fabricate production and inspection gauges, small checking fixtures, and injection, rubber, and foam molds.

How To Use A Resume

WANT ADS

I recommend reading the want ads. In cities with two or more newspapers, one paper usually predominates and gets 95% of all jobs advertised. Of course, some employers will advertise in more than one paper, but typically only about 5% of the jobs will be advertised in the secondary paper and *not* in the primary one. In addition, about 95% of all jobs advertised will appear in the Sunday paper. For the sake of time, read only the primary paper, and read only the Sunday edition. Scan it from A to Z. Some very interesting jobs can be listed with job titles you would never expect.

If a want ad is vague, mail out your standard resume and hope for the best. If the ad is fairly explicit concerning the desired qualifications and experience, you must decide whether to mail your standard resume with a custom cover letter, or whether you will take the additional time to tailor your resume to the position. If you feel strongly enough about a position, and your standard resume does not adequately cover some key points, it is worth modifying the resume. It can double your chances of getting an interview.

Blind Ads

Blind ads are rarely productive, but may be worth trying. A blind ad is a help-wanted ad in which the name of the employer has been omitted, and all you are given is a box number in care of the newspaper. Most are legitimate, placed by companies that for one reason or another want to maintain anonymity. Unfortunately companies sometimes use these want ads to gather salary information and in fact have no position. No one knows how frequently it occurs. The problem is, there is no way to tell which are legitimate and which are not.

Since blind ads usually draw fewer responses than ads that include the name of the employer, you'll have an excellent shot at an interview if your background is ideal.

To respond to a blind ad follow the instructions that each paper prints in the want ad section. If you are concerned about the blind ad being placed by your own company, or merely one that you don't want to receive your resume, follow the instructions for that situation. If you were responding to an ad placed in the Seattle Times you would address your envelope to the Seattle Times and include the box number for that ad. You would also write on the envelope, **Confidential Desk.** That alerts those sorting the mail that there are certain companies which should not receive your resume. Inside the outer envelope you would enclose a second envelope which would contain your resume. That envelope would also have the box number for that ad written on the outside. Also inside the outer envelope would be a separate sheet of paper which would indicate those companies you would not want your resume to go to.

Responding to blind ads rarely gets results because the companies placing them are highly particular and may interview only three people instead of the more typical six to eight. Unless your background is almost a perfect fit for the job, blind ads are rarely worth responding to.

Sources Of Want Ads

In addition to your local paper, other good sources of want ads are the *Wall Street Journal* (Tuesdays and Wednesdays contain the most ads) and the *National Business Employment Weekly*, which carries most of the ads from all four regional editions of the *Wall Street Journal*. Both are found in most libraries. The *National Business Employment Weekly* can be found at some newsstands and costs $3.95 a copy. You can also subscribe—$22.00 for six weeks. *The National Ad Search* contains want ads from all major newspapers from around the country. Read these resources in your library to determine if a subscription would be beneficial to you.

Competition can be fierce when good jobs are advertised. An ad for a good position can draw up to 500 applicants (50-150 is most typical) and rarely will more than eight people be interviewed. Your results will depend on how closely the job matches your qualifications and how much time you spend tailoring your cover letter. If you emphasize accomplishments and potential, you will certainly get a better response than average. According to a Department of Labor study, about 20% of all managers, sales workers, professionals, and clerical workers who answer ads, get their jobs through a help-wanted ad.

UNSOLICITED RESUMES

Unsolicited resumes are frequently sent to employers in hopes that a position may be available at the time the resume is received. Resume campaigns typically result in less than one interview for every hundred resumes sent out. If you use the strategy I'm about to discuss, you should get eight to ten interviews for every hundred resumes you mail.

You must start this type of campaign with an absolutely top-notch resume. Then develop a list of 50–200 employers of the right size, in the right industry, and in the right geographical area. Determine the department in which you would most likely work. Next, making about 20 calls an hour, call each organization and ask the receptionist for the name of the appropriate executive or department head. Be sure to get the correct spelling and title. Then and only then are you ready to send out resumes. Address each cover letter and resume to the specific person who has power to hire you. Addressing your letters to those with the power to hire should double your interviews compared to merely addressing it "Dear Mr. President," "Dear Marketing Manager," or "Dear Personnel Manager."

Usually you will know the typical title of the person with the power to hire you. In those cases simply ask the receptionist for the name of the person with that title. Sometimes you will be told, "We don't have anyone here with that title." Your response would then be, "Can you give me the name and title of the person who would typically hire engineers?" (or, whatever your job title is). If that does not work, ask using a different job title or ask for the personnel department.

If you simply cannot identify who your resume should go to, address it to the president *by name*. The resume may still wind up in personnel, but it is just as likely to be delivered to the most appropriate person.

Decide whether you will follow up with a phone call to each person or simply wait for interview offers. Calling and asking for an appointment will usually result in appointments 30–60% of the time, while waiting for interview offers (assuming you have a top-quality resume and sent it to a specific person) should result in an 8–12% success rate. Of course your actual percentage will be determined by the quality of your resume, the amount of experience you have in the field you are seeking, the impressiveness of your accomplishments and results, the job market, and the care with which you select potential employers.

The decision to call or wait is important because it will affect the wording in your cover letter. If you will be calling for an appointment, you simply state in the letter, "I will call you next week to set up a brief appointment." This statement will cause the reader to pay more attention to the resume, to be prepared for your call, and it likely will be kept close at hand rather than filed or discarded. With the waiting approach, you can end your letter with something like, "I look forward to hearing from you soon."

It's wise to send your chosen batch of employers a second mailing of your resume. A surprising finding, first described by Carl Boll in *Executive Jobs Unlimited*, is that resumes sent to the same organizations, six or more weeks after the first batch, will usually obtain results equal to the first mailing. In other words, if one hundred resumes netted you eight interviews, the second batch of one hundred should provide another eight. Give serious consideration to a second mailing.

FAXING

Do not fax a resume unless an employer has specifically asked you to do so. The quality at the other end looks like a poor quality dot matrix printed resume, and the paper will be typical fax paper. If you do fax a resume, also send one through the mail so the person will see its quality. If you want it there fast, but have not been asked to fax it, use an overnight express service. This approach will have more impact.

References

BEFORE LISTING PEOPLE AS REFERENCES, check with them to make sure they are willing to do it. Then ask them what they would feel comfortable saying about you. More than a few job seekers have been surprised to learn that an expected glowing recommendation turned out to be anything but. You can also suggest things you would like your references to say about you. Most will be happy to accommodate you.

References should virtually never be listed on a resume, even when those references are well-known people. Some people, however, like to write at the bottom, "Personal and Professional References Available Upon Request." My recommendation is to leave it off.

References are nearly always required on application forms, so you should have a list of your references ready. Each reference should include the person's name, title, name of organization, address, and phone number. You might want to type up your list of references and make four or five copies. That way, if it seems appropriate, you can give a copy to an employer during an interview.

References usually go into one of two categories—personal or professional. Although it is generally assumed by employers that personal references will say nice things about you, they are still often contacted. Therefore, choose your references carefully. John may say great things about you, but if he speaks in a monotone, gets easily flustered, and often lacks tact, I would choose someone else. Personal references should be those who know you well or have observed you for several years. It doesn't help your cause when someone says, "I don't know her well, but ..." Use influential people as references only if they can speak first hand about you and know you well enough to answer personal questions about you.

Your most important references are former bosses. Although companies are increasingly refusing to provide more than dates of employment—due to a rash of defamation of character suits in the 80s—those who really want information can usually get former bosses to reveal something. So while company policy may require your former boss to refer such calls to personnel, your boss may still supply information—good or bad.

With former bosses that you had good to satisfactory relationships with, you should at least call them and tell them that they may get calls from prospective employers. Explain what you've been up to since you worked together and thank the person for any positive contributions the person made to your career or personal growth. Find something positive to discuss, even if overall, it was not a good experience for you.

Cover Letters

THE COVER LETTER is merely a letter which introduces you to an employer. All resumes sent through the mail should be accompanied by a cover letter. The cover letter personalizes your resume and gives it greater flexibility. If your resume does not contain an objective, the cover letter is the place to express it. A cover letter gives you an opportunity to share points that are not easily covered in a resume. So a resume plus a cover letter represent the ideal vehicle to get across all of the key ideas and points that you want an employer to know about you.

A resume which arrives without a cover letter gives a jolt to the receiver and makes a loud statement about the sender—the person could not even take a few minutes to make a personal statement or sign his or her name. It begs the question, "Is this the type of person we want to hire?"

When answering a want ad, specify the exact job title in the cover letter. It is not necessary, however, to specify the source of the ad or its date. The exact title will provide all the information personnel needs. When a want ad explicitly requests certain types of experience which you have, but which are not adequately covered in the resume, use your cover letter to fill in the details. The alternative would be to rewrite your resume slightly to include the necessary details. A highly specific cover letter with a modified resume will always provide better results.

If an ad does not provide a name and you are unable to obtain the name of the person with power to hire, it is generally accepted that it should be addressed Dear Sir/Madam. If you are sending your resume and cover letter to personnel you could address it, Dear Personnel Manager, but do your best to get the name of the person.

View your cover letter and resume as a team. Each performs a different function, but they must work well together. Cover letters generally consist of two to four short paragraphs and seldom total more than twenty lines. The first paragraph should open with a strong statement about you that arouses interest and curiosity. Devote a middle paragraph to an accomplishment that will further arouse interest. The accomplishment can come from your resume but should be slightly reworded. When I write cover letters, I usually pick the strongest accomplishment from the resume and include it in the cover letter. Notice how this can be done:

> I can save money for your firm by utilizing my experience in cost control. At Standard Products I reduced paper usage by 24% and photocopying costs by 30%.

> ❖

> I can help increase the impact of your agency. While at Family Services I wrote a proposal which was funded for $22,000. This allowed us to significantly increase the quantity and quality of our services.

Appeal to the employer's self-interest by indicating that you are a problem solver and that hiring you will lead to increased production, greater efficiency, better planning, less waste, higher profits, and more satisfied customers.

Begin the process of responding to want ads by creating a "standard" cover letter; then modify it for each response. An electronic typewriter or a dedicated word processor will prove very helpful. If you believe that "time is money," you'll save a great deal if you can modify your cover letters yourself rather than going to a word processing outfit each time you want to produce a customized cover letter. You can also rent a computer by the hour at some copy shops and then print out your work on their laser printer. Charges are generally quite reasonable. Most have Macintoshes and offer several word processing software packages. If you have your own computer, but all you have is a dot matrix printer, go ahead and use that for your cover letters but be sure to put it in letter quality mode.

To create an effective response to an ad, begin by writing down or under-lining all of the key points mentioned in the ad. Check off those points which are clearly and effectively covered in your resume. If several points are not covered in your resume, determine whether you should modify your resume, or merely cover the points in your cover letter. If you decide to modify your resume you should make sure the resume covers all of the desired experience mentioned in the ad.

In using the Systematic Job Search methods you will want to meet the person with power to hire, even if no openings currently exist. Indicate in your cover letter that you will be calling to arrange a meeting. Avoid using the word *interview*. Instead say, "I'll call next week to arrange a brief meeting," or "I will call next week to arrange a time when we can meet." The word *interview* is always associated with formal hiring procedures; what you want is a relaxed meeting in which both parties learn more about each other.

Cover letters should be individually typed. Some people, however, print up 200 cover letters and then type in the employer's name and address. It doesn't look good and it does not make a good statement about you. The reader can tell that you said exactly the same thing to everyone who received your resume. Even if you develop a standard cover letter to be sent to 100 or more companies, you can still personalize it. Write the cover letter so you can insert the name of the company somewhere in the body of the letter. With today's word processors and memory typewriters, you can easily do it yourself. Secretarial services can type your letters and address your envelopes for less than two dollars each, and each one will look perfect.

If you know the company by reputation or your research has revealed some interesting information, don't hesitate to include it in the cover letter. This was done quite effectively in the following excerpts from cover letters:

> One of your competitors told me Alpa has the best quality control of any winch manufacturer in the country. The quality control system I established at Braddigan Gear also became recognized as tops in the industry.

❖

> Your recent acquisition of Marley & Sons indicates to me that you could use someone with my international marketing background.

❖

John McNamara at IBM believes you are one of the top management consulting firms in the country.

❖

The recent article in *The Seattle Times* about your rapid expansion was of great interest to me.

Review the sample cover letters, then simply start writing.

March 20, 1993

John Travis, Director
Home Energy Department
N. W. Center for Energy Efficiency
323 Sixth Avenue
Seattle, Washington 98021

Dear Mr. Travis:

Your recent efforts to promote energy conservation are of great interest to me. My experience as Energy Consultant for Seattle City Light would make me an excellent candidate for several positions in your organization.

While at City Light, I have inspected and provided energy savings estimates on over 500 homes. Eighty percent of the homeowners have acted on one or more of my suggestions and have averaged over 17% in energy savings.

I will call you next week to arrange a brief meeting.

Sincerely,

Brad Tolliver

❖

January 11, 1993

Leslie Acosta
Regional Sales Manager
Peoples Pharmaceuticals
5825 146th Avenue S.E.
Bellevue, Washington 98006

Dear Ms. Acosta:

I was attracted to Peoples Pharmaceuticals when I read your annual report. My medical background and my customer service experience make me an excellent candidate for a sales/marketing position in your organization.

While at Danton Instruments, I was a key person involved in the writing and organization of new product manuals. My oral presentations to the sales force were always valuable and well received. District sales managers and the sales representatives themselves consistently expressed appreciation for the sales aids and information given to them. In addition, a large part of my time was spent working closely with our customers, successfully troubleshooting problems, answering questions, and informing them of new products or instrument applications that might better serve their needs.

I will look forward to hearing from you soon.

Sincerely,

Sandra Gulliver

Next is an example where the applicant has spoken to the employer by phone and is thanking the person for having given him some time. There was no opening, so the cover letter is also acting as a thank-you note. Notice that the first paragraph was written strictly for this one letter. The other paragraphs are part of the standard cover letter.

February 2, 1993

Paulette Meyers
National Sales Manager
San Sebastian Winery
San Sebastian, California 95476

Dear Ms. Meyers:

I very much enjoyed our conversation yesterday. As I indicated, I have always been impressed with San Sebastian Winery. At the Blue Panda in Portland, I was instrumental in taking San Sebastian wines from our sixth most popular wine to number two. I totally agree with you that a top sales rep must be highly knowledgeable about wines. I frequently invite wine reps to give wine tastings at the restaurant, both for my own benefit and for the staff. I think you would be impressed with both my knowledge and my palate.

At the Blue Panda Restaurants I have always been a producer. I run what has become one of the most profitable restaurants in the chain, and our wine sales are ranked number one. At each of the four restaurants I've managed, wine sales experienced dramatic increases. I am committed to remaining in the Northwest and am confident I can substantially increase your wine sales in this region.

I will call you in a few weeks to learn about any developments.

Sincerely

Tom Reston

❖

Dear Mr. Ronagen

Your ad for a Western Region Dealer Representative was of great interest to me. I am very impressed with the Mitsubishi Company and the cars it produces. I would very much like to be a part of Mitsubishi, particularly in the area of dealer servicing. I can help Mitsubishi establish the reputation it wants for parts and service.

I know what is required to make service and parts departments run smoothly and profitably. I have always developed close working relations with dealership owners as well as parts and service managers.

In Oregon I worked closely with 16 VW dealerships. Most were poorly managed and barely making money. The service departments were all losing money. Within a year their appearances were tremendously improved, mechanics and service managers had received additional training, and quality control and inventory control systems had been established. Parts sales jumped 85%, and sales of new cars rose 45%.

I am committed to the automotive industry. My experience in Oregon is just one example of what I have been able to do with dealerships. Please feel free to contact me so I can tell you more about my background.

❖

Dear Mr. Swenson:

As a Project Manager and Construction Manager for Danson Construction, I have overseen both large and small projects. As an architect I can design projects or work with an architect to come up with the best and most cost effective design. I have hired contractors and have been very successful in making sure the projects were completed on time and were of high quality.

My degree in architecture, along with four years experience in designing, cost estimating, and managing construction projects, plus nearly one year of drafting, make me an ideal candidate for your Facilities Engineer position. I am a person of high energy, which has enabled me to watch the many details of a construction project and make sure everything was completed correctly. That same energy and hard work will prove most helpful as I oversee projects at your many facilities along the East Coast.

❖

Dear Ms. Glasser:

Since age eleven I have wanted to work as a flight attendant. I've been working in restaurants the last four years because I believed it would give me the best training possible for being a flight attendant.

I moved up into restaurant management so quickly because I proved I could handle the responsibility. I mix very well with customers and make each one feel important. This has increased the number of steady customers at each restaurant I have worked.

I am also a problem solver. At Leo's I helped reduce operating costs significantly. At J. K. Jake's I reduced turnover by working more closely with the staff. At both Wooden Lake and Ashki's I helped lay the groundwork so these restaurants could be successful from the day they opened.

I am very much looking forward to interviewing for a flight attendant position.

❖

Dear Ms. Preminger:

I have had a very exciting nine years in hotel sales, six of those years as Director of Sales. During that time I have developed highly effective techniques for attracting association and corporate business.

I would enjoy very much the opportunity to describe in more detail why those techniques have worked so well, and why I would function effectively as your next Sales Manager.

Marketing Letters

BEING DIFFERENT OFTEN BRINGS POSITIVE RESULTS. Marketing letters are successful for that reason—they're different. The marketing letter presents your strongest accomplishments, usually those with quantifiable results, to entice the reader. Dates and names of employers are seldom mentioned. The marketing letter acts as a substitute for a resume with cover letter. It can even be used when responding to want ads requesting resumes. In essence, the marketing letter is more like a lengthened cover letter than a resume. Compared to resumes, marketing letters are more personal in tone and more like business correspondence in appearance. Consequently, they are rarely screened out by secretaries.

Less than 5% of all job seekers use marketing letters, yet nothing I know of can lead to more appointments and job interviews. By sending only the marketing letter, your resume is held in reserve for later use. The key to success is addressing it to a specific person and informing that person that a phone call will follow. Your goal is to meet as many people with the power to hire as possible, regardless of whether any openings exist at the moment. This is accomplished by requesting just fifteen minutes of their time.

The use of marketing letters has revolutionized the way my clients find jobs. In the past I had clients cold call potential employers to ask for brief appointments. They understood the importance of the calls, knew they would work, and had practiced what they would say. However, some failed to make their calls, and those who did call, often procrastinated. Sending a marketing letter makes placing those calls easier now. Knowing that a person is expecting your call and is already convinced that you have something of quality to offer, makes a substantial difference psychologically. Using the marketing letter should get you in to see people with the power to hire, 40–80% of the time. Those needing to speak to presidents of companies should expect to make appointments 10–20% of the time. Notice the impact of the following marketing letter and you'll begin to see why these letters get results.

The following marketing letter is especially strong because each accomplishment has been quantified. Marketing letters always have more impact when results are quantified, and most people can easily come up with at least four solid accomplishments. You sense that an employer would want to meet such a person even if no position currently existed.

1121 65th S.W.
Red Rock, California 92006
(916) 456-9874

January 20, 1993

John Campbell
Executive Vice President
Diversified Products Inc.
440 5th N.W.
Redding, California 96001

Dear Mr. Campbell:

When I joined my current employer two years ago as Production Superintendent, our quality control department was rejecting 6% of all printed circuit boards. Today that figure is less than 1% and continuing downward.

You may be interested in a person who has broad experience in solving production problems. Here are some other things I've done:

Reduced absenteeism 42% and turnover 31%. With less turnover we were able to invest more in training, with a corresponding increase in quality and productivity. While rejections dropped from 6% to less than 1%, productivity increased 22% per employee.

Introduced an idea program with incentives. The number of suggestions that were implemented grew from 11 in 1989 to 65 in 1992. In 1992 bonuses cost $15,000 while documented savings amounted to $197,000.

Implemented an inventory control system. We increased production 34% with only a 6% increase in inventory. Production delays due to unavailable parts dropped from 72 in 1986 to 11 in 1988.

Instituted a company-wide safety program. Lost time due to accidents was reduced 21% during the first six months. Reductions in insurance premiums will save $85,000 in 1992.

I graduated from the University of Wisconsin in 1968 with a degree in Business. Since then I have experienced rapid promotions during 24 years in manufacturing.

I'll call you next week to arrange a time when we might meet for fifteen or twenty minutes.

Sincerely,

John Gaddly

The next two examples demonstrate the flexibility of marketing letters. While they use a more narrative format and are less quantifiable, they also have a strong impact on the reader.

11918 Northeast 143rd Place
Kirkland, Washington 98034
(206) 821-3830

March 18, 1993

Peter Phillips
Sahalee Development Corp.
2119 Fourth Avenue
Seattle, Washington 98124

Dear Mr. Phillips:

In anticipation of the next development upsurge, you may be looking for a person with a broad background in land development and marketing. I have saved projects from failure, reduced development costs, and increased project marketability.

Recently, at the developer's request, I was retained to save a mobile home project that had been rejected during preliminary hearings. By creating a new marketing strategy, employing a more imaginative design, and representing the client throughout the remainder of the public hearings process, I was able to negotiate the project's approval.

As part of a team of consultants for a 1900-acre/$680 million dollar new town development, I prevented costly delays by reducing agency review time and ensuring project approval with appropriate planning and design concepts. This saved the developer hundreds of thousands of dollars in additional consultant fees and penalty payments for an extension of the land-purchase option.

I have nine years' combined experience in civil engineering, land planning, and urban design. I graduated from the University of Washington with a B.A. in Urban Planning.

I will call you next week to arrange a time when we might meet briefly to discuss my background and your future needs.

Sincerely,

Roger Cricky

❖

1298 N. Rosewood Avenue
Portland, Oregon 97211
(503) 682-9874

April 6, 1993

Don Harris
Vice President, Sales and Marketing
MicroCad
4309 Sepulveda Blvd North
Los Angeles, California 90030

Dear Mr. Harris,

I am currently looking at sales management positions with medium-sized high tech manufacturers. During the last 15 years I have worked for Datacomp and Syngestics and am currently district sales manager for a major manufacturer of teleprocessing equipment.

I was given a mandate three years ago to strengthen the Pacific Northwest district. During that time we have increased sales an average of 35% annually, the highest rate in the region. I'm known as a motivator. I work closely with my staff to develop marketing strategies and I give them the independence they need to be effective.

I've been successful in both sales and sales management. As a senior account manager for six years with Datacomp, I took my territory from a ranking of 19th nationally to 5th and exceeded quota each year. I got my start in the industry with Syngestics. As a field marketing support rep for two years, my district exceeded its sales quota each year. Then as area supervisor for three years, I supervised six field marketing support engineers. The staff was rated number one in the region for providing technical support, two years in a row.

With a history of success behind me, I believe I can contribute to the further growth of MicroCad. I am strong in marketing, sales training, staff recruiting, and staff development. I will call you next week to learn about your future plans.

Sincerely,

Paul Sanderson

Writing an effective marketing letter requires that you first have a results-oriented resume. Once the resume is complete, the marketing letter almost writes itself. In fact, the results statements used in the marketing letter can come almost word for word from the resume.

The primary portion of any marketing letter is a description of your results and experience. To write a strong marketing letter, review your resume and think through how you want to summarize your background. If you have four to six key projects or results that can be quantified, simply describe them, as was done in the first sample marketing letter. If your background does not lend itself to that approach, the more narrative form will work best for you. Although names of companies are usually not mentioned, you can mention them if you so choose. Sometimes people will mention only well known companies. Even dates or time periods can be mentioned, but are not usually necessary.

Remember, the marketing letter is not a resume. The reader is not expecting to know everything about you. Your goal is to have impact. Your letter should cause the person to recognize your value and to remember you when you call. Write like you would in a letter. Let it flow. Take a look at your qualifications statement in your resume. Perhaps it can be included almost as is. If you are going to emphasize results, they can be lifted almost word for word from your resume, although you'll probably want to make some minor changes. Since your resume was written in telegraphic style, with incomplete sentences and certain words removed, you'll need to adapt the resume to the marketing letter. All sentences should be complete sentences.

Lead-ins for your results could be worded:

You may be interested in my labor negotiating experience. Some of my additional accomplishments are:

❖

My six years in customer relations could be valuable to you. This experience includes:

❖

If your advertising department needs a person with strong experience, you may be interested in what I've done.

If you choose to describe past jobs, as in the third marketing letter example, phrases can again be lifted from the resume. Since this is a marketing letter, you may choose to describe only the last three jobs, even if in the resume five were described. Don't be concerned if your resume and marketing letter have similar phrases in them; no one will notice.

A good closing paragraph for your marketing letter might include a summary of your background, such as the number of years in your field, and information about your degree and alma mater. The final paragraph then prepares the reader for any follow-up contact you might make. In most cases this will be a follow-up phone call.

If the person is local you would usually request a 10–15 minute meeting and indicate so in the letter. If the person is out of state, but is likely to be in your area in the next two or three months, you would request an appointment when the person is in the area. If the person is out of state and would unlikely visit your area, you'll have to sell yourself by phone.

Each marketing letter should be individually typed and addressed to the person with the power to hire. By supplying a word processing service with ten or more names at a time, you should be able to keep your costs down to about two dollars for each letter and envelope. There will be an initial inputting charge for the letter, but after that you'll be paying primarily for printing time, plus the inputting time for the additional names and addresses.

OTHER USES OF THE MARKETING LETTER

The marketing letter is a very flexible tool. It can even function as a substitute for a resume when responding to a help wanted ad. Sometimes, no matter how well written your resume is, it may not work well in response to a particular job listing. Perhaps the job would make an excellent use of your talents, but requires experience you don't have. Traditionally one would write a customized cover letter and possibly even modify the resume. Using the marketing letter approach the entire letter would be geared to the specific job. Of course you would probably keep in major sections of your standard marketing letter, but it would be customized throughout.

Perhaps your most applicable experience occurred five years ago. With the marketing letter you could mention it first and indicate how many years you did that work. The exact dates would not be mentioned.

Although I recommend that you send marketing letters to specific people, with the intention of following up by phone, they can also be used in mass mailings. Even if you do not intend to follow up with a phone call, I still recommend that you invest the time to identify the person with the power to hire. However, if you choose not to do so, address the letter to a specific title, such as Personnel Director, Chief Engineer, or Accounting Manager. Because it is a letter, and does not have the appearance of a traditional resume, it is more likely to be delivered to the most appropriate person. With this approach it is easy and fast to send out the same mailing two months later if you have not accepted another position by that time. Your success rate will be lower with this method than if you followed up by phone—quick and easy is its main selling point. Please, however, do not use this method just as an excuse to avoid the more productive and effective follow-up methods discussed.

Part Two
Finding The Job
That's Right For You

The Systematic Job Search

MANY PEOPLE ARE STARTLED to discover that only three of every ten job openings are ever advertised or listed with employment agencies. The other seven jobs have become known as "the hidden job market." This fact of life necessitates a job-finding strategy far different from those used by the average job seeker. The typical job-finding strategy consists of mailing out dozens of resumes, visiting a handful of employment agencies, and religiously reading the want ads. While 30% of all people do find jobs this way, there are many for whom this strategy simply does not work.

Finding a job that provides growth and satisfaction requires the right strategy. It takes considerable thought, time, and energy, but the payoff is tremendous.

In order to find such a job, you're going to tap into the hidden job market with the Systematic Job Search strategy. These are the requirements:

Focus - Know exactly what type of work you want and the type of organization you want to work for. Identify your strengths so you'll know you can do an outstanding job.

Resume - Develop a resume that really sells you, one that accurately describes your accomplishments and potential.

Employer Research - Develop a list of 50–200 prime organizations that match your requirements for industry, location, size, growth, and any other key factors. When an interview is arranged, learn more about the organization and go prepared.

Contacts - Send your resume to friends, relatives, and business contacts. Then talk to them about the type of position you're seeking. Your network of contacts will keep their eyes and ears open for you; when positions open up in their organizations (or in their friends' organizations), they can supply you with the names of people to contact.

Calls - In the first week, call each of your top 20 organizations and ask for the name of the person with the power to hire you. He or she will usually have a position one or two levels above the position you would fill. Send a marketing letter to that person. A marketing letter is a letter that outlines your background and acts as a substitute for your resume. (See page 178 for a complete description of the functions and purposes of a marketing letter.) State in your marketing letter that you will call to set up a brief meeting. Call those you've sent letters to and ask for a brief appointment, even if there are no openings.

Appointments - Your calls should result in appointments 40–80% of the time. Before each appointment, research the organization. During the 15-minute appointment you will learn more about the organization and what they look for in their employees. Ask intelligent questions and explain how your background could be helpful to them. Create a favorable impression of yourself so if an opening occurs, you will be given top priority.

Follow-Up - After each appointment send a thank-you note and express your interest in the organization. This causes the person to think favorably of you once again. Three weeks later, call to see if any openings have developed. If not, make a brief call every five weeks. This type of contact has at least 40 times the impact of sending a resume alone.

Interviews - All of your hard work—whether responding to want ads or getting appointments with the people with power to hire you—will result in formal interviews. Because you are ready for virtually any question, you'll shine in the interviews and get more than your share of job offers.

Finding jobs in the hidden job market will require hard work and endurance, but it can be enjoyable and rewarding. There may be frustrations and down times. But remember: your efforts will pay off. Those efforts will directly determine the success of your job search.

FOCUS

First you need focus. Focus means you have narrowed your choices to one or two main fields. Within those fields there may be several job titles to consider, but they will all be interrelated. Occasionally someone can handle as many as three or four fields, but that requires a lot more effort than most can devote, and often dilutes energy. The person looking at four different fields may spread himself too thin and not do justice to the job search in any of them.

People looking for the same type of job with a different company or a promotion to the next level in their field, already have this basic kind of focus. The person making a career change or the person who has merely held jobs but never a career, often lacks this type of focus. Their tendency is to depend on the want ads as their only source of job leads. An attitude of, " I don't know what I'm looking for, but when I see it in an ad, I'll recognize it" will rarely lead to a high quality job. Professional career counseling can help such people develop focus.

Some people are fortunate enough to discover at a fairly young age what type of work they like to do. Others fall into a job somewhat by accident and find that they enjoy it and do it well. Some find it very difficult to select an occupation they really like and bounce from job to job. Still others have been in one field for several years but realize they need a change—the challenge may be gone, their specialty may have become obsolete, or perhaps their values have changed. The last two types of people have the most difficult time achieving focus in their job search.

If you are a person who has had jobs but never a career, or if you've had a career which now must be altered, you are the best candidate for professional assistance. I suggest you read *The Three Boxes of Life* by Richard Bolles to start. *The Three Boxes of Life* will take you through the steps of making sound career decisions. After reading it you may want to consider taking a career exploration class at a community college or work through your exploration with a private career counselor.

Talk

Once you've narrowed your choices down to a few occupations and done your reading, begin talking to people who already work in your chosen field. Learn the positives and negatives about the field, get advice, find out which are the best companies to work for, and get referrals.

People are generally easy to talk to and they like to be helpful. If you wanted to be a buyer for a clothing store you could begin by calling a store and asking for the name of a buyer, or you might simply ask for the buying department. Explain that you are seriously considering buying as a profession, have done some reading about it, and need to talk to several buyers before you can make a final decision. Then ask for twenty minutes of their time. If you are pleasant on the phone, I guarantee that ninety percent of the people you call will give you some time. Of course some will be more helpful than others.

Normally you will want to meet these people at their place of business to get a feel for the environment. At times, however, a conversation over the telephone will provide everything you need. You'll mainly ask questions and listen to their answers. Your questions should revolve around issues left unanswered by your reading. Ask what they like or dislike about their occupation, how they got into it, and what their background is. Ask for suggestions regarding job finding strategies for that field. Ask about salary ranges. (Be tactful about salaries, though—people will not want to reveal how much they make. A good approach is, "With my education and experience, how much do you think I should expect to be offered? I know it's hard to say exactly, so maybe you could just give me a range.") Ask which are the best companies to work for. Finally, ask if they can give you the names of people to talk to.

EMPLOYER RESEARCH

Employer research is one of the most important yet most neglected aspects of a job search. Researching employers consists of two stages: 1) using directories and other resources to develop a high-priority list of 50–200 employers; 2) gathering specific information about each organization before an interview, and conducting in-depth studies of organizations that offer you a job.

Stage One: Developing Your High-Priority List of Employers

Begin with a stack of one hundred 4 x 6 cards and find a directory that will lead you to the types of organizations you're interested in. Examples of these directories include the *American Banking Directory* and the *Thomas Grocery Register*. As you come across appropriate organizations, write down whatever information the directory provides. They typically provide the name of the organization, its address and phone number, the number of employees, its products or services, and its sales volume. All of that information should go on the front side of the card, leaving space on the back to write information that you obtain from people or from newspaper articles. The card system is also useful because it makes prioritizing easier.

Most directories will contain key information such as an organization's industry, products, size, and location. At this point, that's all the information you need. You'll use this information to identify the organizations that would be most likely to hire you to do what you want to do.

In metropolitan Seattle there are 30,000 employers. Since it's difficult to work effectively with an employer list over 300, a system must be devised to enable a job seeker in the Seattle area to screen out all but 100 to 250 employers. By selecting 1-10 industries, limiting the search to a 30-mile radius, and by limiting the selection to organizations of 10-250 employees, a list of about 200 employers will result.

Begin this process by deciding which industries and products you'd like to be involved with. The Standard Industrial Classification (SIC) coding system was created to help you do that. Because every business functions in one or more industries, each is assigned one or more industry codes. This coding system will help you find your prospects quickly. In those directories which segregate organizations by SIC, you will find a list of the industries with their codes. If you really want to dig into the different industries, use the *Standard Industrial Classification Manual* found in most libraries.

Next, decide what size of organization you want to work for. Since the greatest amount of new job creation in the last ten years has been in organizations of under 50 employees, do not overlook smaller organizations. The work some people do is available only in organizations of over 100 employees. These people would target companies with 100 or more employees.

Next, decide the maximum distance you are willing to commute. If the maximum commute you'd accept would be 35 minutes each way, you would use that as a guide to select organizations. For a truly outstanding company you might be willing to accept a longer commute, but there would be relatively few exceptions.

Once you've made your decisions, you will be ready to utilize the many directories available in your library.

Resources

The Yellow Pages. One of the most useful directories is available in your own home—the Yellow Pages. Most organizations in your area will be listed somewhere in the Yellow Pages even if they don't advertise. The "space ads" in the Yellow Pages can be particularly useful. Those ads can give you an excellent idea of what the businesses in a particular industry do. Using the Yellow Pages will give you companies to consider that you might have easily overlooked if you relied solely on other resources.

To use the Yellow Pages, go through the listings from A to Z. Scan each page and look at each of the specific categories. Rather than assuming that you don't want to work in a particular category, start with the opposite assumption. Give each category or industry serious consideration unless you can come up with a good reason why you should not. This technique opens you to possibilities that you might otherwise have been closed to.

Librarians. Make use of the business or reference librarian at your library. Tell the librarian precisely what types of organizations you are trying to locate, and mention which directories you intend to use. Then ask the librarian if there are other directories you should use. The library will probably have several local directories that could provide exactly what you need. Don't hesitate to ask for help—that's what librarians love to do.

Industry-Specific Directories. Some industries have their own, specialized directories. To locate these directories, use the *Guide to American Directories* or *Directories In Print*. A good example of a specialized directory is the *World*

Aviation Directory. It provides names, addresses, and phone numbers for every airline, airport, airplane or parts manufacturer, aviation insurance company, and dealer in the United States. For some people, a specialized directory is the only resource they need.

Associations. Determine whether there is an association that represents your field or industry. The *Encyclopedia of Associations* and the *National Trade and Professional Associations* can provide this information. You'll also find local associations listed in the Yellow Pages under "Associations." Associations are usually formed to give an industry or profession more political clout, as well as to provide a forum for new ideas. They generally publish membership lists and news magazines, hold conventions and meetings, list job openings, and distribute free literature.

The Sunday Paper. Another way to build up your employer list is to review the back issues of the Sunday newspaper in your area that has the most want ads. Read through the want ads quickly to see if certain organizations seem to be hiring. Add them to your list even if you don't know much about them.

Stage Two: Researching Your Top 20 Employers

Once you have compiled and prioritized your list of 50–200 employers, it's time to do some preliminary research on each of your top-20 organizations. To research companies, your first step is to visit the nearest major library. Many libraries will have such resources as clipping files, house organs, and annual reports. These resources will be described in detail on page 194.

As valuable as written resources are, information gathered from people is often the most helpful. Talk with people who work for or have worked for your target company, people with competitors or suppliers, and people who work for a customer of the target company. All of these people can add to your insights and information about a company.

REASONS FOR RESEARCHING AN ORGANIZATION

There are four main reasons for researching employers.

1. **To determine whether the organization is right for you.** Try to discover all the pros and cons you can. Research may reveal a serious problem that might cause you to eliminate the organization, or it may reveal some outstanding opportunities that will further encourage and motivate you.

2. **To impress the interviewer.** Because so few people bother to research a company, you'll stand out in a very positive way if you've done your homework and go armed with information. Weave your information into the conversation appropriately. Some employers will ask, "What do you know about us?" Most people will hem, haw, and fail this question miserably. But you will shine. Even when asked this question, however, don't overwhelm the interviewer with your answer. Give a thorough but concise response.

3. **To discover problems you can help solve.** Problems you have the ability to solve could come to light before or during an interview. If you discover them before the interview, you'll have time to prepare and perhaps even develop a proposal. Otherwise, listen for clues to such problems during the interview. An employer may come right out and describe problems, but will probably only allude to them. Careful listening can help you match your abilities or experience

to the problem area. By all means emphasize those strengths that can help solve the organization's problems.

4. **To identify questions that must be clarified by the employer.** An annual report or a magazine article may have mentioned an exciting new product being developed by your target company. If the interviewer doesn't mention it, you may have to ask if you would have a role in developing, marketing, or selling it. If an inside source told you that a strike could cripple the company, you might ask about the effects of such a strike. If the company has lost money three years in a row, you might ask what the company is doing to reverse the losses.

Interviewing is a continuation of your research. Keep your detective cap on and discover all you can. Ask yourself if you would enjoy working for this person. Will you respect this boss? Do your management philosophies match? Will you like each other? These are some of the important questions that can be answered, in part, by the research you conduct during interviews.

Do some research before each interview, even if it's the third or fourth interview with the same company. This is particularly important if you feel really good about the job, your potential boss, and the company. Discover all you can. Answering questions effectively and asking the right questions could make the difference between being the number-one choice and the number-two choice.

RESOURCES FOR EMPLOYER RESEARCH

Employer research takes place in two stages: 1) Obtaining a list of 50–200 employers, and 2) gathering information about employers prior to the first interview, as well as more in-depth research after a job offer is made. A survey of professional recruiters indicated that knowledge of the company was one of the three most significant factors in successful interviews. "What do you know about us?" is a favorite question of many employers.

STAGE ONE—EMPLOYER LIST

In stage one, you'll be using various resources to develop your list of 50–200 employers. As with any resource that lists key company officials, always call to confirm that that person is still there and holding the position listed in the resource.

Local Resources

People with no desire to leave their current geographical area will get better results with local, rather than national resources. It would be impossible, of course, to list all local resources, but I can help you find them. The best place to start is in the business reference section of your library. In this section you'll find *Yellow Pages* and many other directories.

After you've scouted out the reference area, talk to the reference librarian and ask about resources. You'll find reference librarians very helpful. Some libraries will have a list of useful resources and directories.

If you are looking for government, nonprofit, or social service agencies, ask the reference librarian for help. United Way generally publishes a booklet describing the agencies it funds. For state, city, or county governments there may be a telephone directory with names of departments, key staff people, and their phone numbers.

Virtually every chamber of commerce publishes information on local companies. Most of their directories cost between ten and twenty dollars but they should also be available at your library. As an example, the Seattle Chamber of Commerce produces a resource which lists the 800 local companies with over 100 employees. For those wanting to or needing to work for larger organizations, that can be the perfect resource.

State Directories

Every state publishes a list of manufacturers operating in that state. The alphabetical section gives names, telephone numbers, addresses (including divisions and subsidiaries), key executives, SIC codes, products manufactured or services provided, number of employees, locations of branch offices and/or plants, whether they are importers and/or exporters, annual gross sales, and year established. State directories also have SIC and geographical sections. Ask your reference librarian to help you find your state's directory.

National Resources

Some of the national resources listed below cost over one hundred dollars per year and are found only in libraries with a major business section. Go to your nearest library first to find out what local and national directories they have. Eventually you may need to visit a larger library.

National resources are useful primarily for those who want to work for companies over 500 employees and are willing to relocate to do so. If you want to remain in your metropolitan area, or at least in your state, there will virtually always be local directories which will be more helpful than the national directories.

Dun and Bradstreet—Million Dollar Directory. This publication lists 160,000 companies with a net worth of $1,000,000 or more. The alphabetical section includes company names, names of parent companies, addresses, telephone numbers, SIC numbers, sales figures, number of employees, principal officers, and whether companies are involved in importing and exporting. Dun and Bradstreet also has geographical and SIC sections.

Dun and Bradstreet—Middle Market Directory. Same as above except it covers companies with a net worth between $500,000 and $1,000,000.

Standard and Poor's. This directory includes 37,000 corporations, with names, addresses, telephone numbers, products made, number of employees, and sales volume. Volume 1 has an alphabetical listing, volume 2 has biographical information on 75,000 key officers listed alphabetically by last name, and volume 3 lists corporations by SIC and geographic area.

Dun's Directory of Service Companies. It lists 50,000 organizations in the following categories: management consulting, executive search, public relations, engineering and architectural services, business services, consumer services, research services, repair services, hospitality, motion pictures, amusement and recreation. All have more than 50 employees.

Mac Rae's Blue Book. Mac Rae's lists 50,000 firms and is primarily used by purchasing agents. It provides addresses, primary products or services, telephone sales offices and distributors, and cities and phone numbers for sales reps or outlets. Volume 1 has an alphabetical listing plus about 100,000 brand names listed alphabetically with name of company. Volumes 2 through 4 are arranged by product with manufacturers of that product listed below each heading. Volume 5 contains the catalogs of over one hundred companies.

Thomas Register. This directory is like *Mac Rae's*—it was designed primarily to assist purchasing agents locate companies that offer certain products or services. Volumes 1 through 6 list over 50,000 products and the companies that produce them. Volume 7 indexes these products by the pages they can be found on; it also lists 72,000 brand names and the companies that own them. Volume 8 is an alphabetical list of United States manufacturers. It provides names, addresses, telephone numbers, dollar values of tangible assets, subsidiaries, and affiliated companies. Volumes 9 through 14 contain the catalogs of over 800 companies.

Industry Directories

Thousands of directories exist which are helpful to job seekers. As an example, the *Whole World Oil Directory* lists all oil and gas companies, drilling companies, oil well services, and refineries. It may be the only resource some people would need.

Several resources are available to help you locate useful directories. Most libraries will have either the *Guide to American Directories* or *Directories in Print*. Both list and describe over 5,000 directories that are divided into over 300 categories. They are quick and easy to use. They have an alphabetical section and a subject section. They will also tell you what the directories cost and where to order them. Most directories cost $15–30 but some cost in the hundreds. After you identify a useful directory, check the card catalog to see if the library has it. Even if your library does not have it, an interlibrary search with the help of your reference librarian, may help you find a library which does.

A sampling has been included to give you a feel for what's available: *National Trade & Professional Associations of the U. S.; Directory of Management Consultants; American Apparel Manufacturers Association Directory; American Bank Directory; Official Directory of Data Processing; Environmental Organizations Directory; American Electronics Association Directory; Directory of Frozen Food Processors; Directory of United States Importers; National Machine Tool Builders Association Directory.*

STAGE TWO—OBTAINING INFORMATION ABOUT THE ORGANIZATION

Once you've landed an appointment or an interview, it's time to shift into high gear and get prepared. Since knowledge of the organization is critical for interviews, researching an organization can enable you to go in armed with knowledge. This knowledge will give you added confidence in your appointments and interviews. Avoid overwhelming the interviewer with your knowledge about products or financial figures, though. Instead, keep your information in reserve and use it only when appropriate.

The following resources will provide valuable information.

Moody's. *Moody's Industrial Manual*—Provides financial information, history, subsidiaries, products and services, sales, principal plants and properties, executives, number of employees. One to two pages are devoted to most companies. All of the *Moody's* manuals concentrate on large companies.

Moody's OTC (Over the Counter)—Same format as above but covering smaller companies.

Moody's Municipal and Government Manual
Moody's Bank and Finance Manual
Moody's Public Utilities Manual
Moody's Transportation Manual

Clipping Files. Many libraries maintain files of news articles and feature articles about local businesses clipped from local papers. While most articles are short news releases, you will also find highly informative feature articles about new developments within target companies.

House Organs. Companies publish house organs (in-house newsletters) as internal public relations vehicles and will have such things as a letter from the president describing past achievements and future goals, pictures of the bowling team and those retiring, and usually a feature article about a person, department, or a new product. House organs are especially helpful. Check with your library to see if a file of house organs is maintained.

Annual Reports. If the company is publicly owned (stock which is publicly traded), it is required by law to publish an annual financial report. Understanding the financial jargon is unnecessary. The past year's failures and achievements will be summarized along with descriptions of new products and future goals.

Recruiting Brochures. Major companies which recruit at college campuses produce recruiting brochures. The brochures describe the history and background of the company, training programs, company benefits, and desired training and characteristics of employees. College placement offices will have many on file.

Indexes. In addition to clipping files, you will want to use one or more indexes to locate articles in magazines or newspapers. First look up the company by name. If you don't find the listings you want, you could read articles about the industry that your target company falls in and possibly find a reference to your target company in that way. The indexes can also be used to research a topic, a product, a new technology, or an entire industry.

Encyclopedia of Business Information Sources. Lists trade associations, periodicals, directories, bibliographies, and an abstract index of recent articles. An outstanding resource.

Readers Guide to Periodical Literature. Lists articles found in over two hundred popular magazines, giving the periodical, date, and title of article. This is the same green-covered resource you used in high school when you did research reports.

Business Periodicals Index. The *BPI* uses business periodicals which are generally not covered in the *Readers Guide to Periodical Literature*. Examples: *Human Resource Management* and *Automotive News*.

The Magazine Index. An automated system found in many libraries which indexes articles in about 400 general interest magazines. It is published by Information Access Company which, in a similar format, also publishes: *National Newspaper Index*, *Business Index*, and *Legal Resource Index*.

Infotrac. A computerized data base found in many libraries, it indexes 1,100 magazines, going back ten years. With the help of a librarian it takes under five minutes to learn how to use. With it you can research industries, products, new technology, and companies. The business index provides information about the companies themselves, including address, products, number of employees, etc., and articles written about them. With most articles you can also read an abstract, which is a short version of the article. Both the abstracts plus the information about the article such as the name of the periodical, date, and page number, can be printed out so you don't have to write them all down.

ABI Inform. Same concept as *Infotrac,* it abstracts 700 business journals.

F & S Index of Corporations and Industries. Lists articles on industries and companies, including mergers, acquisitions, new products, and emerging technology. Lists trade journals, addresses and their costs.

F & S Index Europe. Same format

F & S Index International. Same format. Covers Canada, Latin America, Africa, and Asia

Wall Street Journal Index. The first section is alphabetical by company; the second section is alphabetical by subject and peoples' names.

New York Times Index. Same format

Chicago Tribune Index. Same format

Los Angeles Times Index. Same format

Washington Post Index. Same format

Libraries which carry these indexes will probably also have the newspapers on microfilm.

CONTACTS

Friends, relatives, acquaintances, and business contacts can all provide useful leads if you approach them in the right way. Before they can help, people must know what you're looking for and what your qualifications are. About 26% of all jobseekers find positions through such leads. This number could be increased substantially if people made better use of this method. Include your banker, barber, broker, and butcher. Every person who has an interest in your success can be helpful.

Begin by sending your resume and a list of your top 60–80 prospects to everyone you know. Enclose a note stating that you will call in a few days. Ask your contacts to review the list carefully and to indicate if they know anyone who works for any of the organizations. Underline the word anyone. You truly want to talk to anyone whether it is a janitor, secretary, or purchasing agent. By talking to that person you can learn if it is a good organization to work for, what it's problems or strengths are, and even get inside information about the person who has power to hire you. Tell your contact what your strengths are and ask the person to call you if he or she hears of any openings. Tell the person that all you need is someone to contact and that you will take care of the rest. You are not asking for any great favors. You would certainly do the same for them.

Speaking to contacts is one of the most valuable things a person can do in a job search, yet few job hunters are willing to expend even the small amount of energy this strategy requires.

CALLS

In this phase of the process, it is crucial to meet the person who has the power to hire you. Determining who that person is and getting an appointment requires a well-planned strategy.

Determining Who Has the Power to Hire

The person with the power to hire you normally holds a position that would be one or two levels above you in the department or functional area you have focused on. Often this person will be a department head. When calling, ask for the name of the person whose job title indicates that he or she has the power to hire you.

Once you have your list of organizations, begin identifying the people who do the hiring. Getting their names is easy because nearly every business has a receptionist. Call and ask for the person's name, being sure to get the correct spelling and title. Most receptionists are so busy that they won't bother to ask you why you want to know.

Occasionally, the receptionist will not know the proper person, or will hastily connect you with personnel. Don't be startled, just ask your question again with confidence and assertiveness. If the receptionist or personnel clerk asks why you are calling, the most simple response is, "I have some material to send to your purchasing manager." Typical responses might be like these:

Receptionist:	Dearborn Insurance, may I help you?
Steve:	Hello, can you give me the name of your claims manager?
Receptionist:	Yes, that would be John Yaeger.
Steve:	Would you spell his last name, please?
Receptionist:	Sure, Y A E G E R.
Steve:	Thank you very much.

❖

Receptionist:	Medico, may I help you?
Sally:	Hello, can you give me the name of your EDP manager?
Receptionist:	EDP?
Sally:	Yes, Electronic Data Processing. Do you have someone in charge of computer programming?
Receptionist:	I think you probably want Bob Benson.
Sally:	What is his title?
Receptionist:	He's vice president of operations, but I think he's in charge of our three programmers.
Sally:	Okay, thank you very much.

❖

Receptionist:	Continental.
Kevin:	Can you give me the name of your purchasing manager?
Receptionist:	Just a moment.
Personnel:	Personnel.
Kevin:	Can you give me the name of your purchasing manager?
Personnel:	That would be James Townsend.
Kevin:	Thank you.

❖

Receptionist:	Malco, may I help you?
Holly:	Could you please give me the name of your advertising manager?

Receptionist:	Just a moment.
Personnel:	Personnel.
Holly:	Could you please give me the name of your advertising manager?
Personnel:	What is this concerning?
Holly:	I have some material to send and I want to make sure it gets to the right person. Could you give me the name of your advertising manager?
Personnel:	That would be Janet Lynn.
Holly:	What is her title?
Personnel:	She's director of marketing.
Holly:	Thank you.

Whether you list 70 or 250 organizations, I would recommend going through the entire list in two or three days to get the names of all the hiring authorities. You can then check off that activity as being completed. You'll also need the names of hiring authorities when you send the list of your 70 preferred organizations to friends and relatives.

Calling the Person With the Power To Hire

Once you know the names of the people with the power to hire in your organizations, start setting up appointments. This part is more challenging than just getting the names. Your first task will be getting past the person's secretary. One of the secretary's duties is to protect the boss from unnecessary calls, and some exercise this duty with a vengeance. Don't be afraid, though; you can get past even the toughest secretary. Once you get to your potential boss, you must present yourself quickly and ask for an appointment. With a polished opening, you should be able to get appointments 40–80% of the time.

Getting Past Secretaries

When talking to a secretary, present yourself as a confident businessperson with legitimate business reasons for calling. Give your name immediately since the secretary will invariably ask for it. You'll also sound more authoritative. If, after trying all the styles given below, you just can't get past the secretary, try calling very early in the morning or after 5:30 p.m. A busy executive will often answer the phone when the secretary is not there. One of the techniques below will usually work:

Receptionist:	Glasgow and Associates.
Polly:	I'd like to speak to Marilyn Shelton.
Receptionist:	Just a moment, please.
Secretary:	Marilyn Shelton's office.
Polly:	This is Polly Preston. I'd like to speak with Marilyn Shelton.
Secretary:	What is this concerning?
Polly:	Don Drummer of Polycorp suggested I speak with her.
	or
	I have some advertising concepts I would like to discuss with her.
	or
	I have some personal matters to discuss with her.
	or
	I have some business matters to discuss with her.
Secretary:	Just a moment, I'll ring her office.

Avoid Return Calls

If the person is out when you call (or so the secretary says), avoid leaving your phone number. Say that you will be in and out yourself and ask for the best time to call back. It is much better for you to initiate contact. If the employer returns your call, you may be caught unprepared. If you have been calling several people, you may not even recognize the person's name at first. This can be very embarrassing. Furthermore, by leaving your name and number you lose control of the situation. Once you leave your name and number, you are basically obligated to give the person two or three days to return your call. If the person never calls, you've lost three days. When you finally do get through, more days will have passed since the person read your marketing letter. The dialogue below illustrates how to handle this situation.

Secretary:	Janet Spurrier's office.
John:	This is John Bradley. I'd like to speak with Janet Spurrier.
Secretary:	I'm sorry, she's in a meeting now. Can I have her return your call?
John:	No, I'll be out most of the day. What do you think would be a good time to reach her?
Secretary:	That's hard to say, but probably about 3:30.
John:	Thank you.

What Do You Say After Hello?

After your future boss answers, you have 20–30 seconds to sell yourself. A prepared script can give you added confidence and just the right words to make a great first impression. Since it is so easy to say "no," make it easy for the employer to say "yes" when you ask for a brief appointment.

To sell yourself, you must quickly summarize your background and present evidence that you are a highly desirable person. Upon concluding your pitch, ask for an appointment. Ask to "get together" or have a "brief meeting," but never call it an interview. You are *not* seeking a traditional job interview.

Practice by first making a few of these calls to low-priority firms. Your voice should convey self-confidence and enthusiasm. Your words should convey potential. Naturally, if you are reading from a script, you won't want the employer to sense this. Practice until you speak in a normal conversational tone. After a few calls you should keep the script by you for reference, but you should begin varying your words slightly each time to provide a sense of spontaneity. You might even record your first few calls to check your enthusiasm level. Record your portion of the call on a portable recorder. Be sure to project enough enthusiasm so that it is conveyed to the person at the other end of the line.

In the first sample script below, a recent college grad is making a cold call. It takes only about ten seconds to complete the call. Notice that the introduction is brief but sufficient for the purpose.

Mr. Crenshaw, this is Brian Dawlar. I just graduated from the University of Washington with a degree in business, emphasizing marketing. I realize you may not have any openings at this time, but I would appreciate setting up a time when we could meet for 10 or 15 minutes.

In the next example, Sandra is reminding Mrs. Garner that a marketing letter was sent. Sandra is hoping Mrs. Garner remembers, but even if she does not, Sandra will still provide only a brief summary of her background and then ask for an appointment. If the person has not received the letter, there is no need to tell the person that you will send another copy of the letter—once you have the person on the line, go for the appointment.

The example below demonstrates how a marketing letter works. It is followed by the script from Sandra's phone call.

7/22/92

Roberta Garner
District Sales Manager
Salvo Corp.
1878 116th N.E.
Bellevue, Washington 98004

Dear Ms. Garner:

I have a strong sales personality. During six years as an educator teaching French and history, I have sold programs and ideas to school administrators, teachers, parents, and community leaders. Selling comes naturally to me. Because of this ability, and a desire to achieve a high income, I am now looking at sales opportunities.

I am a high-energy person with real initiative. I make things happen. I am quick to take on responsibility and I succeed at whatever I put my heart into. The people I know in sales all say I will be successful. I believe them.

I will call you next week to set up a time when we might meet briefly.

Sincerely,

Sandra Bennett

Having read the marketing letter you can see why Sandra is confident as she calls Garner and seeks a brief appointment.

Mrs. Garner? Hi, this is Sandra Bennett. I wanted to confirm that you received the letter I sent a few days ago describing my teaching background in French and history...Good...I've been teaching for the last six years, but all my sales friends tell me I'd be a natural in sales. I realize you may not have any openings at this time, but I would appreciate arranging, oh, a 10- or 15-minute get-together. I'd like to tell you a little more about me and at the same time learn about some of the directions Salvo is headed. Would early next week work for you?

Read Sandra's spiel again and notice what she did. As she introduced herself she mentioned her letter which had described her background in teaching French and history. We all know that teaching French and history are not prerequisites for a career in sales. Nevertheless, she mentioned her teaching because it would act as a "cue" for Garner. Providing a cue is an important part of making the marketing letter and the phone call result in an appointment.

Your marketing letters that are sent to local people should go out on a Friday. You can be quite certain that a letter you mail on a Friday will arrive on Monday. To allow for a delay in the postal system, or in case the person was out of the office on Monday, you should begin calling people Tuesday afternoon. If you send out 10–20 marketing letters each week, that means Tuesday and Wednesday will be your heavy telephone days. By waiting until Tuesday to call, you can be quite sure that the person will have received it, but not so much time will have elapsed that the person is likely to have forgotten it. If you send your marketing letter any other day of the week, you will not be so certain about its arrival time. Also, by beginning your calls on Tuesday, you have the rest of the week to call the people that you were not able to reach on Tuesday and Wednesday. Even those you reach on Friday should not have forgotten you.

There are some cases in which a marketing letter may not be necessary. In the example below, Jim Thomas decided not to use a marketing letter. He has a strong background in sales and is accustomed to setting up sales appointments over the phone. By dispensing with the marketing letter he saves time and money, and he'll end up with just as high a success rate as he would if he sent a marketing letter. Anyone who feels confident in their phone skills should give consideration to skipping the marketing letter and simply making direct contact with the hiring authority.

> Hi Mr. Bradley, this is Jim Thomas. I've been selling radio advertising for the last six years and I'm seriously considering changing stations. I've been in the top 15% in sales for the last three years. I'm not in a rush to leave, but I would like to set a time when we could get together for 15 minutes or so.

Each of the scripts presented here as examples can be said in 10-20 seconds. When you've just reached a stranger on the phone, and the most the person has said is "Hello" or "This is Crenshaw," twenty seconds is quite a long time.

Below is an example of a more complete script where the applicant is going to ask for a 15-minute appointment. The employer will respond by saying he doesn't have any openings. That will be the most common response, even though you will have just said something like, "I realize you may have no openings at this time, but I would like to meet briefly with you for perhaps 15 minutes." Either employers don't hear that statement, or they choose to ignore it. Those who ignore it do so, I believe, because they know that by stating that there are no openings, 90% of all job seekers will lose interest in coming in. By asking for a meeting you'll demonstrate that you're not like all the rest.

The key to the success of this technique is that you are making such a reasonable request. Initially, you ask for 15 minutes. If that does not succeed, you make a second request, but drop the time down to ten minutes. When asking a third time you would ask either for just five minutes or for two minutes just to introduce yourself. Notice how skillfully this is done in the following example.

Jay: This is John Jay.

Sur: Mr. Jay, this is Bob Sur. I was calling to confirm that you received my letter which describes my 15 years in purchasing, including purchasing all the steel, glass, and concrete for the Columbia Center in Seattle.

Give the listener a cue so he can recall you from among the 10–30 letters received in the last few days. In this case, the Columbia Center project mentioned in the marketing letter served as the cue.

Jay: Yes, I believe I saw that yesterday.

200

Sur: I'm glad you had a chance to review it. I do have a strong purchasing background. For Maynard and Wyatt Construction I implemented a very effective just-in-time program. I realize you may not have any openings at this moment, but I did want to set up a time when we might meet for 15 minutes or so. I'd like to tell you a little more about my background, and at the same time learn more about some of the directions you're moving in. Would early next week work for you?

Make it easy for the person to say yes.

Tell the person exactly what you want him to do for you.

Ask for a time in the next few days but do not try the worn out sales technique by saying something like, "Would Wednesday at four or Thursday at one work for you?" Let the employer select a time.

Jay: Bob, I'm sure you have a very good background, but I simply don't have any opening at this time and don't anticipate any for at least six months.

Sur: I can certainly understand that. I really didn't expect that you'd have any openings. What I did want to do is to just set up a time, even ten minutes, when we might meet briefly. Would late next week work for you?

Show that you are not like other people. As soon as most people discover there are no openings, they are no longer interested in an appointment.

If necessary, make it even easier to meet: reduce the requested time from 15 minutes to 10.

Jay: Bob, I just don't have any openings. I'm in the middle of developing my budget and it just wouldn't be worth my time or your time.

Sur: While I have you on the line Mr. Jay, perhaps I could just take a couple minutes to tell you more about my background.

(Gives a two minute summary)

As you can see Mr. Jay, I do have a strong purchasing background. And I really do understand your situation. It's always helpful to me, however, when I can meet a person face-to-face. It enables them to remember me better in case something would unexpectedly develop. Or you may hear of something elsewhere and be able to refer me. Could I stop by next week to introduce myself. I promise I wouldn't take up more than two minutes of your time.

Be tactful but be persistent. Asking for just an additional two minutes of time on the phone allows the person to relax; he or she realizes that the conversation is coming to a close.

Provide a two minute summary which sells you. This summary must be concise and have impact, so work on it carefully.

This is such a reasonable request. Everyone understands the value of face-to-face contact. And you're only asking for a couple minutes.

Jay: Well, I suppose we could do that. Stop over at my office at 11:55 on Friday.

Ideally the person with the power to hire will immediately arrange a time. This happens surprisingly often. You must also be prepared, however, for any objections the person might raise. The example below illustrates my point. Objections are often raised, so you must be prepared.

Employer: We won't be hiring for at least six months.

        (How does she know? An employee may quit tomorrow.)

You: I can understand that. Actually I'm not in a hurry to leave my present job. It would certainly be beneficial to me if we could meet for just ten minutes.

Employer: I'm really tied up for the next three weeks.

You: That's fine. Would the Monday following that week work for you?

Employer: Probably you should go through personnel and fill out an application.

You: I'd be glad to at the appropriate time. But really my goal is just to meet you and introduce myself.

Employer: Right now we're laying off people in your field.

You: I can appreciate your concern. I know the economy is rough right now. I think that makes it even more important that we get together. My company went through a similar situation a year ago. My money-saving ideas helped turn the company around.

Employer: I really don't think you have the right experience.

You: It is a bit unusual, but really, the problems I've dealt with are not much different than the ones you are undoubtedly facing. My new procedures at Silco created a 7% increase in productivity.

It's unlikely you will face all of these objections from one person, but be prepared for them. Make it easy for the person to say "yes." Asking for only ten minutes is a very reasonable request. Most people can spare at least that much time. And because you have much to offer, the interview will prove mutually beneficial. At the very least, such a meeting can give the employer a pleasant and relaxing ten minutes.

Below is an outline of the procedure you should follow when making your phone calls.

1. Speak to the person with power to hire and ask for a 15-minute meeting. Indicate that you realize there may be no openings.

2. If the person responds by saying there are no openings and therefore doesn't want to meet with you, explain again that you understand there are no openings, but that you want only ten minutes to talk about the field and your background.

3. If the person counters by saying there is a freeze on hiring, or gives some other reason why he thinks a visit would be a waste of time for both of you, say something like this: "I can sure appreciate the tough economic climate in this area. Since I have you on the phone, let me just take a minute to tell you a little more about myself." Then give a one- to two-minute summary of your strengths and experience.

4. When you finish your summary, ask once more for an appointment. Ask for a five-minute appointment, or just two minutes for an introduction. You might approach it in one of the following ways:

Mr. Belquez, I can certainly understand your situation. I'm working at this time, and what I'd really like to do is meet you and tell you a little more about myself so when openings do develop you'll be able to keep me in mind. I promise I won't take more than five minutes of your time.

❖

Ms. Baum, that gives you just a sketch of my experience and abilities. It's certainly not uncommon these days for a company to have a hiring freeze, and I can understand your reluctance to take time out of your busy schedule. But it would be very helpful to me if we could meet for just five minutes.

❖

Mr. Baker, as you can see, I have a strong background in purchasing. It would really help me if I could merely introduce myself to you. It wouldn't take more than two minutes.

At that point you will have asked three times for an appointment. Don't give up with just two tries; many people relent on the third request. The first two requests were based on your merit. You're a very capable person and you requested an appointment because most people in management continually have their eyes open for new talent. Make the third request on the basis of a favor. When you appeal to their desire to help others, many people will consent. You should also reduce your request for time by asking for two to five minutes.

5. If you still don't get an appointment, you may yet get some valuable information if you hold the person on the phone another two to three minutes. Remember, you worked hard to get this hiring person on the phone, so don't give up too easily. Consider these: "Mr. Bledsoe, when you *do* have a position open, what can I do to make sure I'll be considered?" "Mr. Bledsoe, when you have openings in your marketing department, what do you look for in candidates?" "Mr. Bledsoe, I've briefly described my background. Is it the type of background you'd be looking for?" "If someone quit, would they be replaced?" As you are getting responses to your questions, jot notes down on the back of your 4 x 6 card. Asking whether a replacement would be hired if someone quit is particularly important. If a replacement would not be hired, that organization should go to the bottom of your priority list.

6. In addition, you could ask about the size of the department, particularly the number of people who do your type of work. Ask about turnover. If no one has left in the last four years, that certainly tells you something. You may want to assign that company a lower priority because of the unlikelihood of an opening. Or you may give it a higher priority because low turnover often indicates employee satisfaction. You're the best judge of priority.

7. By this time you've probably convinced the person that you are a highly desirable employee. The person may know of something happening in other companies. Do not ask the person if she knows of any openings. Instead, try this: "Mrs. Kelsoe, I think you have a pretty good feel for my background. What other companies do you think I should be contacting?" The reason for not asking about specific openings is that referrals are more important to you than knowledge of specific openings. And besides, the phrasing of the question will surely cause her to tell you about any openings she knows of. If the person says "Nothing comes to mind right now," she may need some help to jog her memory. Your response might be, "Basically, I'm looking for a progressive firm like yours in the electronics industry. I realize you may not know of specific openings, but your advice on good companies would sure be helpful." If she names some companies, ask for the name of a person to contact in each. Then ask, "Do you mind if I say you suggested I call?" Nearly always you will be given permission. You would simply say, "Beverly Kelsoe at Utalco suggested I call you. During the

last five years, I've been purchasing microcircuits. I realize you may not have any openings, but I would like to set up a time when I could meet with you for about 15 minutes."

8. Thank the person for his or her time. If no appointment was made, indicate that you'll be sending your resume, and that you'll be staying in touch. If the person asks you to simply talk to his or her secretary, respond with a thank you. This employer is implying that the secretary will know in advance if any positions become available. Send a brief thank-you note with your resume to confirm your appreciation.

Your goal is still to get in and see as many hiring authorities as possible. A personal meeting always creates a much stronger and more lasting impression than just talking by phone. But think of it this way: if *you've* been unable to make an appointment, virtually *no one else* is going to, either. When you got the person on the phone, you made the most of it and sold yourself. The employer was impressed. Once the person receives your thank-you note, resume, and a follow-up phone call, you'll undoubtedly be one of the first to be informed when a position becomes available.

Your primary goal in using this strategy is to locate job openings in the hidden job market. While personal meetings with employers increase your chances of finding such positions, your telephone conversation, resume, thank-you note and follow-up are the next best things.

Let's look at an additional benefit of this telephone strategy. During a period of high unemployment, you may get appointments only 25–40% of the time, compared to the 40–80% rate most experience during better economic times. When you don't get an appointment, chances are great that it will be because there really are no openings, and when vacancies occur, they are not filled. So an appointment really would have been a waste of your time. While the employer is saving only ten minutes, you'll be saving the two to three hours it would take to research the organization, drive there, meet the person, and return home. When you get a turndown, be thankful that you just saved yourself three hours, and then go ahead and call the next person on your list.

In your phone calls, use humor whenever possible. My clients report that making the employer laugh has significantly increased their ability to get valuable information, even when they do not get in to see the person.

Produce 40 Times The Impact

Meeting a hiring authority in person has many times the impact of merely sending a resume. A resume, no matter how good it is, is just a piece of paper. You will always be more impressive in person than on paper.

Your goal is to meet hiring authorities in person, even if it is for only ten minutes. Lasting impressions are made from person-to-person contact, not from resumes or even telephone conversations. The person meeting you will associate your name with a face, a voice, a personality.

In each meeting, create a lasting, positive impression so that when a job opening occurs, you'll be the first person considered. Suppose five weeks ago you spent 15 minutes with Mrs. Johnson, a key hiring authority in one of your most desired companies. No opening existed at the time, but you had a pleasant conversation. You learned more about her organization and you shared some of your accomplishments. Mrs. Johnson told you she was impressed with your background, and even mentioned three companies she felt you should look at. Two days later Mrs. Johnson received a nice thank-you note, and she once again remembered you and recalled your potential. She also felt good about herself because she knew she had been helpful. Three weeks later you called her and had a one-minute conversation asking if there had been any job developments. Not surprisingly, there had been none.

Two weeks after your call, however, someone informed Mrs. Johnson that he was leaving the company for a better position. What could Mrs. Johnson do? She could have informed personnel immediately and asked them to place an ad. She could also delve into her file cabinet and review the hundred or so resumes she has accumulated over the last six months. Instead, she thought of you. She picked up the telephone and called you for an interview.

Consider for a moment why the strategy of meeting hiring authorities works so well. During the first twelve weeks after mailing your marketing letter, you will have eight high-quality contacts. The average job seeker has one low-quality contact—a mediocre resume. These eight high-quality contacts produce at least 40 times the impact of mailing a typical resume. The eight contacts include: 1) mailing a marketing letter; 2) following up with a phone call and obtaining an appointment; 3) meeting the person face-to-face; 4) leaving a copy of your resume; 5) sending a thank-you note that evening; 6) following up with a one-minute call three weeks later; 7) a second short call five weeks later; and 8) mailing an interesting article five weeks after that. From that point on, a call would be made or an article sent about every five weeks.

Going through the strategy step by step will show you how this combined approach has at least 40 times the impact of a resume.

An excellent first impression is created when the person reads your marketing letter. The marketing letter is a nice touch because it is different from what employers are used to receiving. While your background may not be so powerful that the employer calls you on the phone immediately, a favorable impression has been created, nonetheless. The person will notice that you've indicated that you will call in a few days. While not necessarily excited about taking your call, particularly if there are no suitable openings, the person will probably speak with you. You may have to call several times because such people are often in meetings, out of the office, or out of town. But when you speak to the person you are going to come across as very confident and capable. Most people will agree to meet with you.

When you meet the person, you will have prepared a monologue. You'll use it if the first thing the person says is, "How can I help you?" Frequently the person will not even remember why you are there. The person may only know that your name is on his schedule for a fifteen-minute appointment. The "How can I help you?" question, or any one of its derivatives, are cordial ways of getting down to business right away. By having a five- to seven-minute summary of your background and strengths prepared, you'll be ready to sell yourself. When you leave the meeting, this person should be thinking, "If I had an opening, this is the type of person who could really help us."

As you leave, you will give the person your resume unless the person had already asked for it. Some people prefer not to bring a resume with them. Instead they tailor the resume to the situation after they get home. If you really do intend to tailor each resume, then this is a good strategy.

That evening you would compose a personal thank-you note. Although many notes are no more than four lines, they can be considerably longer if you want to supply additional information about your background or strengths. The person who met with you will receive the thank-you note a day or two later and think favorably of you once more.

Three weeks later you will call and reintroduce yourself so that the person will remember the conversation, if not your name. Then you will ask if there have been any developments (which there probably have not) and then state once more your interest in the organization. There is no need to feel that you are impinging on this person's time because you will take only a minute. Then five weeks later you will make yet another one-minute call. While you are only taking up one minute of the employer's time, it has probably taken you at least ten minutes to prepare and make several calls before getting through. That's okay, though. You are making an impression.

For your next follow-up, I recommend finding an article that your hiring authorities would enjoy reading but are fairly unlikely to have already seen. You would simply write, "Thought you might be interested," and then sign your name. Once again this person will think of you and realize that you are really serious about working there.

When you add up the impact of those eight contacts, I believe it has to be at least 40 times the impact of a resume alone. Let's face it, most resumes are not well written, and they have little impact. Rarely does a person read a resume and say, "We've got to have that person." When an employer speaks to a potential employee, however, and the person is self-confident and enthusiastic, and follows-up by contacting the employer again and again—that has impact.

Tips For Appointments

Your preparation for appointments will be key. Developing a five- to seven-minute summary of yourself is especially important. Some appointments consist of genuine conversation, but if the employer has no openings and wants to keep the meeting short, he or she is likely to say, "How can I help you?" When you get such a questions, respond with something like, "Mrs. Klevinger, I really do appreciate your taking time to meet with me. And I understand that you don't have any openings at this time. Perhaps the best thing I can do is simply share my background and describe some of my strengths. Basically I . . ." Then you'll give your summary.

Seven minutes may seem like a long time to talk nonstop, but it really isn't. It gives you just enough time to summarize your work history and education and then have a couple minutes left to share some strengths. Of course, while you are describing your work history you should briefly mention some of your accomplishments. This will give the employer an excellent overview of your background. It will also allow the employer to ask some questions if he or she is so inclined.

Often the employers you meet with will have no questions for you. Assuming a fifteen-minute appointment, half of your time will be gone when you've completed your monologue. If the person does not ask you to clarify or expand on anything, you should ask some questions. For instance, you might ask questions like: "Do you see any expansion in the next six months?" "Do you think there will be any openings in the next few months?" "When you have openings, what skills, qualities, and experience are you looking for?"

After the person has finished answering your questions, your time will be almost up. You should indicate the appointment is drawing to a close by saying, "Mr. Klucewski, I don't want to take up any more of your time. Maybe I should just summarize what I think my strengths are." You would then share some of your key strengths. This would all be part of a two-minute summary you should have practiced numerous times. In addition to recapping your prepared summary, you would also cover some of the points the employer mentioned just minutes earlier in response to your question about desired qualities and skills. Some of the words you use might be identical to the ones the employer used, some you would paraphrase. All the while, however, you'd be showing that you possess those skills and qualities. After sharing your points, you would then thank the person for the meeting, stand up, and say goodbye. Whenever possible, you should be the one to terminate the conversation to show that you are a person of your word: you asked for fifteen minutes and you got your fifteen minutes, so it's time for you to leave.

Unless the employer is truly keeping the conversation going, you should terminate it at the set time. This is a crucial point. Sometimes conversations go on for an hour, and I'm sure that, in most cases, the employer gladly gives the additional time. I also know that sometimes a person walks out the door and the employer is saying, "She asked for fifteen minutes and she stayed almost 45 minutes. Now I'm really behind in my work." No matter how impressive the person was, no matter how well she sold herself, and no matter how good some of her stories were, this person will be remembered primarily as the one who did not keep her word.

The way to avoid this potential problem is to be aware of time. If you sense time is drawing to a close, you should very deliberately look at your watch. Do it in an obvious way. By doing so you are demonstrating that you are concerned about taking too much of this person's time.

If you really are hoping for some additional time, and it appears that the employer is enjoying the conversation, and perhaps even keeping it alive, you might say, "Mr. Barratt, I appreciate the time you've given me. I did ask for just fifteen minutes. Do you have an upcoming appointment?" If he wants to terminate the conversation you have provided a perfect out, with the person probably saying, "Well, I do need to get back to my project in about five minutes." Or, the person may say, "No, that's fine, I've got another fifteen minutes."

If the person is clearly directing and continuing the conversation, then you may continue past the allotted time. After the appointed time has passed, however, be very alert for signals that the meeting has gone on long enough. If you notice the person looking at a clock or watch, looking away as if bored, or fidgeting, quickly draw your comments to a close and thank the person for the time.

If the person begins asking you specific questions about your experience, the appointment has probably turned from an appointment into an interview. A person who has no openings and knows there will be no openings in the next few months will rarely ask those types of questions. One of the few exceptions would be if the person were considering referring you to someone who has or may have an opening. In any case, being asked questions is a very positive sign.

The reasons why an employer would ask you questions include: 1) The person has no openings but will remember you and probably offer you an interview if something opens up; 2) the person will refer you to someone else if he learns of an opening; 3) the person is thinking of creating a position in a few months and may move that date up if a really capable person comes along; 4) the person thinks someone is about to quit; 5) the person is considering firing someone, but may do so only if the replacement is ready to be hired; 6) the person is always looking for people who can make money or solve problems for him.

During your appointment, do your best to get the employer involved in a true conversation. The more involved the person is, the more likely the person will want to talk beyond the requested ten or fifteen minutes.

FOLLOW-UP

Following up begins the same day as the appointment. Between appointments or when you get home, write a brief, typed or handwritten thank-you note. The five minutes it takes to write a thank-you note could be the most valuable time you spend. It will cause an important person to think favorably of you once more. A successful job search includes doing all the little things right.

The note can be anywhere from three sentences to two pages in length. The note might read like this:

Dear Mr. Mathews,

I really appreciated the time you gave me yesterday. After talking to you, I'm even more sure that personnel is the right field for me. I'll keep you informed of my progress.

Sincerely,

John Stevens

❖

Dear Mrs. Kelser:

Thank you so much for seeing me yesterday. Our conversation confirmed what others have told me--that Dalco is an exciting company to work for. Of course, when I first called you, I did not expect you to have any openings. Since our conversation, however, I am convinced that I could be a real asset in the accounting department. Through my auditing and computer programming background I think I could really contribute to Dalco.

I will stay in touch to check on any developments.

Sincerely,

Ron Sakulski

❖

Dear Mrs. Madison:

I really enjoyed today's interview and I appreciate the fact that I was invited from among so many candidates. I just wanted to say again that I am quite excited about the prospect of working for Sentry, and especially within your department.

Sincerely,

Roberta Marsh

The first note was in response to an informational interview, the second an appointment in which no opening existed, and the third, a formal job interview. Any of these letters could have been longer, but that is usually unnecessary. Write a longer note only if you have a definite purpose in doing so. For instance, you may want to write a proposal describing a problem you discovered during the interview, along with your proposed solution. Or, if you did not have an opportunity to make an important point during an interview, a letter provides you with an excellent opportunity to cover it, even if it extends the letter's length to more than a page. If an objection was raised during the interview, and you missed it, didn't handle it adequately, or simply want to attack it from another angle, you can do so in a letter. Unlike shorter thank-you notes which may be handwritten, proposals or lengthy letters should be typed.

Everyone you interview with should get a thank-you note, so whenever you have multiple interviews or a panel interview, ask for people's business cards or write their names down when you meet them. For multiple interviews where you will meet three or more people in separate interviews, ask the person who is coordinating the interviews to supply you with the names and titles of the people you'll be meeting.

Most of your appointments will be with employers who do not have current openings. Your process of following up with them can last weeks or even months. Three weeks after your first appointment, call to ask if there have been any developments. Don't worry about bothering the person; you'll only talk for a minute. When you get the person on the phone, introduce yourself, indicate when you met, and briefly describe what you talked about. Do not assume the employer will remember you. He or she may have met 40 people in the last three weeks and will probably need a reminder.

Odds are there is still no opening. In closing, emphasize your interest in the company, and perhaps bring the person up to date on your efforts, particularly if you have contacted any of the people you were referred to. If you had not received referrals before, this would be a good time to ask for the names of organizations that this person thinks you should contact. If you think the person may have a position fairly soon, however, avoid asking for referrals. By not asking for referrals in this type of situation, you will be indicating that the organization is one of your top choices.

A follow-up call might go like this:

Bob: Hi, Mr. Benson, this is Bob Phillips. We met about three weeks ago when I came in to talk about microprocessors and the directions Microdata is taking. I just wanted to find out if there have been any new developments in your marketing department.

Benson: Bob, I remember you and I still have your resume, but there haven't been any openings.

Bob: I really appreciated your taking time to see me. The more I hear about Microdata, the more excited I get. I did call Mr. Jensen at Datasoft. He was very helpful. I'll probably talk to you again in four or five weeks. Thanks again.

When making your follow-up calls, you will frequently talk to a secretary if the person with power to hire is out or unavailable. You will generally be asked to leave a message and your number so the call can be returned. Instead, ask when a good time to call would be. After three or four unsuccessful calls, you might explain that you saw the person three weeks earlier and that you just need to talk to him or her for a minute to ask a couple questions. If the secretary has been brushing you off, that may help. *Always stay on good terms with the secretary.* On the second or third call, ask the secretary's name. You may talk to the secretary six or seven times, so you'll want to maintain your composure and sense of humor. Try to get to know this person. Make him or her want to help you.

After your first follow-up call, call every four to five weeks. Try to create and maintain enough interest so that if any openings occur, you'll be notified. Even if they don't call you, you're never more than five weeks away from discovering the opening through one of your calls. In the hidden job market, jobs frequently stay open for six to ten weeks.

If the person asks you to speak to the secretary in the future, that's okay as long as the secretary will know of openings as they occur. One advantage to you is that the secretary will be readily available. Seek to get to know this person and exchange pleasantries each time you call.

Another method of follow-up is to send a note accompanying an article the person may find interesting. This would usually occur after you have made two follow-up calls.

You should also follow up with your contacts. Every six weeks you'll need to call them to let them know about your experiences and your progress. If they referred you to someone, tell them what happened. Make them an integral part of your search and make them feel valued. This kind of follow-up will counter a psychological fact—with every passing week their ears become duller. In the beginning, you'll be notified if they hear of a job that remotely resembles the one you want. But by seven weeks, your contacts may assume you've found another job. By nine weeks they may hear about your perfect job but fail to even think of you.

OPTIONAL STRATEGIES

In addition to the main strategy I've described of meeting hiring authorities face-to-face, there are other options which deserve consideration. When using these next two options you will still eventually contact the people with the power to hire. The advantage of these two strategies is speed. In a few days, you can contact 100–200 organizations to learn if they have any immediate openings in your field. If they do, you may get some interviews that you might otherwise have missed.

Try A Large Mailing

Because I believe it is more effective for you to meet as many hiring authorities as possible face-to-face, I rarely recommend that people rely on the mass mailing of resumes. There is, however, a place for large mailings. On the chance that there may be an immediate opening with one of their 150 target organizations, some people send out resumes or marketing letters to their prospects during the first week of their job search. The attitude these people have is that they do not want to miss any immediate opportunities as they begin the long-term process of sending out 10–25 marketing letters each week.

A marketing letter, or a resume with a cover letter, have impact in and of themselves only if they arrive two weeks before or after a job has officially opened up. If your material arrives sooner, it usually ends up in a file cabinet somewhere. If it arrives later, it receives no consideration because the candidates for interviews have probably already been selected.

So, with all of this in mind, give consideration to a large mailing. This strategy still requires that you develop your list of 75–200 employers, and that you determine who the person is with the power to hire you.

Either a marketing letter or a resume with a cover letter can be quite effective. Be sure to invite the employer to call you if an opening exists.

Once you have the names of the hiring authorities, decide how the letters will be produced. If you have your own computer and "mail merge" software with your word processing software, you may want to key in the names and addresses yourself. Mail merge software enables you to merely type in the names and addresses of your prospects all at one time, then the software joins, or merges, those names and addresses with your letter. It can save hours of typing.

If you don't have your own computer with mail merge software, you should take your letter and your names and addresses to a secretarial service. It will cost you under two dollars per letter for them to type the letter and the accompanying envelope. All you will need to do is sign each letter and mail your material.

Once your materials go out, you would begin concentrating on sending marketing letters to your top-twenty group of employers. You would continue sending out about 20 each week. If you get some invitations for interviews based on your resume or marketing letter, great. If not, you'll soon be getting appointments as a result of following up on your marketing letters.

Call Your Prospects

Calling your prospects is another strategy that has the advantage of speed. This strategy works most effectively when the companies you're interested in are large and have personnel departments. Once you have your list of prospects, call their personnel departments and simply ask if they are currently looking for people with your background. If the personnel manager is unavailable, a personnel clerk will usually know what positions are open. When speaking to someone in personnel, briefly describe your background, and suggest one or more job titles that might be suitable for you. Using this strategy you will learn only of those openings that have been made known to personnel. With whatever information you have garnered, thank the person and move on to the next one.

This strategy has several advantages over just sending a resume. Two negative things can happen when you mail a resume—a rejection or no response at all. In either case, you still don't know what the real situation is. A quick call, on the other hand, can give you a great deal of information. Whether you get a clerk or the personnel manager, ask questions. If you learn that there are no suitable openings, you could confirm that the company does in fact have the types of positions you're interested in. You can also discover whether the organization is growing, and if so, whether there are any plans to expand in your specialty.

At a rate of eight calls per hour, you can get through your entire prospect list in three to five days. With this strategy, do not expect lots of interviews. Think of it instead as a way to gain some additional information about the firm. It is another way to ensure that you are not missing out on any opportunities as you begin the longer process of meeting hiring authorities.

AN IMPORTANT JOB FINDING OPTION

I typically recommend that job seekers develop a list of at least 70 potential employers and seek face-to-face meetings with the hiring authorities. There are exceptions, however. In some types of positions, particularly office and clerical jobs, you are actually better off calling the personnel department of larger companies or the office manager of smaller companies. The reason for this is that clerical people work in almost any department of an organization, so there may be many people who hire clerical staff. If you use this strategy you could still identify 10–20 organizations that you are especially interested in and meet the personnel manager or office manager. Simply walking in and meeting someone in personnel can also be effective.

When using the calling strategy, you would begin by introducing yourself, briefly explaining your background, and asking if any openings currently exist. You should be able to average 12 calls an hour. If you have 120 organizations on your list and call once a week to learn of openings, your total time expended is only ten hours weekly. The strategy should yield two to three interviews each week. Although 120 may seem like a lot of organizations, when using this strategy you need large numbers. Even 150 is not too many. If you are looking for office positions and you live in an urban area, there will probably be over 150 potential organizations within 15 minutes of your home.

If personnel informs you that no openings are currently available, carry on a conversation similar to this:.

Personnel: Personnel, may I help you?

Carol: This is Carol Prescott, I have a diploma from Harrington Business College and two years of clerical experience. Do you have any clerical positions available at this time?

Personnel: No we don't.

Carol: Do you anticipate adding any office staff in the next month or two?

Personnel: It's highly doubtful that we'll be adding any positions in the next four months.

Carol: If someone quit, would the person be replaced?

Personnel: I'm sure they would.

Carol: Approximately how many clerical positions do you have?

Personnel: Counting bookkeepers, probably around 30.

Carol: What kind of turnover do you have?

Personnel: It's nothing unusual, I'm sure it's about average.

Carol: Thanks a lot for your help, who am I speaking to?

Personnel: I'm Betty.

Carol: Betty, you've been really helpful. I plan to call once a week and if it's all right, I'll probably just ask for you. Is there anything else I can do to learn of any openings?

In less than two minutes, Carol learned so much more than if she had hung up after hearing that no openings existed. She also has a person to talk to in personnel. In a short time, Betty may actually recognize Carol's voice, and because Carol is friendly and courteous, Betty may actually go out of her way to help her. Of course, don't feel you can only talk to one person. If your regular person is unavailable, ask questions of whomever happens to be on the line. Also, notice what Carol did at the end of her call. Although she stated her intention to call periodically, she specifically asked if there was anything else she could do to ensure that she would learn about all potential openings. Although she plans to call weekly, she is prepared to do anything else that will help her.

This strategy is fast and gets excellent results—but don't use it as a shortcut if you are one of those who should be talking with the person with the power to hire.

MAKING THE SYSTEMATIC JOB SEARCH WORK

The people who succeed with the Systematic Job Search strategies become detectives. Successful detectives never get discouraged. They follow up on each lead until the case is solved. Dozens of leads may dead end, but eventually one pays off. Remember, it only takes one good job offer, and you'll never be able to predict where the lead will come from.

The number-one cause of failure in job hunting is inaction, and the number-one cause of inaction is fear of rejection. Many people are not technically inactive; in fact they may be very busy. But they're inefficient, spinning their wheels, and making no headway. Such ineffective tactics can lead to a vicious cycle. It usually starts like this: when people lose their jobs, they start looking at the want ads. They throw their slightly revised resume around with very little success, but finally an invitation for an interview is offered. Since most people "wing it" in interviews with no research, practice, or forethought, the first few interviews go very poorly, leading to a string of rejections. Eventually, many people reach what Richard Bolles calls "Desperation Gulch," that feeling of hopelessness and depression that can lead to giving up.

By all means, avoid the vicious cycle. You will do that by: 1) following the strategy as it has been described; 2) keeping busy and using good time management; and 3) enjoying several low-stress appointments each week.

A New Definition Of Success

I have one more thought to offer you. I'd like to give you a new definition of success. For most job seekers the only success is getting the right job offer. That's *all* wrong. You can experience success each day and should reward yourself for it by feeling good about yourself. I believe success is having one or more pleasant experiences every day. Success is talking to someone who opens up to you and tells you everything about a field you're interested in. Success is completing your employer list. Success is getting in to see an employer and having an interesting conversation. Success is getting a good lead from a friend. Success is being a finalist among 50 applicants.

If you have at least one success each day, that ultimate success—a job— will come about as a matter of course. Start your day as if you had a full-time job. If you're used to getting up at 6:30 a.m., continue that habit. Put in a solid six-hour work day. You're different from the rest of your competition. While they're complaining about their rotten luck, you're doing your employer research. While they're sitting next to the telephone waiting for interviews to be arranged for them, you're on the telephone setting up your own appointments. While they're watching soap operas and game shows, you're meeting hiring authorities and getting job leads. While they're hoping for a lucky break, you're creating your own breaks.

Relaxing is one of the most difficult things for an unemployed job seeker to do. Turning your job search into a full-time job is the best medicine. If you're busy with research and appointments, you won't have time for negative thoughts. If you spend six full hours each day on your job search, you've done your job for the day. When you were employed, you didn't try to finish big projects in a single day. You knew you would get part of it done each day. In a job search you can't do it all in one day. That's what tomorrow is for. Monday through Friday stay busy between 8:30 a.m. and 4:30 p.m., then call it a day. You've done all you can do. Relax. Enjoy your family. Read a book. Go to the health club.

REAL EXPERIENCES

The following examples demonstrate some of the many ways people find out about their new jobs. These weren't just lucky breaks, the people created these situations.

I had spoken to someone in each of my top-ten companies, but there were no openings. I then developed a new list and was starting to talk to key people. One of the firms had no openings but suggested that I talk to someone in a very young but growing firm that I had never heard of. Sure enough, this firm was expanding and I got there at just the right time. The training I'm getting is excellent, and the income potential is excellent, too.

❖

I was just calling people to get information. I spoke to one person who thought his company was looking for a person with my background. The next day I went in for an interview and got the job.

❖

After I clarified what I really wanted to do, I contacted a former co-worker who had moved into the field I was interested in. We talked by phone and later had several meetings. He needed someone to assist him and he knew I had the ability and the background. We're now working together.

❖

A former supervisor went to work for a new company, and when an opening occurred he recommended me to his boss. I was hired after several interviews.

Part Three
Winning At
Interviewing

Winning At Interviews

INTERVIEWING PRINCIPLES

Effective interviewing is an art which can be learned, and the payoffs can be tremendous. You'll work so hard to get each interview that it would be a shame to go into an interview unprepared. By knowing what to expect and by preparing for all of the difficult questions you'll encounter, you will greatly enhance your chance of receiving the job offer. The following fourteen principles provide you with an overview of things you should consider before going into an interview.

1. An interview is simply an opportunity for two people to meet and determine whether an employer-employee relationship will prove beneficial to both parties.

2. Interviewing is a two-way street. You're not begging for a job, you're an equal.

3. The employer is actually on your side. He or she has a need and has every reason to hope you are the right person to meet it. Keep the employer on your side. This requires active listening. Try to detect what the employer's real needs are.

4. An objection is not a rejection, it is a request for more information. If the employer states, "You don't have as much experience as we normally want," the employer is not rejecting you. In fact, the person could be totally sold on you but for this one concern. Your task is to sell yourself and overcome that objection. You will do this by emphasizing your strengths, not by arguing.

5. Let the employer talk. You listen. The longer the employer talks at the beginning, the more you can learn about the organization. This will help you formulate positive responses.

6. Increase your chance for a second interview by dressing properly, being on time, listening intently, demonstrating potential and enthusiasm, appearing relaxed, providing brief, well thought-out responses, and asking a few intelligent questions.

7. Hiring decisions are based mostly on emotion. Do I like her? Will we get along? Will she accept criticism and be a good team worker? Being liked by the employer is just as important as having the qualifications.

8. Concentrate on giving examples of your accomplishments. Accomplishments demonstrate your potential. Stress how you can benefit the organization.

9. Be yourself, but also be your best. If you tend to be overly aggressive, consciously tone it down during the interview. If you have strong opinions on everything and like to express them, keep them to yourself. If you tend to be too quiet and reserved, try to be a little more outgoing and enthusiastic during the interview.

10. Use examples to back up any statements you make. Be prepared for questions like "Are you good with details?" "Are you a hard worker?" "Can you handle difficult people?" You can begin your response with, "Yes, I *am* good with details. For example ..."

11. Be able to explain any details included in your resume, such as accomplishments or job duties. You can use your resume to predict many of the questions that will be asked. Practice describing your job duties in the most concise way possible.

12. Showing confidence in yourself will create a favorable impression. Such confidence can come only from truly knowing yourself and recognizing your own potential.

13. Send a thank-you note the evening of the interview. Some employers have never received a thank-you note, yet this simple courtesy frequently makes the difference between selection and rejection.

14. Relax and enjoy your interviews.

Interviewing Secrets

OVERCOMING OBJECTIONS

Performing well in interviews requires an ability to recognize the important difference between rejections and objections. Virtually everyone must overcome several objections during the interviewing process before a job offer is made. People who perceive an objection as a rejection, however, may become defensive or simply give up and assume all is lost. Thus, the failure to understand objections and differentiate them from rejection can cause some interviewees to sabotage their own success in an interview.

An Objection Is Not A Rejection

An objection is *not* a rejection. It is simply a request for more information. Good interviewees, like good salespeople, must learn to anticipate objections. It is important to anticipate an objection because once an objection is stated, it is much more difficult to neutralize or overcome.

The first step in overcoming objections is predicting what they will be and developing appropriate, effective responses to them. The following circumstances are likely to give rise to some types of objections: you were fired from your last job; you appear to be a job hopper; there is a major gap in your work history; you're changing careers; you don't have a college degree and you're applying for a position that normally requires one; you have three or more years of college education but never received a degree; or you have too little or too much experience. The list could go on. Objections can also arise if you lack a certain type of knowledge or experience the employer is seeking.

When overcoming an objection, don't argue with the employer. If the employer states, "You really don't have enough experience in this field," a good response might be:

> I realize there may be others with more years of experience, but I really feel the quality of my experience is the key. Because of the variety of things I've done, and the level of responsibility I was given, I think my five years are equivalent to most people with ten. There's no question in my mind that I can do an outstanding job for you.

Another way to deal with this concern is to describe all of your *related* experience. Related experience is similar to what the employer is looking for, but not exactly the same. Your challenge is to get the employer believing that your experience is close to what they need. The more successful you are at making the employer see this similarity, the more likely you are to overcome the objection and get the job offer.

PROJECT ENTHUSIASM AND POTENTIAL

Enthusiasm and potential will land you more job offers than any other qualities. The two are inseparable.

Enthusiasm

Employers seek enthusiastic people who really want to get involved in the job. You should demonstrate genuine enthusiasm—enthusiasm for yourself, enthusiasm for the job, enthusiasm for your future boss, and enthusiasm for the company.

Suppose the field has been narrowed to two equally qualified people. The employer will ask many questions to determine who is the best choice. A common question is "If we offered you the position, would you accept it?" Notice the difference in the following two responses.

> Sandra: Yeah, I definitely would accept it. The job seems interesting.

> Susan: I'm excited about this job. I like the philosophy of top management, I like the steady growth of XYZ in the last five years, and I really look forward to working for you. This job will utilize my strengths and interests. I'm ready to get started.

If the choice came down to these two people, there is little question as to who would be hired.

The best way to appear enthusiastic is to genuinely *be* enthusiastic about the job. If you've considered your long- and short-term goals, and this job would help you attain those goals, it will be easy to demonstrate enthusiasm.

Enthusiasm is not demonstrated in just one response to one question, however; it must be demonstrated throughout the interview. It starts with listening. Really listening to the interviewer shows respect as well as enthusiasm. You can also show enthusiasm by speaking positively about previous jobs or supervisors. Describe how you put all of your energy into a job and describe the results you've achieved.

I am convinced that enthusiasm has gotten more people jobs than any other single quality. But because of the stress of interviews, most people tend to speak in a monotone and to appear unenthusiastic. Some reduce their level of enthusiasm even further because of the mistaken notion that they should play "hard to get." At the end of an interview, if you truly want the job, tell the interviewer so. Be enthusiastic. When it comes down to two people who are equally qualified, the person most enthusiastic about the job will almost always get the offer.

Potential

Your potential is your future worth to an organization. Demonstrating enthusiasm without demonstrating potential will seldom lead to a job offer. The two must go together. Your enthusiasm will give the employer confidence that you want the job and that you will work hard at it. But if you don't also demonstrate your potential, you will not receive an offer.

Although companies occasionally use elaborate personality tests to determine potential, past success is still the best predictor of future success. If you are a top salesperson at your present company and you are interviewing for a new sales position, your past success will give the sales manager the confidence that you will continue to sell well. If you've been fired from four sales positions because of poor results, you'll have your work cut out for you as you try to convince a sales manager that you really do have potential.

Potential is best demonstrated by telling the employer about your accomplishments. For example, consider Paula, who is returning to work after 20 years out of the job market. She is applying for Administrative Assistant with a small association that represents pharmacists. Membership in the association has dropped because pharmacists feel they have not been effectively represented. In walks Paula, with no paid work experience and only one year of college, to compete with college graduates who have experience working with associations. Even with this competition, Paula lands the job, thanks to her one-year term as president of the PTA. During that year, attendance at meetings increased 60% over the previous year, and fund-raising activities brought in twice as much money. Paula also organized a banquet that people are still talking about. And she was considered to be the primary lobbying force for new state legislation that benefited her school district. By sharing these accomplishments, she proved that she could help turn the pharmacists' association around. That's potential.

Selling potential can get you job offers when others have more direct experience. Tim, who has been the chief financial officer of three companies, states that among the 30 or more people he has hired, he has never hired the "most qualified" person. He is quick to say he always hires qualified people. In fact, candidates are not even interviewed unless they have demonstrated competence in all key areas. But after narrowing the field down to two or three, he usually finds himself drawn to the person who shows great drive and desire. That person has never been the one with the most direct experience. It seems that those with the most experience generally fail to fully demonstrate enthusiasm and potential.

MASTER THE ART OF STORY TELLING

Aloof as they may seem, employers are actually begging you to get them excited. Show that you can make or save them money, solve their operational problems, or ease their workloads, and they'll be thrilled to hire you. Merely saying you can increase productivity or get staff members to work as a team isn't enough. You must support your claims with vivid examples. People remember best those things that are stored in their minds as pictures. In fact, the latest brain research reveals that memories are stored as holographs, or 3–D pictures. That means that if words pass from your mouth and do not create any images or emotions in the minds of employers, those words will literally pass through one ear and out the other—there will be no impact or long-term memory.

Consider what happens when a person is asked to describe himself. He may declare that he is hard working, energetic, a true leader, and a person who can successfully juggle multiple tasks. The problem here is that he is trying to sell too many things at once and doesn't do a good job with any of them. Because he doesn't back up any of the claims with examples, none of the points will be remembered after he leaves the interview.

Using anecdotes to describe job skills is a highly effective interview technique. In less than three minutes, you can tell a powerful story that will make interviewers remember you favorably for days, weeks, or even months after the interview. Since employers know that the best predictor of future success is past success, tell stories which vividly describe your successes.

Stories are important because they can say so much about you in an evocative, concentrated way. Paul Green is the founder of Behavioral Technology in Memphis, Tennessee, a firm which teaches corporations how to utilize behavior-based interviewing. Paul gives an excellent example of how telling stories in an interview can make a difference. While he was conducting an interview he asked the candidate for an example that would demonstrate a strong commitment to completing tasks. The candidate described a time when he had had his appendix removed on a Thursday and was back in the office on Monday—to the dismay of everyone. His explanation was that work was piling up and he might as well do everything he could, even though he could not work a full day for the first week. The story provided strong evidence that he was a driven, hard-working person. The memory he created was that he was "the appendix guy." To this day, when Paul Green thinks about this person, all he has to say to himself is, "the appendix guy," and a flood of memories and emotions return. The beauty of stories is that they can evoke a recollection of many skills, qualities, abilities, and characteristics.

When telling stories, provide all of the key information. Describe the situation and the challenges you faced. Then describe your analysis and the recommendations you made. Next, describe what you implemented and the results you obtained. Look for interesting tidbits and details which, though not crucial for understanding, will provide a stronger visual image of what you did.

A client shared a story with me that included vivid details and tidbits; it is a story I'll never forget. Ron had worked for 25 years in the management of seafood-processing plants in Oregon, Washington, and Alaska. Because of his reputation for working effectively with unions, he was asked to take over a plant in the Caribbean which was experiencing serious labor unrest. Always one for a challenge, Ron took it on. One day, about a week after he arrived at the Caribbean plant, he found himself surrounded by about ten workers. When they began accusing him of trying to destroy the union, he simply faced them down and reiterated the changes he felt needed to be made. When he finished speaking, he walked through the crowd and began heading back to his office. As he walked away, he knew that one of the leaders had pulled out a gun and had pointed it at his back. Although his heart was racing, he kept walking and did not turn around. He was sure that at any moment he was going to have a bullet in his back. He had never been more frightened in his life. When he got back to his office he realized he had been so scared he actually wet his pants. He said it with laughter, of course, and we both laughed together. I heard that story over three years ago, yet I still recall it most vividly.

Whenever I recall this story, I have very strong memories about Ron. The story didn't end there. Ron showed the workers that he could not be intimidated. The workers began to end their work slowdown, and they began to have confidence that he would be fair with them. Within six months the unrest was a distant memory and the plant began making a profit again. I'm not necessarily suggesting that in an interview Ron should always mention his incontinence, but I'm pointing out how this detail makes the story more memorable and amusing. Actually there were several vivid details which made this a memorable story. By imprinting vivid images in the brains of employers, you will be better remembered and more highly regarded.

Most people require practice to be able to tell vivid, effective stories. Once you have recalled 10–15 accomplishments, write brief descriptions of them. Then practice giving a three-minute version, a two-minute version, and a one-minute version of each one. With the longer versions, you can add details which provide a greater richness and make each story more memorable. The shorter versions take the most effort because you must decide which information is most crucial. Then, tell a story into a tape recorder. When you play it back, ask yourself: Is it a well-told story? Is it interesting? Does it create mind pictures?

Software engineers and other technical people tell me that their projects simply don't translate into colorful stories like the one described above. I agree with them to some extent—few of us have such dramatic stories to tell. But anyone can still tell a vivid story by emphasizing the challenges faced and by graphically describing how the problems were overcome. It's the details of a story that create strong visual images and strong emotional memories.

When telling stories that demonstrate how you've solved a problem or overcome an obstacle, create before and after pictures that highlight your impact on the situation. Paint the before picture as bleak as you can. Make the employer feel how bad the situation was. If you were dealing with a quality control problem, you might describe how angry your customers were and describe how some threatened to stop buying from your company or how some actually did. Don't exaggerate, but give the employer the full sense of the problem. As you complete your story, describe how smooth or effective things became. Create the strongest contrast possible without exaggerating. Bruce shared this story about his experience with a mobile home manufacturer:

> Before I took over the parts department, it was taking a month from the time we received a dealer's order until the dealer actually got the part. Because of this we had two problems—most dealers simply obtained their parts from other sources, while those who did order from the factory got their kicks out of yelling at me and telling me to get the parts to them pronto. The problem was simply that no system had been established. Orders either got lost or they didn't get down to the traffic department for days. And no one even knew if the parts were in stock. When they weren't in stock, no one bothered to notify the person who had placed the order. After a week on the job, I decided things had to change.
>
> The first thing I did was create forms for recording orders, something which had never been done even though the manufacturing facility had been operating for four years. My predecessor either wrote things down on scraps of paper or tried to remember things in his head. He was really a smart guy, but he couldn't remember everything. I established a hookup with the warehouse so our two computer systems could talk to each other. This system told me immediately whether the parts were available.
>
> Next, I got the warehouse and the shipping and receiving managers together and we found ways to help each other rather than squabble over turf. Within four months we got our delivery times down from four weeks to five days. We haven't lost an order for at least two years. Now I'm not wasting time tracking down lost or late shipments. And my hearing is getting better since people don't yell over the phone anymore. The best thing is that parts sales to our dealers have increased from $12,000 per month to over $60,000. Our dealers are happy, so they don't need to go to other suppliers anymore.

Didn't you actually picture this person on the phone getting his ears burned? Did you imagine the orders getting written down on scraps and then getting misplaced? Could you visualize these three managers who were working at cross purposes? If so, the story was successful. But you were not merely left with a picture. You were left with a result. It wasn't just that Bruce didn't get yelled at anymore, but that sales increased dramatically. Remember that employers get excited when you demonstrate that you can make money, save money, solve problems, or reduce the boss's daily stress and pressure. Bruce demonstrated through this one story that he could do all four. The final point he made was that he could make money. After all, sales increased from $12,000 per month to $60,000. That did some very nice things to the company's bottom line.

Begin by describing the situation as you entered it. If the situation was something that existed before you became involved, describe all of the negatives. If you are describing a project that you oversaw, describe the problems or challenges in the most graphic terms possible. Describe your analysis of the situation and whatever research you applied to it. Then describe your recommendations or the conclusions you came to. Next, explain what you implemented and developed, and paint a picture of what things were like after they improved. If it was a project, concentrate on describing those parts of the project which met or exceeded objectives. Complete the story by describing how your work benefitted the company. As you end the story, remind the interviewer what skill or strength the story demonstrates, and you might add another two or three points as well. This could be done by stating: "So I really do believe that experience demonstrates my ability to manage projects effectively (the originally stated strength), as well as motivate employees and find solutions to really difficult problems."

Many questions neither invite nor demand a story. Questions such as "What did you like best about your supervisor?" or "What frustrates you about your current job?" do not invite examples. While one could use specific examples for these questions, typically a person would answer them in a very brief and straight forward manner. If you had indicated that your supervisor often did not keep his staff well informed, the interviewer might possibly ask for a specific example, but that is unlikely. There are other questions which would never require a story, such as asking what public figure you most admire.

Even though many questions do not invite stories, you need to be prepared so that when an opportunity to tell a story presents itself, you'll be ready with the best example possible.

Most people speak in generalities when asked about their strengths. Five minutes later, the interviewer will not even remember what was said. When you take advantage of the opportunity to tell a story, you will create impact and cause the interviewer to know a great deal about you. Your challenge is to bring in stories whenever they are appropriate. Any time a question is asked about a strength or asset, back up what you say with an example. If you've never done exactly what they are asking for, you might start with "That's not too different from what I did at..."

To tell effective stories:

1) Provide all of the key information.

2) Describe the situation as you came into it—problems and challenges included.

3) Describe your analysis and recommendations.

4) Describe what you implemented and the results you obtained.

5) Create vivid images.

6) Provide interesting details, but keep the story concise.

7) Make the story interesting.

DESCRIBING ACCOMPLISHMENTS

By now you should recognize the importance of telling stories. The next step is to identify your best stories and write about them. Writing about them will enhance your memory of what occurred. It will also enable you to make each story as vivid as possible. Start by writing about 12 of your accomplishments. An accomplishment is anything you've done well, enjoyed doing, or received satisfaction from doing. If you have several years of work experience, you should write on your 12 top work-related accomplishments. If you are trying to break into a new field, choose your 12 top work-related or nonwork-related accomplishments that best demonstrate your ability to handle the new job.

It is always best to describe accomplishments in terms of dollars or percentages. One of my clients was able to tell employers that in the two years since she had taken over her territory, she had increased the sales of shoes by 54% and profits on her sales by 68%. The company had been marketing in that area for 20 years. You can see how impressive this would be to an employer.

Other examples include: "I received a $600 bonus from Boeing for suggesting an idea that saved $6,000 the first year." "I developed a simplified computer program for a client which reduced the computer runtime by 40% and saved over $17,000 per year."

Dollar figures and percentages are so valuable in accomplishments that you should even estimate them when necessary. The computer programmer in the example above had to estimate or guesstimate the dollar savings. She knew the runtime was reduced by 35–45%, so she chose 40% as her figure. She knew how frequently the program was run, and she knew the cost of the computer time. Thus, the $17,000 figure was calculated using simple arithmetic.

While not all accomplishments can be quantified, many can. When I'm talking with people to gather information for their resumes, I'm frequently told, "There's really no way to estimate it, I just improved it." I will then ask questions from different angles and we invariably arrive at a figure we can use.

See pages 25 to 32 for more on accomplishments. The ideas expressed there for resumes are just as applicable for interviewing.

Once you list your accomplishments, practice sharing them out loud. This will help prepare you to select the most appropriate accomplishment during an interview—the one that shows you doing work closely related to the job you're interviewing for, or one that demonstrates some of your most desirable characteristics.

SELL YOURSELF

KNOWING HOW TO SELL YOURSELF is the key to successful interviewing. Building credibility and projecting a winning personality are the first steps.

Credibility

To interview effectively, you must convey your credibility. You accomplish this by showing that you are truthful, sincere, and genuine. The great benefit of credibility is that, once it's established, whatever you say from that point on tends to be believed. In fact, what you say will be believed unless you give the employer a reason to doubt you. That's why you should do nothing to jeopardize your credibility. Consider, for example, how you might answer the question, "What is your biggest weakness?" Job hunting books frequently recommend that you work out your answer so that your weakness really comes across as a strength. One recommended answer runs something like this, "I'd have to say that my greatest weakness is that I work too hard. My wife complains that I'm not around enough, and I guess sometimes I work my people too hard too." The employer was supposed to think, "Well, isn't it nice that if this guy is going to have a weakness it would be something like this." The problem is that the answer is so planned and contrived that it is difficult to make it seem sincere. And lack of sincerity can damage your credibility.

Once you lose your credibility, everything you said before and everything you say after will come under greater scrutiny and there will always be an element of doubt about you. This is not the way to start a relationship. So do everything possible to establish credibility, and then do nothing to lose it.

Project And Sell A Winning Personality

On a conscious and subconscious level, employers will be evaluating your personality and asking, "Do I like this person and will we work well together?" When considering two people with equal qualifications, the one with the most pleasing personality will always be hired. A job is similar to marriage—the two of you may "live" together for many years. Work will be a lot more enjoyable if you like and respect each other.

In order to adequately sell yourself, you need to know your personality skills. Such skills include being appreciative, cooperative, and energetic. Employers highly value such qualities. Even someone seeking a CEO position must sell personality skills. Some of the most desirable characteristics or personality skills are friendliness, cheerfulness, tactfulness, sincerity, maturity, open-mindedness, loyalty, patience, optimism, reliability, flexibility, and emotional stability. There are others, of course, but these are among the most important.

During an interview you won't just rattle off claims to each of these characteristics—you will demonstrate each one. In just twenty minutes, a perceptive interviewer can accurately assess you in each area—both by what you *say* and by what you *are*. The famous saying, "Your actions speak so loudly, I can't hear what you're saying," is especially applicable to the ways in which employers assess a job applicant's personality during an interview.

Imagine you are interviewing with a company that just fired an employee because he was uncooperative. You might be asked, "In this organization cooperation and teamwork are absolutely essential. Are you a cooperative person?" You might respond, "Yes, I am very cooperative. When we were developing prototypes I would have to coordinate the project with people from four or five different departments. We always got the project completed on time. None of us got our way on everything. We worked out our differences and we felt good about the results." This example, which would be expanded upon in an actual interview, clearly illustrates that this is a cooperative, team-oriented person.

Your goal during the interview is to reveal as many positive attributes as possible. While your competitors are busy merely *describing* their technical strengths, you will be selling your personality skills as well as your technical skills.

There is a saying that sales are made on emotion and justified with logic. When most of us go to buy something, we start by liking it at an emotional level; we then look for ways to justify spending the money on the purchase. This process can be so subtle that few are even aware that it's taking place.

Hiring decisions are very similar. Your challenge is to get the employer to like you and to begin "leaning" your way. You do this by projecting enthusiasm, potential, and a winning personality. The employer has an emotional reaction—she begins to like you and feel comfortable with you. She senses your potential. Once you have hooked the employer emotionally, she will find a way to justify hiring you.

To identify and become more acquainted with your personality skills, rate yourself on the following 42 key skills. Rate yourself on a scale of 1–10, where 10 is excellent and 1 is poor. Be sure to give yourself a range—not all 8s, 9s and 10s. Avoid over-analyzing here—go through the list as quickly as you can.

Appreciative	Energetic/Stamina	Optimistic
Assertive	Enthusiastic	Patient
Cheerful	Flexible	Persistent
Compassionate	Forgiving	Practical
Considerate	Frank	Real
Cooperative	Friendly/Nice	Reliable
Curious/Inquisitive	Generous	Responsible
Decision-making	Goal-oriented	Resourceful
Decisive	Growth-oriented	Risk-taking
Discreet	Honesty/Integrity	Self-confident
Easy-going	Insightful	Sense of Humor
Effective Under Stress	Joyful	Sincere
Efficient/Productive	Loyal	Sound Judgment
Emotionally Stable	Open-minded	Thorough

Writing about your personality skills will prepare you for interviews. So once you've rated yourself on all these skills, pick out your top ten personality skills and write a short paragraph on each one describing how you are that way. This is a quick exercise; you're not trying for polished writing. Using your own shorthand, list an example for each skill. The example should illustrate your ability to use that skill at a high level. Your descriptions might read something like this:

> Although some may say I seldom get excited, I do have a high degree of <u>enthusiasm</u> in many areas. It is not a gushy enthusiasm, but a strong, deep enthusiasm that comes from conviction. Example: Motivating the team on the Baxter project.

> I am very <u>efficient</u>. This quality has been my worst enemy where I am now working. A difficult, demanding job appears so easy because I am efficient. No one fully recognizes my worth. Example: Cut the time it took to get month-end reports out from 8 days to 3 days.

Selling Personality Skills

Once you've identified and described your personality skills, it's important to consider how you might best sell these skills. There are four primary ways: 1) State the skill and then give an example to back it up; 2) State the skill and describe how you use it; 3) While selling a skill using a specific experience, describe the experience so vividly that some of your other personality skills are clearly evidenced; and 4) *Be* it. That is, demonstrate that you possess the skill.

State the skill and give an example. During an interview you might be asked to describe your strengths. You could respond by saying,

> I'd have to say that one of my strengths is my ability to work effectively under stress. A good example would be when I was working on the Otis account. Out of nowhere our client told us that they needed a new ad campaign for a product that was not doing well. We had only two weeks to develop a campaign that would normally have been a two-month project. My staff and I practically lived at the office, but we got the campaign out. It was a very successful campaign for the customer.

If warranted, you could expand on this by taking two or three minutes to explain the details of the project.

State the skill and describe how you use it. Sometimes providing an example is not possible or not appropriate. Instead of giving an example you might say, "I have a reputation for being reliable. People at work know that if a tough project has to get out on schedule, it should be given to me. When I agree to take on a project, my boss knows it's as good as done. I'll get it done no matter what." In this instance a specific example was not used, but the person did everything possible to prove she is extremely reliable.

Describe an experience so vividly that other skills are evident. You may have indicated that one of your strengths is your flexibility and then offered an example which clearly illustrates your flexibility, but reveals other positive traits as well. When you describe your experiences vividly, even a half-way perceptive person will pick up other positive qualities without your having to label them.

At other times it's best to point out what those other skills are: "So I think that's a good example of how I'm flexible. I think it also shows that I'm very resourceful and work well under stress."

Be it. Don't just say it, show it. For instance, you can demonstrate your energy level through the way you walk and talk, your body language, facial expressions, and your voice inflection. I can sense a person's energy level within the first minute we are together. Cheerfulness, insightfulness, joyfulness, open-mindedness, optimism, self-confidence, enthusiasm, sense of humor, and sincerity are all traits that can be demonstrated.

Practice. Practice telling your stories. Only by doing so can you really hone them down to their most important points. Describe the experiences so vividly that the interviewer forms a mental image. Mental images can last for weeks or months in an employer's mind, mere words may last five minutes.

Sell Exposure

If you know you lack certain skills or experience, look for ways to sell your exposure. In an interview your order of priority is: 1) Sell the experience you have that is identical or nearly identical to what is being sought; 2) Sell your related or similar experience; and 3) Sell exposure. Exposure means you have observed that task or skill being done by others, you worked closely with people who used that skill, or you assisted someone performing that skill on one or more occasions. People don't get hired *because* of their exposure to certain skills, but exposure can tip the balance scale just enough to make the difference. When all you have to sell is exposure to a skill, do not apologize. Rather, move straight ahead and make the most out of what you have to offer.

Show What You Can Do For Them

One of the biggest turnoffs for employers is the candidate who seems self-centered and cares only about what the company can do for him or her. Employment is certainly a two-way street and there must be give and take, but during the interview the emphasis *must* be on how you can benefit the organization.

Excite An Employer

You can genuinely get an employer excited about you. You do so by demonstrating that you can do any or all of the following: 1) **make** money for the organization; 2) **save** money for the organization; 3) **solve** problems the employer is facing; and 4) **reduce** the level of stress and pressure the employer is under.

It's fairly easy to show how you have helped a company make money, save money, and solve problems. You do this by describing actual examples. Less obvious, but just as valuable, is demonstrating that you can reduce the stress and pressure your prospective boss is facing. Start by selling your reliability, responsibility, and resourcefulness. By having confidence that responsibilities can be delegated to someone of your caliber, your prospective boss will actually visualize a life filled with less pressure.

QUESTIONS TO
BE PREPARED FOR

I SEE A LOT OF PEOPLE who only do a passable job in interviews, and the cause is almost always lack of preparation. Since nearly every conceivable question can be anticipated, you can have a real edge over others by being ready for them.

Below are 76 questions which are frequently asked or cause great difficulty for interviewees. Write each question on a sheet of paper, and then briefly list the points you would like to make in response to them. Do not write out your responses word for word and try to memorize the answers. In an interview you may forget parts and stumble. Besides, your answers would sound "canned." Instead, briefly list the main points you'd like to cover, then practice speaking the answers. This will help prepare you to give thoughtful but spontaneous-sounding answers.

1. Tell me about yourself.
2. What is your greatest strength?
3. What can you offer us that someone else can't?
4. What are your three most important career accomplishments?
5. What is your greatest weakness?
6. What kind of recommendations will you get from previous employers?
7. What are your career goals?
8. Describe your perfect job. *Be general (creative)*
9. What is most important to you in a job?
10. Why do you want to change careers?
11. Why do you want to get into this field?
12. What do you really want to do in life?
13. What position do you expect to hold in five years? *decision general organization coaching*
14. Why would you like to work for us?
15. Why do you want to leave your present employer?
16. How long have you been out of work?
17. Why did you leave?
18. What actions would you take if you came on board?
19. How long will it take before you make a positive contribution to our organization? *immediately (how so?) I'm a great prob solving*
20. What is your opinion of your present (or past) employer?
21. How long would you stay if we offered you this position?
22. What do you like least about this position? Most?
23. What personal, non-job-related goals have you set for yourself?
24. What do you know about our company?
25. Are you willing to relocate?

looking for new challenges done will that I could at the rest

26. Can you supervise people?
27. Can you work well under stress?
28. Do you prefer to work individually or as part of a team?
29. Are you a team player?
30. Tell me about your duties at your present job.
31. What frustrates you about your job?
32. Describe your relationship with your last three supervisors.
33. Are you willing to travel overnight?
34. How do you feel about overtime?
35. What jobs have you enjoyed most? Least? Why?
36. What are your supervisor's strengths and weaknesses?
37. What have you learned from your mistakes? What were some of them?
38. What do you think determines a person's progress with a good company?
39. How would you describe yourself?
40. Why did you pick your major?
41. What kind of grades did you have?
42. What courses did you like most? Least? Why?
43. How has your schooling prepared you for this job?
44. Do you feel you did the best work at school that you were capable of doing?
45. Why should I hire you?
46. Who has exercised the greatest influence on you? How?
47. What duties have you enjoyed most? Least? Why?
48. What kind of supervisors do you like most? Least? Why?
49. Have you ever been fired or asked to resign?
50. Why have you changed jobs so frequently?
51. Describe the biggest crisis in your career.
52. Why have you been out of work so long? What have you been doing?
53. What public figure do you admire most and why?
54. What are your primary activities outside of work?
55. Would you have any concern if we did a full background check on you? What would we find?
56. What qualities do you most admire in other people?
57. Tell me about the last incident that made you angry. How did you handle it?
58. How has your supervisor helped you grow?
59. What did your supervisor rate you highest on during your last review? Lowest?
60. What are the things that motivate you?
61. How do you handle people that you really don't get along with?
62. Describe your management philosophy and management style.
63. What is the biggest mistake you ever made?
64. How many people have you hired? How do you go about it? How successful have the people been?
65. How many people have you fired? How did you handle it?
66. How would your subordinates describe you as a supervisor?
67. Some managers watch their employees very closely while others use a loose rein. How do you manage?
68. How have you improved as a supervisor over the years?

69. What kind of supervisor gets the best results out of you?
70. What have you done to increase your personal development?
71. How do you feel about your career progress?
72. What is unique about you?
73. What types of books and magazines do you read?
74. Starting with your first job out of college, tell me why you left each organization.
75. What is your boss like?
76. How would your supervisor describe you?

DISTINGUISH YOURSELF FROM THE COMPETITION

Ultimately there are twelve key things you can do to get more job offers. All of the tips and all of the techniques covered on interviewing are incorporated in these twelve points. Tell yourself that you will do everything necessary to fulfill each of these points on every interview you attend.

1. Demonstrate enthusiasm and potential.
2. Tell vivid stories.
3. Exude confidence.
4. Be prepared.
5. Sell yourself.
6. Come across as a real and genuine person.
7. Listen intently.
8. Show you can solve problems.
9. Be interesting.
10. Know things about the organization.
11. Know yourself.
12. Build credibility.

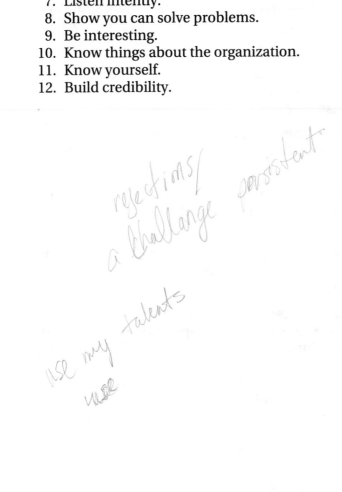

rejections/
a challenge   persistent

use my talents
use

Professional Editing

WRITING A TOP-QUALITY RESUME is one of the most difficult parts of an effective job search. As I prepare clients for their job search I advise them on resume writing and then assist them by editing their completed resume. With the help of *Resume Power* most write a very fine resume which would get excellent results. If I edit what they've come up with, effectiveness is often increased twenty to fifty percent.

By following the advice of *Resume Power* and by spending six to ten hours writing and editing, you should produce a top-quality resume. If you feel that professional editing could strengthen it, however, I would like to help. The cost of the editing service is $45.00. I typically devote an hour to each resume. I will review your resume and look for ways to improve the layout and the writing. If you have specific questions about a portion of the resume, I will make recommendations. Perhaps you're not sure if you should include certain information. Give me your thoughts—pros and cons—and I'll tell you what I think and why.

What You Need To Do

1. Send me your <u>double-spaced</u>, typed final draft. It's okay if you've made a few final corrections on it. Send your resume only when you believe it is the best you can possibly do.

2. Include your job sketches. They must be as complete as possible and legible. Be sure your sketches have included all possible results and accomplishments.

3. List any questions you have. Perhaps you're wondering if you should include a seminars section or a particular job duty.

4. On a separate sheet, write your name, address, and phone number. Give me the best times to reach you by phone, including a daytime number. Indicate whether we can talk freely if I reach you at work. I do not typically call, but sometimes it is essential.

5. Enclose a check or money order for $45.00 made payable to Career Management Resources. Address your envelope to Tom Washington, Career Management Resources, 1750 112th NE, C-224, Bellevue, WA 98004.

What We Will Do

1. Within 48 hours of receipt of your material I will have your resume heading your way by first class mail. Send only copies of your job sketches since I will not return those to you. Be sure you have a copy of your resume, but send me the original.

2. I will review your job sketches and resume. First I'll look at any possible ways to improve the layout and eye appeal of the resume. Next I will review each portion of the resume, sentence by sentence. I might, for example, recommend an objective with more punch, or a way to combine two sentences to make them more concise and more clear. I will recommend better words and will make sure everything is spelled correctly and is grammatically correct. If I feel a statement is unnecessary or detracts from the resume I will scratch it out and explain why.

3. If necessary I will call you so I can gain a better understanding of a particular job or experience.

4. I will return your draft with my suggestions and will keep a photocopy for my records.

Notice in the example below how the job description was strengthened through editing.

For this equipment manufacturer,

REGIONAL MANAGER - 7/89-Present. ^Responsible for the total

operation of the Midwest Regional Office providing sales and service

to customers through local field representatives. Supervise 11

(not necessary, assumed to be part of hiring)

salespeople and 12 office personnel with responsibility for ~~interviewing~~,

₽ = delete comma   *Work*

hiring, and training all regional personnel. ~~Travel extensively, working~~

closely with field representatives to promote sales to end users,

(this is assumed and is not

dealers, and original equipment manufacturers. ~~Supply information to~~

a powerful or needed phrase)   *(a number is better   4-6 trade*
than various)

~~Corporate as requested and~~ Represent the company at ~~various trade~~

annually

shows. Improved office efficiency and morale by opening lines of

—%

communication between management and staff. Increased sales

%

and reduced expenses by realigning sales territories and job

^ (adding another point will strengthen
this statement

responsibilities, *as well as by . . .*

(Do the necessary research to determine as exactly
as possible what the increase in sales and the
decrease in expenses actually was.

Bibliography

Career Planning

The Three Boxes of Life, Richard Bolles, Ten Speed Press, 1981

The Truth About You: Discover What You Should Be Doing With Your Life, Arthur Miller and Ralph Mattson, Ten Speed Press, 1989

Job Finding

Career Satisfaction And Success: How To Know And Manage Your Strengths, Bernard Haldane, 1988. Available only through mail order at $9.25: Wellness Behavior Northwest, 4502 54th Ave NE, Seattle WA 98105

The Complete Job Search Handbook, Howard Figler, Henry Holt & Co., 1988

Go Hire Yourself An Employer, Richard Irish, Anchor Press, 1987

Guerrilla Tactics In The Job Market, Tom Jackson, Bantam Books, 1991

How To Get a Better Job In This Crazy World, Robert Half, Plume, 1990

The Hunt: Complete Guide To Effective Job Finding, Tom Washington, Mount Vernon Press, 1992

What Color Is Your Parachute? Richard Bolles, Ten Speed Press, 1993

Who's Hiring Who, Richard Lathrop, Ten Speed Press, 1989

Interviewing

How To Make $1000 a Minute: Negotiating Your Salaries and Raises, Jack Chapman, Ten Speed Press, 1987

Sweaty Palms: The Neglected Art Of Being Interviewed, Anthony Medley, Ten Speed Press, 1992

Headhunters

How To Get A Headhunter To Call, Howard Freedman, John Wiley & Sons, 1986

Career Building

Skills for Success, Adele Scheele, Ballantine, 1979

About The Author

Career Management Resources — (206) 454-6982

Tom Washington holds a master's degree in counseling from Northeastern Illinois University and is the founder of Career Management Resources (1979), a career exploration and outplacement counseling firm in Bellevue, Washington. He has personally written over 800 resumes and edited hundreds more, with most clients receiving 10-15 times more interviews than the national average.

He has shared his resume writing and job finding strategies on radio and television talk shows across the country. He is a frequent contributor to *The National Business Employment Weekly* and other employment related publications. In 1992 he received the **Ten Best** award from *The National Business Employment Weekly, a Wall Street Journal Publication,* for producing one of the ten most practical and timely articles of the year. Mr. Washington is also the author of *The Hunt: Complete Guide To Effective Job Finding,* a 1992 job finding guide.

Mr. Washington speaks to college audiences, career and job finding professionals, associations, job fairs, schools, and professional groups. He covers a wide range of topics and always instills a motivation to conduct an effective job search. If you would like him to speak to your group, please call him at (206) 454-6982.

Career Management Resources provides outplacement assistance to people throughout the Puget Sound Region who are terminated or laid off. Organizations desiring to provide job finding assistance to their employees can reach Mr. Washington at CMR.

Career Management Resources
1750 112th NE C-224
Bellevue, WA 98004

What Satisfied Users Are Saying About *Resume Power*

Congratulations on your outstanding book, *Resume Power: Selling Yourself On Paper*. Among the many resume books I have seen, yours is the most practical one I have encountered.

> *P.R.   Chico, California*

Resume Power has been easy to read, easy to follow, and filled with practical and workable information which can benefit readers of all ages who work in many wide-ranging occupational industries.

> *T.R.   Arlington Heights, Illinois*

This spring I will be teaching a course in career planning. *Resume Power: Selling yourself On Paper* is an excellent resource for practical resume information.

> *N.G.   Fargo, North Dakota*

I found your book *Resume Power* both enjoyable and extremely informative. It is, by far, the best book that I have read on the subject of resumes and job search. I will recommend your book to everyone.

> *N.B.   Auburn, Indiana*

Resume Power is a must for job seekers . . . I have recommended your book to my friends, relatives, students, and business contacts.

> *R.S.   Auckland, New Zealand*

Thank you for your wonderful book, *Resume Power*. From it I have gained valuable insights into job searching and resume construction.

> *A.W., Employment Coordinator   Anchorage, Alaska*

Your book *Resume Power* is the best thing that has ever happened to me. Wow! Thanks a million for writing it. It has given me so much more confidence!

> *R.A.   Rough and Ready, California*

I wanted to write and thank you for coming out with the book *Resume Power*. I responded to ads in the *Chicago Tribune* if I had at least 50% of the credentials requested. I received the most interviews of any similar period in my working life, approximately 12 interviews. There is no question the format of the resume was critical. I learned from each interview and built on the experience. After accepting my last offer, I feel almost as giddy as my first major success in a serious job search.

> *D.W.   Chicago, Illinois*

I operate a small typing service from my home. More and more my business is specializing in resume writing. Your book, *Resume Power*, has become my bible. From it I have learned many techniques that have improved my resume writing, thereby bringing me more referrals and increasing my business.

> *K.L   St. Clair, Michigan*

Since I and several of my direct reports will be searching for new jobs, due to the relocation of our present operation, we need effective resumes. I reviewed over twenty books on writing resumes and purchased four. After reading all four it was very clear to me that *Resume Power* was by far the best.

A.H. Atlanta, Georgia

Please count me as one of your satisfied customers. I have thoroughly read your book and I have made all of the corrections you suggested. After years of applying for jobs with a poorly written resume, miracles started to happen when I used your methods.

V.R. Friendswood, Texas

In November we ordered three copies of *Resume Power*. We have found this book to be very valuable and useful to the department and would like to order eight additional copies.

S.J., Duke University Durham, North Carolina

I purchased *Resume Power* to help me get my thoughts together on resumes. I will be conducting workshops for those who ask assistance in their job search and intend to have them use your book as a guide in writing. The format of your book is easy to follow and moves along.

M.K., Personnel Director Milwaukee, Wisconsin

I have just finished using your book to revise my five year old resume. I was delighted with my results. *Resume Power* is a treasure of practical gems. Hints and ideas flow freely to inspire and encourage.

C.P. Miami, Florida

I just want to let you know how fantastically successful your book was to me in my search for employment. A total of fifteen resumes were sent out in a two week period and I got four interviews. I accepted a position where I can better my career. Thank you for the tremendous insights into "handling" a very uncertain time in my life.

J.Y. Fullerton, California

I most heartily thank you for writing *Resume Power*. I purchased your book when faced with the task of writing a resume and interviewing after ten years in the Air Force. Your resume writing information and job location guide are the best I've seen. In particular, the interview section helped me prepare for interviews. I have received an offer for every interview I have gone on.

C.C. Ypsilanti, Michigan

Thank you for writing such an excellent book. *Resume Power* is the best book I have read on resumes and I have read at least six others from the library.

S.J. Kent, Washington